BUSIER THAN EVER!

CHARLES N. DARRAH,
JAMES M. FREEMAN,
AND J. A. ENGLISH-LUECK

Busier Than Ever!

Why American Families Can't Slow Down

STANFORD UNIVERSITY PRESS

STANFORD, CALIFORNIA

2007

Stanford University Press
Stanford, California

Library of Congress Cataloging-in-Publication Data
Darrah, Charles N.
  Busier than ever! : why American families can't slow down / Charles N.
Darrah, James M. Freeman, and J. A. English-Lueck.
     p. cm.
  Includes bibliographical references and index.
   ISBN 978-0-8047-5491-0 (cloth : alk. paper)--ISBN 978-0-8047-5492-7
(pbk. : alk. paper)
   1. Family--United States. 2. Family--Time management--United States. 3.
Parenting--United States. I. Freeman, James M., 1936- II. English-Lueck, J.
A. (June Anne), 1953- III. Title.

HQ536.D324 2007
306.872--DC22   2006038221

Typeset at Stanford University Press in 10/14 Janson

To our families:
Janice, Zachary, and Joshua Darrah
Pat and Karsten Freeman
Karl, Miriam, and Eilene Lueck

busy [adj]: having a great deal to do

Contents

PART ONE

Busyness

CHAPTER ONE

A Journey Through Busyness

Bill Allen was coasting along in his truck on the way to a softball game, with two boys seated beside him, when he suddenly realized that one of them wasn't his. Bill's biggest fear had come to pass, forgetting one of his boys. He turned around and raced back to day care to retrieve his misplaced son. The concerned staff chided him, adding to his anxiety and embarrassment.

Why was Bill transporting these children in the first place? He and his wife, Sophia Rodriguez, a data entry clerk in a public sector organization, were committed to providing extra structured activities for the two sons they were adopting, despite the additional commute that it required. Believing that these activities were important for their children's development and demonstrated that they were good parents, they therefore squeezed another commute into a schedule that already was so varied, tight, and hectic that the slightest miscommunication or delay led to disaster.

Each day started with worries, since Bill and Sophia had carefully rehearsed the night before who would transport each of the children to and from school. Who was picking up the children? Who was looking after Sophia's elderly mother, Alicia, who was in declining health and possibly afflicted with Alzheimer's disease? Who was monitoring Alicia's brother and her son, who were both disabled? At whose house were they meeting for the next gathering of their circle of nearly twenty relatives?

Recurring medical issues disrupted their dreams of a happy family. Some of these interruptions were trivial, though stressful, such as finding out that Alicia had not renewed her prescriptions, taking her to buy some more medicine, and finding that she had forgotten where she got it. Others were as distressing as the collapse from a stroke of an uncle at a New Year's celebration, or the unexpected death of a young niece from a brain hemorrhage.

These sudden crises shattered Sophia's relentless schedule. She was unable to relax. She constantly worried about where she was supposed to be, what she should be doing, and what surprises might derail her plans. Unlike her husband, she was the one with the flexible job, making her the person who had to take corrective action when the unexpected happened.

Bill and Sophia's daily lives were tightly scheduled already, and yet they took on even more obligations because of their sense of moral commitment to family and community. Despite his busyness, Bill dreamed of starting a small business to provide employment for "good" people who just needed a break. Their identities as responsible people rested upon seeking out opportunities to act, and it was precisely these activities that plunged them into busyness.

Bill and Sophia are not alone. For many Americans, busyness is like water to a fish; the context in which life is lived that is so obvious that it often passes without comment. This book is about families who are busy because they do lots of things. The demands of jobs fuel their sense of busyness, but this work often merges with the demands of family and community. People get work done wherever and whenever possible, including at home and in their cars. Family chores and personal tasks can also become interspersed at work, making it difficult to tell where work, family, community, and personal realms begin and end.

Millions of Americans spend countless hours coping with various forms of busyness that permeate their everyday lives. For some people, the focus of their busyness is family; for others it is job and career, or church and religious activities. For still others, busyness involves a combination of deeply held values or desired social activities. Sometimes, busyness results from a big event, like the catastrophic illness of a family member or a major reorganization at work, but much of it is the accumulation of many small, seemingly inconsequential demands on time, which collectively can be overwhelming. We search for the best ticket prices on the Internet, are "partners" with teachers in our children's education, and employ a battery of devices that promise to save labor if only we can learn to use and maintain them. Whether it is managing our careers, portfolios, or health, all of us have assumed more and more responsibilities in managing our lives. If shifts in how we spend our time portend change in society, then these busy lives are indicative of deep changes in American society over the past few decades.

Busyness is so deeply ingrained in many of today's families that people often take it for granted. It may seem so obvious as hardly to be worth analyzing. The activities that make up busyness may seem unimportant, but the phenomenon of busyness is anything but trivial. It consumes the lives of countless families. It is transforming America. Busyness reveals issues that reach to the heart of who we are and what we wish to become.

Busyness is at once ordinary and remarkable. Many of us seek ways to develop efficiency in our lives. However commonplace this may seem, we can also see in it something remarkable. Our busyness is more than how to fit everything into the scarce time available. Although we may experience busyness as a lack of time, or as life somehow speeding up, it is about much more than time.[1] A closer look at what we do reveals that many of us put considerable effort into managing our many commitments, and that we try to create buffers of technology and people, which we hope will help us cope. All of this coping and buffering creates hidden work, which we do in addition to everything else.

Busyness is also associated with meaning in our lives. The ways in which we see ourselves are inextricably wrapped up with busyness. Issues of meaning may derive from religious faith, but may equally arise in the context of our hectic days. Busyness involves time, but it is also about creating ourselves as moral beings who live in communities with other people, many of whom are also busy, albeit in varied ways and with different consequences.

This book recounts a journey through busyness undertaken between 1999 and 2001 with fourteen families, each of which has something to teach us about everyday lives filled with commitments and activities. The impetus for this journey grew from research we conducted in Silicon Valley beginning in 1992, which suggested that balancing or juggling the demands of work and family are more complicated than typically portrayed. In most scholarly accounts, time spent at work is deemed a measure of the intrusiveness of work. While the number of hours is important, however, so are the characteristics of industries, employers, and jobs. Some people spoke of long hours, with little personal control over when they worked. Others worked fewer hours but were subject to their employer's demand for constant "accessibility." For still others, work affected home life through a rigorous travel schedule, or simply the challenge of working across time zones. The particular dimensions of work were significant to individuals and the others in their lives.

The details of families and households also required attention. Some people spoke of the difficulties of raising children and how these changed as children grew older. The jobs of spouses mattered too. We found that in families with two career builders, each was typically reluctant to constrain the work habits of the other, since the shoe might soon be on the other foot. Other participants in our study lived in families with one career builder, and the other person often alerted his or her partner when work habits threatened family life. In general, we found that the impact of work on home life was subtle and could not be measured just by the number of hours worked or by counting the interruptions to home life. For example, people brought models and metaphors from the workplace into family life. These included talk about efficiency and productivity, various techniques to manage interpersonal relationships, and tools such as total quality management. Furthermore, despite the emphasis on the impact of work upon family, we heard tales suggesting that elements of family and community life were imported into the workplace. Assumptions and values about how men and women should act, the relationships between family and work, and the responsibilities of superiors and subordinates were often products of family life that played out at work.

As the months passed, we learned more about the complex dance between work and family, but what we found remained tantalizingly incomplete. First, people repeatedly told us they had figured out how to manage the demands of work and family by keeping the realms separate.[2] Yet all too often we saw briefcases lugged home and heard of e-mailing or telephoning interrupting the supposedly separate domain of family. One person, for example, when asked if she and her husband had any rules about working at home, replied, "No e-mailing at dinner." Then she laughed and shook her head. Parents often remarked that they interacted with their children until they could put them to bed and then begin a "second shift" of paperwork to be completed before the morning. Such revelations called attention to the gap between what people said and what they actually did. Second, busy people often told us that their families and friends understood and accommodated to their hectic schedules. We could only imagine what those others really said and how their lives were affected by the busyness of a spouse, parent, or friend. We set out to understand more completely how the juggling act of daily life really occurred.

Our research revealed that busyness was widespread, but it was most transparent among working families with children. Not only did parents have their own obligations at work, but they were also affected by the hectic lives of their children. Children, too, had their own forms of busyness and their own views about it, which often differed substantially from those of their parents.

Our journey with the fourteen families began, as ethnographic ones do, with a commitment to study people on their own turf, doing what was important to them. Although we talked with them throughout the day, we did not interview them using our questions, but rather tried to discover what mattered to them about their lives: we learned *their* questions. The lessons we learned were not always the ones we expected, but they were important to the people in our study.

Our choice was to study a few families in depth, rather than to survey a larger number, so choosing them was critical. We settled on fourteen families whose members said they were middle-class. Within the constraint of a small sample of dual-career families to be studied in depth, we tried to choose ones that would provide a variety of lifestyles. They varied in the number and age of children. Income was a relatively poor criterion of middle-class status in a region where the median house price hovered at about $500,000. Still, the team sought several families whose members expressed middle-class values about lifestyle and education, but who were struggling financially to realize their aspirations. In addition, we sought at least one family whose income and lifestyle placed it beyond the middle class. We also sought families that varied in ethnicity or country of origin.

Our goal was not to seek a representative sample, since this was meaning-less with such a small number. Instead, we assumed that a culturally diverse sample of families would increase the variety of strategies used to manage work and family. We also recruited families that included workers from the public and private sectors, as well as from different industries.

We sought to include families who believed that they had found ways to cope with all the commitments of their time, rather than ones who saw themselves as "dysfunctional"—however defined. Our assumption was that the former would teach us about everyday problems and dilemmas, as well as how to handle them, while the latter would only expand the litany of problems. Above all, we needed families whose members were open and would tolerate our presence.

Families participated for several reasons. Many people valued our willing-ness to spend time with them in order to capture how they saw the world; they contrasted it with the often-glib pronouncements in the media. Many believed that busyness was important, yet overlooked, and they viewed their participation as contributing to their community. Most families, too, con-tained at least one person who reflected on the family's practices and sought to improve its capacity to cope with complex responsibilities. Although we were explicit that therapy was not part of the study, some people undoubt-edly participated in it in order to work through issues within their families.

How to study busy families was also a challenge, for sitting in their homes would likely result in many lonely hours. Family members were mobile and dispersed during much of the day. To provide continuity, we decided that only one of us would study each family and, in fact, we each only met the members of "our" families. Initially, our presence constrained how people acted, but we were soon accepted as part of their lives, someone to be taught the family's way of doing things.

We conducted our fieldwork with each family for about one year, but we did not work with all of them at the same time. Instead, we staggered the study of the different families over a span of three years. We divided our fieldwork into phases that were adapted to each family. First, we shadowed individual family members during their days, often remaining with them for 10–12 hours at a time. This meant arriving early at the family home, ac-companying a family member at work, and then returning home with him or her at the end of the day, often stopping to collect children or dinner on the way. When the focus was on a child, we typically accompanied the child throughout the school day and accompanied him or her to after-school activities. Child and fieldworker then returned home together, usually after being picked up by a parent.

This most intense phase of fieldwork lasted two to four months, and we usually spent four complete days with each family member, resulting initially in 140–70 hours per family. During these hours, we took meticulous field notes either on a laptop computer or, if that was too intrusive, in small notebooks. The second phase focused on more collective "family activities." Then we often began our work when one or more family members arrived home after school, work, or errands. We joined families for dinner and after-dinner activities, such as homework, meetings such as Cub Scouts, watching television, or playing video games. We also joined families on weekends in order to observe activities ranging from running errands or performing chores to hosting baptisms or family reunions. Individual members were asked to think about activities or events that expressed something important or distinctive about the family and to notify us when we could observe these. We remained in touch with family members until the end of the year and beyond, asking about changes in the family and the routines of its members and visiting to capture important activities or events. We continued to receive information from the families after the one-year period of shadowing, and on occasion we met with various family members, who updated us on their lives.

Our fieldwork thus took the form of classic ethnographic participant-observation. Sometimes participation dominated, as when a fieldworker joined a family at a party, Easter egg hunt, or holiday dinner. At other times, especially when a family member was at work or school, observation dominated. The interplay of participation and observation was extremely fine-grained. For example, laws, policies, and practices sometimes constrained us, as when Charles Darrah shadowed a fireman or J. A. English-Lueck, a pair of attorneys. English-Lueck was not allowed to be present during client meetings, and Darrah was instructed where to stand and what to say to observers who might not understand his role. Yet the balance could shift abruptly to participation. Darrah, for example, accompanied someone to a corporate board meeting, signed a nondisclosure agreement, and was admonished to remain silent throughout a meeting that was expected to be tense or hostile. Yet board members soon solicited his opinions about the issues facing the company. Fieldwork often was a roller coaster of involvement and detachment, coolness and intimacy, informality and formality.

Unlike most kinds of social research, ethnographers develop close relationships with those they study. They do not always result in close friendships, but it is difficult to maintain the stance of dispassionate scientist for a year. Initially, families were uncertain about having an ethnographer around, and more than once they asked whether they had to pretend we were not there while they were eating dinner. Even if that had been ethnographically desirable, it clearly violated the rules of hospitality, and we routinely dined with the families. Doing so yielded important data and avoided an awkward situation, but it also meant we broke bread with the people we were studying. Friendships formed, but they were friendships of a special kind and were treated as such by both participants and researcher.

The people we studied were living lives not unlike our own, and it was sometimes tempting to offer advice. For example, a parent might be struggling to find a supervised activity for a child at a particular time, and we might know of a likely possibility because we lived in the same area. If we suggested it, we were helping someone who was helping us, but we would also be shaping the very strategies we were there to observe; so we remained silent. More typical were requests from a family member for advice. A parent might ask us how to improve a child's school performance, because, after all, we typically knew the most about what went on in class, since we spent days sitting in the classroom, chatting with the teacher, and watching kids play during after-school programs. One of us was asked how to respond to negative performance reviews at work, and another to suggest potential nannies for the family.

Underlying the complexity of the relationships is the concept of reciprocity. Although each family was paid a token $1,500 honorarium, this was not intended as payment for information, for what they offered us was beyond remuneration. Besides, once fieldwork began, the logic of reciprocity became evident. While we eschewed the role of family advisor, families often asked us about our own families, and we often answered those questions. Not to do so would have exposed the asymmetry in information about respective lives, and it might have harmed fieldwork in some cases. At the same time, we avoided making judgments and always explained that our way of handling a situation was just one of many alternatives, as was theirs.

Reciprocity thus swept us into the lives of the families. Often the requests were blatant and humorous in their self-interestedness. Sometimes, people scheduled days to be shadowed because they needed another person to get them into a carpool lane during a particularly horrific commute, and the ethnographer would serve. "You might as well be good for something," they would joke. Darrah agreed to meet with a colleague of Eleanor Flaherty's and eventually to serve on an advisory board for an organization she was founding. Eleanor was pleased at being able to "deliver" someone, since it helped build her professional network. She explained that this was how she had built a successful career.

What these and many other incidents show is that, just as we used other people for our purposes, and so had an obligation to protect them from harm, so too others used us. How they did this taught us lessons about how they juggled work and family obligations, and capturing this insider's perspective is one reason for doing ethnography. Each family member understood in his or her own way what we were doing and why we were doing it. Many of them considered what we found out about them to be important and interesting. They, of course, brought their own perspectives to bear. One child, for example, explained to her friends that the researcher was writing her life history for a book, while a middle-school boy from a troubled background explained to friends that the ethnographer was his bodyguard. When Darrah explained to a teenager that the boy himself could choose when he was to be shadowed, so as not to embarrass him, he responded, "There is nothing you can do that won't embarrass me."

The families sized us up and decided what to reveal to us. One man said his family was alone in the region, and only later did we discover that his brother's family lived a few blocks away; he was embarrassed by the latter's success. A child in another family had a criminal record that was not initially revealed. Family members thus sought to control how their lives were represented, and their understanding of what was ethnographically interesting seldom corresponded exactly to how we saw their family. Our individual characteristics also entered into the equation, often in ways we could only see in retrospect. James Freeman, for example, had done his original doctoral research in a temple town in India and for many years taught courses on anthropology and religion. Coincidentally or not, notes about his four families reveal much about their religious beliefs. Darrah and English-Lueck had long studied information technology at work and home, and their notes contain descriptions of personal digital assistants and cellular phone use.

The interpersonal dynamics of ethnography with families could sometimes seem overwhelming, but the unfolding dramas and dilemmas taught profound lessons. Arguably, they were why we were there in the first place, participating in the messiness and ambiguity of daily life, rather than handing people surveys they could quickly answer. Of course, people might lie, but even lies can open the door to deeper conversations about why the lie was told, and why it took the form it did. While it can be tiresome guarding against offering advice or being used in others' agendas, the very fact that people tried to involve us in their lives on their own terms gave us the chance to discuss those lives with greater sensitivity.

As ethnographers, we thus view the very difficulties and limitations of fieldwork as providing additional sources of data. Reciprocity need not be achieved by offering answers to life's imponderables, but rather by providing an opportunity for a particular form of dialogue that is otherwise largely missing from the lives of busy families. Indeed, many families asked at the onset of fieldwork if they would receive a "report card" at the end, but none actually asked for it when the time arrived. Through the reflections and conversations about their practices that they had engaged in over the months, there was no need.

We try in these pages to provide glimpses into the daily lives of ordinary people. While our goal is to be faithful to those lives while using them to develop the idea of busyness, we do not claim to be describing the totality of their lives. We do not provide charts tallying the minutes and hours spent at work or home. Doing so would give the reader both a false sense of precision, while distorting the central lesson our journey taught us: busyness is about our activities and what they mean to us.

We suspect that many readers may have been motivated to pick up this book because busyness is a concern or annoyance in their own lives. Many of the people who contacted us about participating in the study were similarly motivated. We tried to avoid thinking of busyness as a problem unless a family saw it that way. We promise readers neither glib answers nor universal solutions to enhancing their efficiency or productivity, much less how to create a good family or life. But in following the journey of our study, you may come to appreciate why it is so difficult to slow down or pull away from busyness.

Through the stories of the ordinary people in this book, we try to engage the reader in a conversation about the activities in his or her own life. This is a challenge for both you and us, but arguably the result will be more valuable than another set of admonitions about what to do. Anything else would be a betrayal of what "our" families taught us: the dilemmas of busyness are in the details, and so "one size fits all" solutions are irrelevant at best, harmful at worst. Accordingly, we are led to a mindfulness about our obligations and how we fill our days.

In the remainder of Part One, we elaborate the concept of busyness and ask what drives it in the lives of so many people. Then, in Part Two, we explore how people cope with busyness and how that coping comes to constitute a hidden or tacit work that further complicates our days. Coping, however, has its limits, and so in Part Three, we look at how people create buffers of technology and other people that enable them to better cope. Finally, we close our journey with a look back at where we have ventured, as well as ahead to what all this portends for the society in which we live.

CHAPTER TWO

How Are We Busy?

Soon after beginning fieldwork with the families in our study, we were immersed in their everyday lives. Our days were spent scheduling times to be with the families, shadowing family members, jotting down field notes while accompanying them throughout the day, returning with them to their homes, and then driving back to our own homes, where we spent evenings elaborating the day's notes.

The three co-authors frequently met to discuss what we were learning. Obviously, the families were busy, and all of them in some way balanced or juggled competing burdens. But more important, each family was utterly distinct in *how* it was busy. Just how different they were became evident when we tried to do fieldwork with members of two different families in one day. We found this to be quite disorienting. What became clear was that we were doing much more than simply observing different people who did different things. When we participated in various activities with them, we found that each family was in effect a separate universe. To start with, their basic practices of daily life varied widely. So did the assumptions, values, and motivations that guided their actions. Once we understood the former, we saw how the latter often followed logically, sometimes with seeming inevitability.

For example, the busyness of the Carlsberg family began with work. A prominent feature of Alex Carlsberg's work environment was job uncertainty, which led him to present himself as a conscientious employee worth retaining. To make sure that his employers viewed him like this, he enrolled in various corporate training programs so that he possessed the skills needed in new and unforeseeable circumstances. As added insurance in case his main job faltered, he was developing a business plan for his own Internet enterprise. He could not depend on his wife's employment, since it was uncertain, dependent on irregular grants and contracts. The couple assisted their elderly parents, and their family was infused by a sense of volunteerism. They also were heavy consumers of goods and services and systematically looked for the best prices. All this shaped their ideas about the good life and how best to prepare their children for it. In particular, they tried to provide an education that would get them into elite high schools and colleges that they believed led to the social networks that Alex and Pat thought were the key to success, but which they felt they personally lacked. What followed was deep and frustrating involvement in their boys' parochial school and reluctance to "waste time" by punishing their children, assign them too many chores, or deny them material pleasures.

Unlike the Carlsbergs, neither Bill Allen nor Sophia Rodriguez saw themselves as career builders. Busyness for them centered on family. The issue they faced was that their jobs made it difficult to coordinate all of their family transportation obligations. Bill and Sophia were in the process of adopting two children. They had to take these children to their schools and to health care appointments. Sophia also dashed off during lunches to care for two disabled relatives and her elderly mother. She could only relax at work, she joked, and a large extended family was both the site of her social life and the source of most of her stress. In her view, the good life consisted of nurturing a large network of relatives, working at undemanding and predictable jobs that did not interfere with her family obligations, and retiring by the time she was fifty. She and Bill prepared their children for the future by socializing them into the family, making sure they got a basic education, and inculcating the virtues of discipline and hard work

The lessons here are that the challenges of busyness lie in the details, and those details differ from family to family. Often, one or two obligations deemed critical by a family member reverberated through their days and made their family a distinct universe. How individuals and families were busy was fundamental to understanding what they could and could not do, if indeed they even saw busyness as a problem.

Work

MARTIN KLEIN: MERGER BUSYNESS

We begin with the work busyness of Martin Klein, which shot upward when the semi-conductor firm he worked for was taken over and absorbed by a European multinational corporation. Martin was caught up in changes taking place throughout the world, in which certain kinds of work are becoming more global, service-oriented, and infused with technology.[1] In Martin's case, his workplace world was turned upside down. He spent his days coping with changes in corporate strategy, new technologies, modified accounting practices, new personnel decisions, and an endless number of tasks that flowed from these changes.

Martin was assigned to switch data from one computerized accounting system to a completely different one. Complicating this was the fact that the two systems differed in what was counted, how it was counted, and who counted it. Martin worked with integration test consultants and the trainers who wanted to know specifically how information flowed, but they could not trace this with concrete details. It was like writing an essay, Martin said. A person might be able to do it but still be unable to explain how to choose the next word. Furthermore, coming up with an explanation was irrelevant to the task. There were many ways of writing the essay, just as there were many ways of achieving the same end in accounting. By the end of the day, the employees, frustrated with the decisions forced on them by their software, joked that they needed to go back to the pre-computer days of green-lined paper.

Then Martin was assigned to work through the tax dimensions of the software. He described the technical problems connected with this task. The two programs had incompatible character strings. One used twelve numerical characters. The other, which used eighteen alphanumeric characters, automatically added zeroes, and it left-justified, turning data into garbage. Martin had to figure out how to accommodate multiple calendars into the planning software, since each country in which they did business required different customer, factory, transport, and warehouse calendars and had different holidays. He could not get financial data into his models until he worked out the calendars.

To compound the confusion, the new corporate president reorganized how the employees were supposed to conduct business, using ideas that in Martin's view were partly brilliant, partly stupid, but also a rehash of reorganizations he had experienced over a period of fifteen years. Above all, the clash of software systems pushed other business considerations into the background. The old company had used a web-based system that maximized input, transparency, and monitoring, often using Excel. The new company ran on paper reports and a twenty-year-old computing style. They replaced Microsoft Outlook with Lotus Notes as a communications system. Martin adjusted by using both systems, the new one on his desktop and the old system on his laptop. Throughout his workday, he switched back and forth. In the same vein, he used a fiscal calendar for the new company and the schedule for closing the old company.

As the new company brought in new changes, people left for other jobs or were transferred to other workstations; buildings stood abandoned; equipment was scattered everywhere, as were people with the knowledge and skills to use the old system. Numerous consultants tried to solve the myriad problems of merging the two software systems. Martin wandered the halls looking for consultants and workers who had migrated to other cubicles; he couldn't call them because in one of the buildings where he worked neither he nor they had phones.

The uncertain work environment led Martin to worry about loss of data and the accuracy of the calculations he was making, and so he wanted to double-check his figures with an adding machine that produced a printout. He spent hours searching for a workable adding machine. When he went to the repository of adding machines and keyboards, he was disconcerted to find that they were missing keys, cords, or paper. Not a single one was usable. "It is not to be," he sighed, with mounting frustration.

Martin and his co-workers struggled with an uncertain infrastructure and an ambiguous workday. Work was continuous, and as the day ended, Martin still faced the responsibility for integrating two incompatible management systems.

VIC JACKSON: MULTIPLE TASKS, DEADLINES, AND PRESSURES

Vic Jackson's job seemed fairly humdrum until you followed him through a day's work. Vic was an electrical engineer at a large high-tech company, where he tested the safety and reliability of new designs for integrated circuits. He started the day in his cubicle, one of dozens in a vast warren of office spaces and buildings of his firm. There, he engaged in a dizzying kaleidoscope of tasks, some from his workplace and others from his family life. Vic's workplace tasks were so varied and complex that he constantly needed to refer to a schedule to keep track of his activities and the locations where he performed them.

Vic often worked on four projects at once. On this particular day, he checked e-mail and interoffice correspondence, read reports, studied manuals outlining safety procedures, called out questions and joked with employees in nearby cubicles, visited people in distant cubicles to clarify inconsistencies and discrepancies in reports, cleared up inaccuracies, donned protective gear and conducted tests in a high-tech clean room, evaluated the safety and reliability of new products, checked compliance with safety and reliability standards, and, in consultation with company employees and outside vendors, interpreted what was considered safe or reliable. Interspersed with these tasks, Vic called his wife about their sick daughter, filled out his income tax return, using suggestions by fellow employees, applied to take another college engineering class, made an appointment with his dentist, and checked with a real estate agent about buying a house.

Vic and the four other members of their risk-analysis team, two men and two women, had a friendly, easygoing working relationship. They helped one another complete assigned tasks and covered for each other if someone had to take off to deal with family matters. They ate lunch together and discussed new technologies, current projects, former team members who had moved to other jobs in and outside the company, and family issues, from children's education and day care to buying a house. Once a month, after work, they would go out for drinks and food at a well-known restaurant, where other employees of their company and other high-tech companies joined them. Every three months, all of the families of Vic's team would go off for a long weekend. Their favorite trip was to Yosemite.

In essence, they had created a little community for themselves. But underlying this was the realization that their community was both vulnerable and ephemeral. Each of their projects operated with tight deadlines, and as those deadlines approached, so did the pressures to finish on time and demonstrate that the circuit worked properly. They had to measure the safety of the device against the cost of making it safe. When projects failed or were late, both work and research teams faced the prospect of being reassigned or laid off. Testing had to be done both quickly and accurately, and the determination of levels of risk had to be within acceptable guidelines. "If we make a mistake," Vic remarked laconically, "we could blow up the whole building."

The rhythms of daily life profoundly affect families such as Vic's and their busyness. Their regular daily routine is fast-paced and crammed with activities, punctuated by deadlines that must be met by one or more people. Such schedules are stressful. If someone misses a connection, it can have unintended consequences throughout the day. Departures from routines create difficulties, since one person or another will often forget the new plans. The fear of forgetting a critical connection adds an edge to an already busy schedule.

HUMBERTO MENDOZA: DOMAINS OF A FIREFIGHTER

Humberto Mendoza was a firefighter whose work divided along four distinct lines or cultural domains: captain of a fire truck; captain of a hazardous materials truck, requiring specialized knowledge about chemicals and the specific factories, shops, and offices where they were stored; arson investigator, requiring knowledge of law-enforcement procedure and investigations resulting in criminal prosecution; and firefighting teacher. Humberto had to remember at each moment which of the four firefighting hats he was wearing. To appreciate how Humberto worked, it is not enough to add up the sheer number of his tasks. We also must consider their variety and note that they were widely different in each of the four domains.

On top of this, Humberto interspersed family tasks throughout his workday. While driving to another fire station, he stopped off at a tile store to pick up samples for the front entry to his house. His tile setter was another firefighter, who would do the job on a day off. Later in the day, Humberto gave advice about personal financial planning to a junior firefighter. On other days, he gave impromptu financial workshops, cautioning firefighters that their salaries alone would not provide security; they needed sound planning.

Humberto also called his wife at work to give her financial advice. He had been reviewing her portfolio and recommended that she redistribute her investments. Suzanne had been at her computer workstation, organizing a marketing program for her company's latest product. In an instant, she left the world of marketing and put her personal account on the computer screen. She studied this for a moment, and then flicked back to marketing.

What made Humberto's daily activities complex were the variations of the different domains into which they fell, the distinctive tasks, information, and technology that each required, the diverse networks that characterized each of them, and the ways these various domains opened out into larger systems that influenced Humberto's life and the lives of his wife and two daughters. In this, Humberto's family was not alone. Every family we studied revealed a complex tapestry of activities tied to multiple domains that highlighted how these families connected to a wider world.

DAN AND FERN LE: FLEXIBLE AND INFLEXIBLE JOBS

Some people complain that they are overwhelmed by the number and variety of activities that confront them daily. Others find themselves in job situations that they perceive as giving them little flexibility. Not Dan Le. Confident, buoyant, and jaunty, Dan was constantly on the go from before dawn to late evening, doing one of his three jobs, attending to family errands and day care, or shopping for the latest high-tech gadget. In his primary employment as a career noncommissioned officer in a branch of the U.S. military, Dan found a way to maximize flexibility of hours and routines, to make the bureaucracy work for him. A day with Dan was both a story of unending busyness and an exercise in exuberance without letup, with constant new challenges that required his immediate attention. By contrast, Dan's wife, Fern, considered herself overworked in a job that afforded her very little of the flexibility achieved by her husband.

Dan Le began his day at 5:30 AM, still in his pajamas, by turning on the rice cooker for the evening meal and popping frozen waffles in the toaster for his two sons. A few minutes after 6:00 AM, he awakened them. While Fern dressed them, Dan checked over his Dodge Caravan. By 6:30, the boys, sleepy and whimpering, had been hustled into the vehicle for their 30-minute commute to the day-care facility at the military base where Dan worked. The boys had to arrive before the rooms filled up; otherwise they would not be admitted. Dan dropped them off and drove to his worksite nearby, arriving before 7:30. Meanwhile, Fern, in her Mercedes sedan, was commuting to a small high-tech company that formed and resharpened drills used in the manufacture of circuit boards. She worked as an office manager and all-around troubleshooter involved with invoices, inventory, sales to customers, and shipping.

Dan's primary work responsibility was to send out and receive parts for the repair of various aircraft, or order repaired parts from elsewhere, a task that connected him to military as well as private vendors throughout the country and beyond. He worked fast and efficiently, cultivating his contacts so that they responded to his requests in a timely manner. Throughout the day, Dan received or made several calls related to family matters and checked on his sons at day care.

Dan's spheres of activity extended to side businesses. One of these was leasing and selling credit card machines to small businesses in northern California. Fern had actually started this business, but when she lost interest in it, Dan took it over. He stored the credit card machines in his garage. While at his office, he received pager calls from customers, as well as from banks, which charged different rates for processing the cards. He called back on his cellular phone. On occasion, he traveled to the business sites to make sales, install the machines, service them, and sometimes replace them with upgrades that were faster and had more features. During these trips, he usually stopped off to visit friends or shop for parts or software for his home computer or toys for his two sons. If he was gone for long during the day, he called his office on one of his two cellular phones to find out what orders had come in. He called Fern on his second phone to coordinate picking up the kids from day care.

Several months later, the day care closed suddenly. Ben, the older child was sent to a Vietnamese Catholic preschool in another part of town, while Steve, the youngest child, ended up at the house of an elderly Vietnamese woman who provided day care.

Dan also instructed Tex, a young employee in Dan's workplace, in the credit card business. Dan showed him how to manage his money and get out of debt. Tex, who was highly motivated to better himself, responded to Dan's suggestions and encouragement, turning around an $8,000 debt and putting $15,000 in the bank. Dan observed, "I get him started in the business, and I make some money off of that."

Dan also started a small food concession at his worksite, assisted by Tex. During their lunch period, they bought sweet rolls, coffee, sugar, soft drinks, candy bars, and chips at a large discount center, which they sold to the employees for a small profit. Dan instructed Tex how to price the goods so that they sold for less than vending machines but still made a profit. Dan proudly called himself an astute businessman.

Dan explained that he had engineered a trade-off that enabled him to stay away from the office for long periods of time without being reprimanded. Reciprocally, he was on 24-hour call seven days a week. If an emergency arose, he responded, whatever the hour of day or night. His superiors allowed him this arrangement, he said, because, "I work fast. I can do in two hours what takes others a day. I have the freedom to be away because I do the job right. I gave my superiors a choice: either I follow strict regulations or I do the job. They recognized that if I don't get parts on time, repairs don't get done, the rating declines, and my managers lose their rating. So they let me do the job my way."

Dan got what he wanted. Full responsibility for the job rested with him, but at a cost. Dan was in perpetual motion, performing two or more tasks at the same time or in brief consecutive bursts of energy. Rare was the day when he was not shuttling back and forth between tasks, as well as locations.

At home, Dan continued his many tasks. On this day, after picking up the boys from day care, he prepared their meal. Later in the evening, Fern warmed up some take-home Vietnamese soup that she had bought on the way home from her job. The soup was for the two adults. Then Dan cleaned the dishes, straightened up the house, and played with his sons. He admonished them several times to cooperate and share their toys. He had spent countless hours constructing model aircraft, which he had strung from the ceilings of the boys' playroom and bedroom. He would often talk to the boys, describing each plane and their military uses. Near their bedtime, he put on a Rugrats video for the boys, and they watched this in their bedroom. Around 9:00 PM, he sank into a chair and watched television, visibly exhausted from his frenetic daily schedule.

Fern also ended the day exhausted, but for different reasons. Unlike her husband's, her job provided her little freedom, and it required her to take on more tasks than she could handle effectively. When an employee in charge of benefits at Fern's place of work had gone on maternity leave for several months, the office supervisor had told Fern to take over that woman's job and also to assume new administrative responsibilities. Fern had asked him for some training or guidance, but he had never given it. Fern felt overworked and underappreciated. She received no extra money, support, or even expression of appreciation for doing two full-time jobs. In her view, the management of this small company was chaotic compared to the large telecommunications company where she had previously worked. In the main office room, which contained twelve desks with no partitions, there was no friendly chatter, only a moody silence. "I am asked to do several different jobs at once," she said. "This drives me crazy. Everybody wants his job done first. If you do more than your job, you are not recognized, so who cares? You might as well do less. Why do more for the company? Why stay?"

Adding to Fern's frustration and resentment was her company's inflexible policy regarding emergency leave. When her youngest son was in the hospital with a serious illness, the company refused to give her time off to visit him. Her husband, who had created a more flexible work arrangement, was at the boy's bedside. Fern's unfriendly working environment took its toll. After work, Fern returned home tired and irritable, complaining about her treatment at the office.

Soon afterward, she sought employment elsewhere. Within three weeks, she received four job offers, testimony both to her competence and to the hot job market at that time. She moved to a large international consumer electronics company at twice her previous salary. In the next two years, she changed jobs three more times. After that, she took a post in security for a U.S. government agency, and two years after that, she became an insurance fraud investigator for a major company.

The differing accounts of Dan and Fern Le provide another illustration of why it's important to look at the specific activities, the details as well as the time people spend on work. What they do, how they do it, the constraints they face, and how they respond to them vary widely, and thus so do their work experiences, as well as the diverse ways in which busyness enters their lives. It is also important to recognize that not all people seek to minimize busyness in their work lives. People like Dan thrive when they involve themselves in many and varied work activities. This is in marked contrast to people who prefer a consistent and unwavering routine and becomes disconcerted when that routine is upset.

Family

THE HOPKINS/JOHNSONS: FAMILY MATTERS PENETRATE WORK

Home life and personal obligations can have a profound effect on how people work at their places of employment. Even the routine Peggy Johnson followed at work was a direct consequence of a decision that she and her husband, Kent Hopkins, had made about the kind of family life they wanted. Both of them worked in Silicon Valley's high-tech sector, he as a facilities manager and she in business process development. They created an environment in which the house they bought, their jobs, and the preschool for their one son were near one another. But this convenience came with a trade-off. Houses near their work were more expensive than others located further away. For the same price, they could have bought a larger house elsewhere, but that would have come with a long daily commute. They rejected this in favor of a centrally located small house with cramped quarters and no room for the home offices they desperately needed.

Their home-buying decision had a profound impact on how Peggy worked at her place of employment. She did not complete required tasks in a simple sequential order. Instead, she switched from one activity to another. This enabled her to do many things unrelated to her specific work assignments. She attended to home and family affairs, searched the Internet, and even put in time on the development of her own dot-com business. But as the following example shows, Peggy imposed strict limits and guidelines on how far she should go in using the office for her personal life.

On this day, Peggy checked her e-mail and responded to several inquiries from co-workers. Then she clicked a key and suddenly was shopping for a gift for a special friend. The search took an hour. When asked if she did other shopping from her cubicle, such as ordering groceries from an online grocer, she expressed shock at the idea: it would be a violation of her employer's trust, since the purchase of groceries was a regular activity, and that would be wrong.

Later in the afternoon Peggy suddenly switched from desktop to laptop, explaining that the company's desktop was the one she usually used. However, she was enrolled in a graduate program at a nearby university and could not gain access to its library because of her employer's computer "firewall," which prevented unauthorized entry. At first, she had connected her personal laptop to the telephone to use the library, but this had tied up the phone, and her customers, all located within her building, could not reach her. She then asked a friendly co-worker in the facilities department to install another phone line. He did so, and now she had both official and "gray" phone lines. She did not know who paid for the gray line calls, but she needed to be accessible to customers while also working on her graduate degree. This enabled her to be a conscientious employee with a good reputation while continuing her graduate studies to build her career.

Later in the day, while taking her afternoon break, Peggy prepared for a weekly conference call with her incipient dot-com partners, who were located on the East Coast. Retrieving her cellular phone from her car, she headed for the company gym, where she moved between different exercise machines while trying to conduct the conference call.

Peggy used her time in shifting bursts of activity that were difficult to label, much less measure. When she discussed what she was doing, her tone conveyed a sense of self-consciousness, as if she knew she was engaging in an experiment that might backfire. It also conveyed a deep sense of personal morality: she was not trying to "get away" with anything, but rather to fulfill moral obligations to different people, who each had legitimate claims on her time. What is clear in all of this is that Peggy fashioned patterns of busyness that were a peculiar mix of family and work activities, and that this way of doing things was grounded in a larger vision both of work and family, which she shared with Kent.

THE MENDOZA/JONESES: THE MORALITY OF ROUTINES

Suzanne Jones and Humberto Mendoza devoted much time and effort to building a predictable, secure environment for their daughters. They saw this as a moral mandate, the way that their children would learn to cope with the world around them. A central part of that stable environment was the establishment of routines and a daily rhythm, including day care, which Suzanne and Humberto considered indispensable for enhancing the skills and well-being of their daughters.

For Suzanne and Humberto, routines provided continuity and stability in everyday life. Because they were a dual-career family, providing such continuity was a constant challenge. Suzanne, who shared a marketing position in a high-tech company with another woman, remained at home on Mondays and Tuesdays, and went to work Wednesday through Friday. Humberto, a firefighter, worked three 24-hour shifts, separated by days off, followed by four days off. While his workdays were predictable a year in advance, they could fall on any day of the week, thus altering his presence in the household each week.

In contrast, the daily routines of his children remained unchanging: a leisurely early morning of play, followed by drives to their respective day-care providers. They followed this routine even if both Humberto and Suzanne were home for the day.

On this day, the two girls were in the living room at 8:00 AM watching Sesame Street. Two helium balloons left over from Suzanne's birthday drifted around the living room, a sparsely furnished space with a white area rug, sofa and two chairs, and a home entertainment center. Strewn on the floor were a few toys, including two foot-long trucks, a plastic schoolhouse, and a box of blocks.

Suzanne puttered in the kitchen and then asked her daughter Angela to help her clean up a mess of paper clippings scattered on the floor, table, and a chair. She used the broom and coached Angela to hold the dustpan. They repeatedly swept and dumped the scraps. When they finished cleaning up, Angela announced that she wanted to color, but Suzanne replied, "We're going to eat breakfast soon and I'm going to need your help. Would you like to set the table?" Suzanne explained what to do and said, "Nicole, I need your help, too." Together they picked up the blocks on the living room floor. She also asked Angela to help, but Angela protested. Suzanne said, "I've got Eggos (frozen waffles), and I want us to eat together. It doesn't matter who dumped them out, we all help together." Soon the room was clean, and Suzanne said, "Let's go eat Eggos. Who's going to turn the television off?"

After helping Nicole into her highchair, Suzanne gave her a plate of waffles and pieces of watermelon. She asked Angela, "Do you want to put these plates on the table? And you forgot to put the forks out, so you'll have to do that." Angela served herself and her mother, pushing her place mat so it touched Suzanne's.

Suzanne commented that the previous night, she had planned to work for four or five hours after the children were asleep. She had been taking care of them but then fell asleep with them. She laughed, saying that she was still tired.

By 8:45 AM, Nicole and Angela had eaten and taken their plates to the sink. Nicole was walking around watching television in the living room, while Angela was playing with several Barbie dolls and sets of clothes. Suzanne finished eating breakfast. A few minutes later, Humberto returned from his 24-hour shift at a fire station and greeted his wife and children. Suzanne asked Humberto to watch the girls while she finished getting ready for work. Humberto, in the living room, played with the girls while they watched Sesame Street and instructed Nicole in how to count.

When Humberto was at home, each parent drove one daughter to a separate day-care provider. But the night before, while he was on duty, Suzanne had relayed a message to Humberto that an old friend had died in a fire in her home. Now he looked particularly tired, and she told him so. She offered to drive both girls to their day care. While discussing the day's plans, they also agreed to attend Angela's day care in the afternoon. Suzanne explained that it was a "VIP thing to make her feel important, although, I think we do that every day. At least I *hope* we do."

Suzanne and the girls departed at 9:30 for the ten-minute ride to Angela's day care, located in a residential dwelling. When Angela asked to listen to some music, Suzanne reminded her that they did not do so on the way to school, only during the afternoon drive home. The girl quietly looked at a small photo album with pictures of her and Nicole. Suzanne allowed her to look after they stopped and then told her, "We've got to go. Your family is waiting. I mean, your friends," she chuckled.

Inside, eleven children were sitting quietly around a large table eating their morning snack. Suzanne signed in Angela and gave her a hug. An aide greeted Angela, who moved over to her place at the table, and Suzanne departed to drop Nicole off at her day care, also in a house, located about eight miles away. She arrived at 10:00 AM, carried Nicole inside, signed her in, hugged and kissed her, and departed for her nearby job. Nicole joined three other children.

Suzanne had expended much time and effort finding day-care providers for the girls, interviewing eighty by phone and visiting thirty-five over a six-week period. In her view, few were "really good." Suzanne looked for a place that was clean and that explicitly emphasized manners and civility. She insisted that the staff be respectful to the kids and that the environment provide them with sufficient stimulation.

Suzanne had carefully structured her routine. "I spend my best hours with my children. I spend mornings with them." She laughed, "I don't get to work early. I don't rush my children. I *try* not to." She only hurried the girls "if it looks like we're taking an hour to eat our cereal." Suzanne preferred to work at night after her daughters were asleep instead of rushing them out the door in the morning. When she told her co-workers that "my first goal is my family," they were surprised, although not upset, about her priorities.

Hours later, Suzanne returned to pick up Nicole. Her greetings followed the same pattern each day. As she approached the girl, she broke into a broad smile and told her how much she missed her that day. Suzanne hugged her as she signed out and walked with her to the car. Once there she pushed a tape cassette into the player and the sounds of "Baby Beluga" filled the car. Suzanne sang along as they drove toward Angela's day care. "Is the water warm? Is your mother home? Is that the way it goes," she asked rhetorically, prompting Nicole to sing along. After a twenty-minute drive, Suzanne and Nicole arrived at Angela's day care. Suzanne hugged her in turn and told her how much she missed her. When she asked, an aide told her that the day was "a little rough in the afternoon when the mothers come" (to collect their kids). Angela retrieved several stuffed animals, some drawings, and a St. Patrick's puppet she had made, and the trio departed. As Suzanne strapped the girls in their car seats, she said, "Your Papa is home just waiting to see you." The tape deck played children's songs as they drove the few blocks home.

Their daughters' day-care routine provided Humberto and Suzanne with time to pursue projects and tasks during the day with undivided attention, although of course at financial and logistical costs. With the children out of the house, Humberto could complete some needed household remodeling, as well as do his various side jobs, which entailed report writing and reading. He said that when he was with his children, he was *really* with them.

Humberto and Suzanne insisted that day-care routine was an important part of a well-lived life. Routines provided a basis for the focused attention needed to accomplish things and a sense of security that reduced stress both now and in the future. Routines and rituals would enable their daughters to cope with the abundance of stimulation and learning found in contemporary society. "They are seeing kind of a routine where they know where I go to work, and they know what I do. They've been to Suzanne's work and they've seen what she does, write on the computer and work on projects or talk on the phone, play, stay home, or run errands. They also see that there's a time for them to go to the preschool day care [and] for them to be creative."

These routines, argued Humberto, "empowered" his daughters by allowing them to understand that everyone had to contribute to the larger good, thereby conveying a message that everyone had value: "I want the girls, regardless of their gender, to understand that there's some value to each person in regards to what they do."

For this couple then, the routines and rituals that gave their family its distinct rhythm and pace were inseparable from a larger belief in the virtue of acting correctly according to the occasion. That was why they attended mass. There the children learned that there were times to be silent, times to sing, and times to pray. At the dinner table, they learned the ritual of discussing the reasons they had to be thankful. This family prized structure, predictability, repetition, and security. These benefited both children and adults, but were also important in and of themselves as timeless markers of the meaning of being human in a fast-paced world.

Consuming

When we began our fieldwork, little did we expect to spend so much time studying consumption. Families, too, denigrated it, announcing that a particular day would be uninteresting to us because it was just for running errands. Yet we soon learned that consumption could be a significant activity for families, whether it occurred in downtown shops or the mall or via catalogs or the Internet.

THE CARLSBERGS: THE BUSYNESS OF FRUGALITY

Purchasing decisions profoundly influenced the busyness of families and connected them to larger institutions, sometimes with unexpected consequences. For Alex Carlsberg, consumption was neither trivial nor an afterthought, but a skilled activity that highlighted his frugality, his ability to find bargains, and his expertise at negotiating the lowest price. He demonstrated this in the ways he made his purchases and discussed them with his wife Pat, and also in the manner in which he taught consumption to his sons. He saved a lot, but at the cost of spending much time looking for bargains. For this family, the deal on a product was more important than the product itself. Family discussions invariably focused on buying for less.

Alex and Pat, children of Depression Era parents, were skeptical about stock market investments as a way to build financial security. Instead, they practiced the virtues of hard work and thrift, exercised within the constraints of life in a large new house. Even though the house was large, well-decorated, and stocked with abundant goods, the Carlsberg emphasis on thrift was evident everywhere, highlighting the juxtaposition of luxuriousness and frugality. For example, Alex bustled around the kitchen one morning preparing lunches for the boys. He offered James a pasta dish for school lunch, which the boy accepted eagerly. James asked where it had come from, and Alex explained that the previous night at work there had been a meeting of "higher ups," and dinner had been catered. After the meal, Alex had taken the leftover food. He said, "I grabbed it for your lunches."

Alex's co-workers recognized his penchant for frugality. When they asked Alex to recommend a mechanic, they knew he would recommend the least expensive one. Alex and Pat used the credit union his employer provided, at least partially because it could not dispense cash; there was an automatic teller machine (ATM) instead. But Alex wouldn't use them if there were any service charges. He switched banks when they added on new charges. Whenever he went out with a group, he always paid the bill with his credit card and then collected cash from the others. He laughed at them because they paid a service fee for using the ATM. It might be small, he said, but they used the ATM so often that the charges added up.

As a rule, Alex avoided charges beyond those for the goods he was purchasing. He looked for bargains on the Internet. He made many online purchases, but added, "I will not pay for convenience." He looked at the price of the product, including the shipping. He compared it with the price at a store, and he bought it wherever it was cheaper. He observed that Internet deals might look good until you added in the charges for shipping and handling.

Still, he made large purchases over the Internet. The doorbell rang; a driver handed Alex a large carton. Alex laughed as he placed the carton in the entry, saying, "Daddy has his new toy." It was a computer that he had bid on through an online auction service. Pat looked slightly askance and said she didn't know he was going to do this. Alex replied that he had told her, and then added, "I wanted . . . I needed. . . ." Pat laughed at his change of verb. Alex immediately rattled off all the machine specifications and price, $589, which he said was cheaper than the components separately.

Alex looked for promotional bargains on the Internet and used them to obtain free prizes. Sometimes, he succeeded, such as when he visited a medical site to get free sneakers, but at other times, his bargains did not pan out. One year, he bought tulip bulbs at a bargain price, but only one grew. His boys, too, were learning how to search the Internet for bargains. They spotted an offer from a pizza franchise for a free music compact disc that had no shipping charge. Alex said this was a particularly good deal.

The quest for bargains bound the family together. One day, the phone rang in Alex's office. His mother informed him that Penney's was having its "sale of all sales," a "50% off clearance. This is definitely the sale you wait for." She had persuaded the store manager that the discount should be off the lowest price tag on the item rather than the original price. "You don't get it [the discount] unless you say so. And you know how to say so, Alex. I know my rights!" Alex was excited: "I'll have to alert Pat and maybe she'll want to swing by there on the way home." He called Pat and left a message that there was a sale, and that she must insist on the 50% off clearance. He added that she might want to stop there on the way home, "Otherwise I may go over tomorrow."

Alex commented, "I expect to get at least half off at a sale, or it's not a sale." Some of his colleagues bought $40 shirts at Macy's, but Alex said, "I would never pay $40 for a shirt." He bought on sale at Penney's or Target, paying around $8. He might buy a shirt from Macys, but only in the closeout bin. A colleague's more expensive shirt might look better, "but not $32 better."

The frugality of the Carlsbergs was thus part of the discourse of their family life, not a mere accompaniment to it. Everyone in the family looked for deals. They did not deny themselves goods and services, but rather bought them as cheaply as possible, looking for deals first and preferred products second.

The family's consumerism was grounded in Alex's philosophy of financial management and its relationship to the good life. Decisions emanated from a conscious orientation to the world. Alex said: "There are two ways to get ahead. The first is to make a lot of money. The second is to spend less. Most people think of the first way, but not the second." While their incomes were well above the national average and they each spent considerable effort building and protecting their careers, Alex and Pat focused less on making more money than on spending less, without denying themselves goods and services. Indeed, Alex was passionate about managing money. "My particular addiction," he said, "is the time value of money as in quantitative business analysis." He had first encountered this approach during a college class, and he recalled how he had been swept away by the power of the idea that money saved today will grow exponentially in the future. "When I go out to buy something, it all comes down to cost. We set our minimal standards and go out and get it." For example, their Toyota Previa was the cheapest van they could find with air conditioning and good gas mileage. The latter was a long-term cost that he always factored into his decision-making.

The danger of Alex's philosophy was that he might purchase unwanted goods and services. The deal was simply too good to pass up. Countering this possibility was the internal list of desired goods that he maintained and used to scan the world at all times. He used shopping at the local flea market as the metaphor for this scanning. "You can't go *looking*, he says; "you get what's there." "You walk around with this huge inventory of things you want. Actually, you look for opportunities."

Sometimes, this outlook led to unforeseen consequences. Under pressure to complete a project in Oakland, Pat decided to combine work with recreation by spending a weekend at the Oakland facility, while Alex and boys relaxed at a hotel with their favorite amenity, a pool with a spa. The plan was for Pat to drive independently to the facility and hotel, meeting Alex and boys there on Saturday evening. Complicating matters was a school project, a meticulously decorated garden bench, which Alex and Pat had to deliver Saturday morning. "It was due there at ten [AM], so we got it there at eleven," Alex joked. Pat then returned home, packed for the trip and headed to her office several miles away to get other materials she needed for the project. She realized that she had forgotten the access code to the Oakland building at home. When she called home, she could not get through to Alex for an hour: He was on the phone planning the school fundraiser with another school fundraiser volunteer. The busy signal she heard was strikingly different from the familiar one, and she was unable to get an operator to interrupt the call. Alex explained later that he had signed up for a new promotional phone service. "It's free, and if it's free, I like the sound of it. I'll try it." So he signed up without fully understanding when it would begin or how it would work, and he had forgotten to tell Pat. The service began on Saturday morning, leading Pat to wonder whether or not she had called the correct number. Futilely, she called neighbors and family members. By now quite worried, she drove to the house; he was unaware of the turmoil he had created. "She was livid," a chagrined Alex said. After she retrieved the code, she realized that she had been so upset that she had left her briefcase at the office, and so she had to detour there on the way to Oakland. "That was not a real good day," Alex said with a tight laugh.

The Carlsberg family valued shopping, and they frequently visited stores after school. They were keen to acquire the latest toys before anyone else, and Alex described racing around the city for the latest deliveries of Pokemon cards. Alex said, "If you're not there when it first comes out, you don't get it. We've been through this enough that I have all the Toys 'R' Us [phone] numbers on my Palm Pilot." When Robert asked why the store could not sell a product until the release date, Alex explained in detail and showed him how to investigate such matters using company web sites.

The search for deals affected even the physical configuration of their house. Alex said their buying habits included "buying things on sale and archiving them." There were cabinets in the upstairs hallway filled with items bought on sale and dispensed throughout the year as gifts. Sometimes, family members purchased items for specific people; at other times, they bought something simply because it would make a good gift for *somebody*. Alex explained that they did this in part to save money and in part because they could not otherwise manage the holiday season. They had a large extended family, which gave presents to everyone: "We're not one of those families that has a lottery," said Alex. They often bought multiple gifts for one person. If Alex bought a sweater for his niece, then he would buy a skirt, too. By buying throughout the year, this family reduced the burden at Christmas.

THE SMITHS: ETHNICITY AND CONSUMPTION

America's democratic pluralism leads to a particular self-consciousness about the kinds of families and communities that people want to create. Parents frequently develop and articulate ideas that affect their parenting practices and the values that they hold dear. All of the families we studied spent time and effort working together on defining who they were, what they stood for, and how they hoped to mold or guide their children's development. Ethnic identity also influences family consumption activities. In our study, Janelle and David Smith provide eloquent examples of this. They also illustrate another aspect of consumption: that it may mirror the very ways in which families blur the boundaries between work and family.

Because of her distinctive appearance, people often misidentified Janelle Smith. One time when she was walking down the street, someone stopped her and asked if she came from Ethiopia. Others mistook her for a Somali or Fulani. They weren't even close: she was Panamanian African-American, fluent in both Spanish and English. And she was proud of her multicultural background.

In her capacity as a bilingual school speech pathologist, Janelle Smith combined aspects of her personal consumption with that of work. Janelle gave speech instruction to disabled children. She constantly looked for new and interesting activities that encouraged children to speak. One of them, which she found in the magazine *Family Fun*, was resist-bleaching imprints of plants on T-shirts. For Janelle, parenting and working overlapped; activities that enriched her children's lives also helped her clients. She used her professional background in her own parenting. Thus she tested her own daughter, Mardi, on her linguistic abilities. Recognizing her own potential parental bias, Janelle automatically subtracted ten points from her daughter's score.

Janelle's principle was flexibility. She improvised when she saw an opportunity to provide a new learning experience and then found ways to acquire the materials to make these events happen. She went to a department store to get the T-shirts for the activity. She was supposed to consult other teachers about their choices, but she could not reach them, since her husband David had her cell phone. She bought more than she needed and figured the return trip would allow her to buy other items for her daughter's upcoming birthday party. As she walked down the aisle, she glanced at Hawaiian shirts for her husband. When she realized it would take too much time to examine them, she postponed doing so.

Janelle mixed school tasks of preparation, paperwork, and provisioning with her personal parenting. Any errand of consumption might serve the needs of their family, their jobs as educators, and the larger endeavor of working on their identity. For example, Janelle and her children Mardi and Mirella took a walk around the university campus where they lived. At the bookstore, the staff had bought some small children's sticker books with multicultural themes. Mardi looked at three books and chose one that featured an African-American model. Janelle discovered a multicultural cookbook for kids; she told the staff that she was pleased about this recent trend in purchasing. She also bought several Spanish-language books for her speech pathology work at a Spanish-immersion magnet school.

But it was David, Janelle's husband, who was the main consumer in the family. David was the director of a university residence hall and a gifted athlete who had just missed making it in the National Basketball Association. Although from a middle-class background, he often related to African-American students by acting street-savvy, using complicated handshakes when he met them on campus. He was comfortable in multicultural and diverse settings and typically took on a different persona when he dealt with different age groups. One of his personas was bargain hunter par excellence. Whether he was buying bulk toothpaste or finding a surgeon for his wife's eye surgery, David took great pride in his success at finding good deals, at being a knowledgeable consumer.

When the Smiths moved to Los Angeles, they continued to emphasize multicultural worlds. Instead of sending Mardi to the large public-school kindergarten near their home, they enrolled her in a private international school that immersed the children in the Spanish and French languages. They planned to send baby Mirella there too when she was old enough. Janelle and David expected their children to be trilingual and multicultural by the time they entered fifth grade. At home, Janelle, David, and their nanny spoke Spanish to the girls. Their quest to develop and foster a multicultural identity did not just happen. They forged it self-consciously, at considerable time, effort, and expense, and they guided their consumption patterns to reinforce that identity.

Charting a Future

THE TRANS: PREPARING A PATH FOR CHILDREN IN A NEW LAND

When parents attempt to design a path for their children, they often impose an enormous burden of busyness that involves not only themselves but also the children. Time, physical effort, financial expenses, and worry may take their toll on everyone in the family. How much more difficult it is when surprises derail parental visions or the children refuse to cooperate or wish to pursue plans of their own that contradict those of the parents. Several families in our study reveal such conflicts. But even when the children accept the vision of their parents and succeed in making it a reality, as the Tran children have done so far, the effort remains substantial.

Binh and Sheila Tran knew exactly what kind of future they wanted for their children, and they set about specifically to make this happen. They exercised extremely tight control over their children, devoting an extraordinary amount of time, effort, and thought to reinforcing their family ties, shaping a family that could succeed in the American educational and economic environment and still retain core Vietnamese values.

To accomplish their goals, Binh and Sheila laid out numerous family tasks and after-school activities for their children, among them that older children take care of younger ones. To pursue their catering business, Binh and Sheila often had to leave the house before their children awakened in the morning. The burden of responsibility for maintaining the morning routine fell squarely on the eldest son, Ron, 16, and to some extent on 11-year-old Ginny. Even if Binh and Sheila had not needed to leave early for work, they would have expected the children to help each other. Binh and Sheila felt confident that their children could take care of themselves in the morning because they had instilled into them the importance of maintaining their routines.

Each weekday morning, Ron helped his younger siblings get ready for school. Ron arose around 5:30, washed, awakened his brother and sister, and made them a breakfast of cereal, bread, and eggs. At 6:40 AM, he walked to school, arriving before his 7:00 AM class.

Ginny was up and dressed by 6:30. She ate cereal for breakfast. She said: "If I haven't finished my homework, I do it. I watch TV while eating. From 6:00 to 7:00, it is the news; from 7:00 to 7:30 *Arthur*; from 7:30 to 8:00 *The Puzzle Place*; and at 8:00 I walk to school."

Because 14-year-old Paul had Down Syndrome, Ron helped him in the morning, usually cajoling his younger brother to get ready and giving him breakfast. After Ron left for school, Ginny looked after Paul until Paul's bus arrived, usually between 7:00 and 7:30 AM. Paul attended a special education class in a school several miles from his home. Ginny remained at home alone until she left for school.

Binh and Sheila were usually at home by the time their children arrived. The children rested for an hour. Then Binh drove them to their martial arts school, about ten miles from home. Binh took lessons with his children. At home, Sheila prepared their meal. Binh and his children returned home around 6:00 PM.

After dinner, Ginny helped with the dishes, did homework, and, practiced perfunctorily on the new piano her father had bought for her. Ron did his homework, and at bedtime led Paul and Ginny in evening prayers.

Sheila devoted her Saturdays to doing things for her children. She drove them to martial arts classes, church youth activities, and sometimes to a large flea market. She used these occasions to reinforce her role in the family as the nurturing parent who sacrifices for her children, creating an emotional bond that the Vietnamese refer to as being "at ease" or "comfortable."[2] What Vietnamese refugees miss most in America is that feeling of being at ease, a sense of support and security, which their families gave them in Vietnam, even during times of war and disruption.

Occasionally, the Trans used their weekends to visit other families or attend church camping trips, in which the parents organized games, religious activities, and dramatic events that focused on famous incidents and people in the history of Vietnam. All of the Tran children were expected to be part of these events, including Paul, who, despite his disability, was always included in all activities.

The guided routine of the children included more than religious training and family activities. All three children were expected to learn and speak Vietnamese. Ron described what this routine meant to him.

> Mom and Dad made me learn Vietnamese. I had to read out loud. She'd hit me with a stick every time I mispronounced words. She'd give me five to ten seconds to get it right. I'd spell it out in my head so that I wouldn't get hit. I was ten to twelve years old at the time. I joined Vietnamese language study and the youth group at the church. Father tells me, "If you don't know your mother's language, you would not have a better education."

Ron continued, "Discipline in the house is Dad. All three of us are afraid of him. He acts seriously. He has a stern look. Mom doesn't do it like that. Mom talks to us, just to make us do things right. They tell us, 'Don't hang around with bad people.'"

When Ron was fifteen, Binh made up a schedule of activities for his children on nonschool free days. He restricted television watching, assigned them household chores, and put them to work in his vending business. They would attend various ethnic festivals, where they sold frozen yogurt.

Binh stated that these rigid routines were to prepare his children for the adult world in America, while maintaining elements of Vietnamese culture.

He did not expect them to rebel, but to follow parental directions. "I never ask my kids if they like or dislike anything," said Binh. Their submissiveness and obedience resulted partly from what they saw happen to their uncle, Binh's younger brother. For a while, he had lived with them, but when he started staying out late, would not account for his activities, and refused to change, Binh threw him out of the house. This lesson did not go unnoticed by Binh's children, who liked their uncle.

Sheila also expressed her approval of filling her children's hours with disciplined and focused activities, and showing them role models to emulate. She said, "On Sunday, I go to church. People teach about good behavior. They do this in a good way. Sometimes if parents teach, it's not as much fun, not happy. While they go to the Vietnamese youth group to learn proper ways to behave, I go to the choir." Sheila told her children to use the children of Binh's older brother as role models. All of them had become engineers and dentists. "The oldest son taught his younger brother and sisters, so all are well educated. Learn from that family."

Once in a while, the Tran children said they did not want to visit relatives or participate in family activities. Sheila and Binh would respond, "If you play with a bad person, you get bad. If you are with a good person, you will become good." Added to this were vague threats of impending doom for the family if the children didn't do as they were told, buttressed with stories about failed families that confirmed these beliefs.

Behind this loomed a larger issue. Binh and Sheila's strategy of child control came at an enormous price, both for them and their children. Binh and Sheila worked with quiet desperation to fend off financial disaster. They also spent a great deal of their time and energy outside of and sometimes during their employment hours attending to child-care issues. The children in turn were constantly beset with various activities arranged for them, goals they had to meet, and pressures they had to cope with to satisfy their parents' expectations. Binh and Sheila knew from experience how hard life could be, and they tried to shield their children from suffering as they had. They did this by utilizing adult-sponsored activities for their children in the fervent hope that this would hide the economic straits this family had fallen into. More important, they expected their guidelines to lead their children along a path of educational and economic success at the same time as they reinforced strong family bonds.

THE SCOTTS: EXECUTIVE FUTURES

The Scott family charted a future grounded in professional development. Both Roy and Michelle Scott were successful top executives, and their vision of what the future would hold derived in great measure from the successes they had achieved in the workplace.

Roy Scott was born in southern central California, into a working-class family. His father ended up working in the oil industry. Neither of his parents had finished high school; both came from large families. He said, "My parents met when they were picking cotton, which is how they were supporting themselves, and their families." They had come as children from Oklahoma and Missouri in the Dust Bowl era. Roy was the first among his cousins on both sides of his family to graduate from college. His education and career directions removed him from his family origins. He remarked dryly, "There's a big social gap, to say the least."

In the mid-1970s, Roy studied physics at the University of California, Los Angeles. He had worked at computer programming, but he was not great at what he did; he did not "eat and drink programming." When he recognized that the opportunities for leadership in that field were limited, he left it and took a job in computer sales in Boston, before eventually taking over the company's territory in Silicon Valley. He became the chief executive at a couple of small software companies, moving back and forth among large companies as a sales vice-president.

After that, Roy took a job at a networking company, which was doing poorly and had undergone massive downsizing. His challenge was to reorganize the company to make it profitable and salable. Here again, he showed his versatility by moving into a new industry and becoming a leader in that one as well. At first, he took on whatever tasks needed to be done: controller, debt collector, finance officer, office manager, and "general flunky," emptying garbage cans and placing sales calls. He found smaller, cheaper space, hired new staff, created a new name, renegotiated debts, and found new financing. He had little time for normal business and managed his family time carefully.

Roy's successes came at a cost for his family. They were, in essence, his hidden infrastructure, for his wife and children had to accommodate to his changes, as did a secretary, who moved from job to job with him, helping him in innumerable ways as he made the transition to new settings.

Still, something had to give, and it was his wife, Michelle, a southerner from a middle-class family. Previously, she had been an executive in a large electronics company. To more easily juggle parenthood and work, she now took a job in a lower-pressure nonprofit forecasting research company as chief financial officer. The pressure at her new job was less, but not her busyness. Along with her duties as a financial officer, she also was in charge of human resources, space management, and Internet/intranet articulation with payroll.

One day, Michelle was so engrossed in working with a new formula to simplify payroll accounting that she forgot to pick up her daughter Crystal from day care. She looked up, chagrined, and remarked: "That was so fun! That was why I forgot all about my daughter." Late pickup cost twenty dollars for each five-minute increment beyond the deadline. Crystal was almost always the last one picked up.

Their lifestyle was hectic, but both Roy and Michelle flourished in their executive worlds. Moreover, they had an optimistic view of the future. Given his long record of successes, Roy assumed that he could always find a job quickly. The Scotts moved to southern California and bought a large house. Their timing could not have been worse. The recession of 2000 had begun, and he could not find employment. They sold the house and moved into a smaller one. Neither he nor his wife had a job yet. Roy became a consultant and Michelle trained to become a nurse.

THE SCHWARTZES: TO THE BEACHES OF NORMANDY

Linda and Arthur used their successes as affluent, highly educated attorneys to emphasize certain values for their daughters: Jewish ethnicity, community involvement, professional prowess and a passion for education were what mattered. Linda often told a cautionary tale to Sonya and her six-year-old sister, Hettie. When Linda was in high school, all girls were required to take a course in home economics. Two girls in the class, none too bright in Linda's view, had painted their fingernails with white correction fluid and later dropped out to be teenage mothers. Their plight became the crux of a Schwartz family joke: either you go to college or you become good at saying "Do you want fries with that?"

The values conveyed were more than those of financial independence;

they were also preparation for a fulfilling life. After school, Sunny (Sonya), the older daughter, studied Hebrew, music, and karate and played sports, while Hettie, the younger daughter, was poised to begin these activities. Of course, all this increased the family's busyness. A nanny took them to various scheduled events. Even the selection and instruction of the nannies reaffirmed the family's values. The best nannies, according to Arthur and Linda, were those training to be teachers, who could both do household work and offer larger lessons in education, art, and culture.

Nannies allowed the family to pack in the activities that were both personally fulfilling and linked to creating a desirable future. They insulated the family members from each other's busyness, until breaks in routines compelled them to pay closer attention. When Reta, the nanny, had an ulcerated eye and could not drive, a parent had to fetch the Schwartz children from school. At 1:30, Arthur picked up Sonya and took her to his office; at 2:30 he returned for Hettie. But this interrupted Sonya's tight sequence of activities: soccer practice from 4:00 to 5:30, followed by half a session of Hebrew school, not to mention that she missed her piano lesson. She had to make this up on another day, along with her karate lesson. Further complicating family logistics, her schedule conflicted with that of her sister. Hettie had soccer practice with Arthur until 5:30, while Sonya's karate continued until 5:45.

Linda commented that it was hard "being so busy and trying to make sure that when Sunny has conflicts . . . I'm scheduling around them getting alternatives." When Hebrew school conflicted with soccer, Linda hired a private tutor for Sonya. She also had to take Hettie to basketball at 6:00, then Hebrew school thirty-five minutes later, resulting in an incomplete basketball practice. Once home, she prepared dinner for Hettie. Linda sighed: "That stresses me out, but she likes to do it so much. I don't let her know how much it does [stress me]. I just do it. I get it done."

Schwartz family values were reflected not just in activities but in their home as well. The family room displayed vibrant colors, tribal masks, and Mexican folk art. The windows contained succulents and Mexican pottery. Masks from Native America, Mexico, Africa, and Indonesia hung from one wall, along with a Purim-style mask made by Hettie. Linda's mother was an artist, and Linda herself collected art. In addition to the dining table, the room contained an eight-foot-tall stylized ostrich and raven totem pole. Displayed throughout the house were other artifacts, which portrayed a family that was engaged in world cultures, art, and issues. Talk within the family confirmed that these were important for individuals to understand.

Religion, too, played a large role in family life. Arthur, along with 50 percent of America's Jews, had married outside the faith.[3] Linda converted upon marrying and became a leader in the local Jewish community, visiting her daughters' classrooms to do annual presentations on Hanukkah. The girls studied Hebrew and regularly attended Sunday school. Sunny's Bat Mitzvah was a major event in all their lives.

Before a European vacation that included a trip to Normandy and its relics of D-Day, they rented *Saving Private Ryan* and watched it together. Although ordinarily Linda and Arthur would not allow their children to watch such a movie, they wanted Sunny and Hettie to prepare for the journey and to understand the invasion. Once there, they stayed at a friend's house in Normandy and rented a Mercedes to drive around France. Linda said that when she and Arthur stood on the beach in a solemn moment they were also struck that such a beautiful place had been the sight of such carnage in 1944. The two girls were playing in the bunkers, making Linda and Arthur feel uncomfortable. Later, when they took the girls to the cemetery, the couple was stunned by the thousands of grave markers. Sunny said she did not see why this was so important to them, and Arthur replied, "These people died so that this Jewish family could drive across Europe in a Mercedes." At first, Linda and the girls thought that Arthur was delivering another of his dry, satirical jokes, but then the impact of his words sobered them. Their affluent and worldly life rested on the sacrifices of the soldiers at Normandy. Their vacation was another opportunity to place their family in a larger context of world history and to learn lessons for the future.

Conclusions

The families we were studying, like many in America, had no difficulty in expressing that they were both busy and overwhelmed with work and family commitments. But when asked specifically how they were busy, the people we studied seemed to be perplexed by the very question. We suspect that others would respond similarly.

Being busy seems to state the obvious, a brute fact of life. When someone asks us "How are you?" we often reply without thinking, "Busy, busy," as if that said it all. Sometimes, we think of being busy in spatial, geographic terms, as having a finite "length" of time before us as we puzzle over how to "fit" everything "into" it. Or we may join in a conversation with friends or co-workers in which we nod sagely and complain that life is speeding up, even though what is moving faster is unclear.

All of these expressions presuppose that busyness is a single phenomenon shared among all families, and initially that is what we thought. After a while, we realized that while people spoke a similar language of busyness, the facts of *their* busyness were distinctive. While work and family obligations were important, these obligations differed significantly among families. Put differently, what people thought of as work or family varied widely. Some people defined "family" as having to do with caring for aged or ill relatives, while for others it was dealing with a child's school. One family might define dealing with school and homework as an intrusion into family time, while others saw this as an exhibition of family commitment or solidarity. Often families defined a particular activity, such as watching rented movies on Friday nights, as their quintessential family activity. They would insist that if we were to understand them, we had to observe that activity. They might discourage us from accompanying them on Saturday since they were simply running errands, which they didn't see as a family activity, even though they spent more time together doing this than at any other time during the week. Family, family obligations, and family time provided a common language for people to discuss their lives, but this language concealed as much as it revealed.

Thus busyness was not so much a unitary, brute fact of life as something that had distinct rhythms or textures in different families and among different individuals. The common language was misleading, for it allowed people to talk as if their experiences were identical, with the implication that the solutions to busyness were shared. But this was far from the actual situation. Families are busy in distinct ways, general solutions to busyness are unhelpful, and any understanding of busyness must be based on what we learn in detail about how *we* are busy. We are never busy in general, only in particular ways, with particular consequences, which are ours alone. In this sense, busyness unites us, but at the same time it signals the differences among us. It makes each of us the author and actor in our own stories.

CHAPTER THREE

Why Are We Busy?

Fieldwork provided a deep, richly detailed view of people's obligations and commitments and how they translated into daily tasks. Of course, we were delighted to watch as they performed those activities, and we listened attentively as they explained what they were doing. The picture that emerged provided glimpses into everyday life not available from quantitative research, which, while certainly useful for some purposes, largely reflects what the researcher deems interesting and important. For example, John Robinson and Geoffrey Godbey speak of four types of time as fundamental: paid work, household/family care, personal time, and free time.[1] Classifying specific activities under these headings is comfortable and familiar. It also allows researchers to formulate commonsense questions to ask people about what they do. But it also places their answers in procrustean categories. Even if we measured the relative proportions of each "type" of time, we would fail to grasp fully the experiences of people as they make their way through daily life. We would be overlooking both the meaning of their activities to them and the complex interdependencies and contingencies of their days. It would also eliminate from study what people do but lack the vocabulary to describe.

We were learning something different: How people saw their lives and what really mattered about them—and to them. Capturing these perspectives was at the heart of our fieldwork, and it is at the heart of this book. Yet how we looked at families had consequences for how we portrayed their lives. We naturally focused on individuals. After all, we spent our time shadowing and chatting with them. Our descriptions reflected how they accounted for their lives and activities, and they did so largely by talking about the choices they made. But regardless of how people spoke of their decisions, we also saw that they were constrained in their choices. Alex Carlsberg might *choose* to enroll in all of his employer's training classes to become a more versatile middle-aged worker, but that employer had laid off most of his co-workers and was threatening to relocate its operations to another state. Kent and Peggy Hopkins/Johnson *chose* to purchase a small tract house near their workplaces. Still, the house was exorbitantly priced in the region's red-hot housing market, and they could have found a cheaper one farther away. But that decision would have lengthened their commutes and reduced their time with their preschooler, Sam. What we were observing were the internal responses of people to external constraints, but once people responded to these constraints and made choices, these in turn created other constraints.

Choices such as those made by Alex, Kent, and Peggy were commonplace, but lurking behind them were what we call drivers of busyness, which are both self-created and externally imposed on people. Often members of the families were astute in their assessment of the consequences of these drivers for their daily lives, while at other times they did not see them constraining what they chose and how they made choices.

These drivers of busyness suggest that busyness is about something more than individual lives and experiences; it is also about the society we have made. We do not live in isolation, and the contours of busyness in our lives are not just matters of personal choice. Individuals may feel the weight of commitments or obligations on their shoulders, but they bear those loads within a particular society. Busyness can thus not be understood just by talking to people and watching them in different settings. To understand the drivers of busyness, we need also to connect the minutiae of people's daily lives to the larger contexts in which they are lived.

Looking for Drivers

Because we had conducted studies in Silicon Valley during the booming 1990s, we were not surprised to find that work loomed large in the families. People worked long hours, often at home after their children were asleep. In addition, people frequently used work and jobs as metaphors. For example, a teacher might explain to her students that their obligation to learn was their "job." So we wondered if the importance of work was distinctive to Silicon Valley or if it represented a broader phenomenon.

There is, in fact, a large literature about the changing importance of work, and its relationship with family lies at the core of busyness. Understanding this relationship is the focus of an emerging interdisciplinary field that has involved universities, the government, and private foundations.[2] Specialists in work-life policies and issues have their own professional associations and conferences, and they are employed in the human resources departments of many companies to advise on corporate policies and create programs for overworked employees.

Over the years, they also have disagreed on some fundamental issues. The economist Juliet Schor argues that Americans are increasingly working longer hours, a thesis that seemed intuitively correct until subsequent research questioned these results and spawned a national debate.[3] Jerry Jacobs argues that the average workweek of Americans has remained relatively constant for the past thirty years. Men in the labor force worked an average of 43.1 hours in 2000, versus 43.5 hours in 1970; the corresponding figures for women were 37 hours (2000) and 37.1 (1970).[4] Similarly, Robinson and Godbey claim that the increase in reported leisure activities is not consistent with Schor's thesis. There are just not enough hours in a week to account for both increased leisure and hours at work.[5] Jacobs points out, however, that the constant average number of hours at work masks an increasing split in the workforce between managers and professionals, who work more hours, and others who work fewer.[6] For some workers, hours at work have increased, partially explaining the palpable sense of time pressure. The fact that many workers are multitasking only complicates how we interpret hours spent at work.

The intersection of families and work also reveals sources of busyness. Beginning in the 1970s, greater numbers of women, including those who were married, entered the labor force, and this led to a dramatic increase in the work of parents. In 1970, dual-earner couples collectively worked an average of 52.5 hours a week. and almost two-thirds (63.4%) worked fewer than 70 hours a week. By 2000, that average had increased to 63.1 hours, and only 53.7 percent were working fewer than 70 hours. Close to 10 percent (9.3%) were working over 100 hours a week. Furthermore, dual-earner couples comprised 35.9 percent of all couples in 1970, but 59.6 percent in 2000, making them more common in 2000 than male-breadwinner couples were in 1970.[7]

The increase in dual-earner families and nonstandard work hours ultimately affects the busyness of households. In 1970, 38 percent of mothers had paid employment; by 2000, that participation in the labor force had risen to 68 percent. For mothers of the youngest children (birth to age 3), labor-force participation increased from 24 percent to 58 percent during the same period.[8] Given their time constraints, families find it increasingly difficult to do routine domestic chores. In 1965, mothers did an average of 32.1 hours of housework a week, a figure that had dropped to 18.6 hours by 2000. Fathers increased their housework from 4.4 to 9.5 hours during the same period. In 1965, mothers put in 7.3 times the number of housekeeping hours fathers did; in 2000, they spent only twice as much time on it.[9] In effect, since the 1970s, many couples have been doing the work of two paid employees and a domestic assistant.

Child care has also been affected. In general, time with their children has remained fairly constant for mothers, while among married fathers, it has increased noticeably.[10] For fathers in 1965, an average of 24 minutes a day were devoted to activities in which child care was primary (mothers spent 90 minutes). By 1998, it had increased to 60 minutes (102 minutes for mothers). Time spent with children in any activity rose for fathers from 2.8 hours a day in 1965 to 3.8 in 1998. Mothers spend more time with children than fathers, but the gap has narrowed. For example, in 1965, fathers spent half as much time in any activities with children as did mothers, while in 1998 they were spending almost two-thirds as much.[11] An implication is that time devoted to housework, especially by mothers, has been reduced to maintain time spent with children.

Both work and family have also undergone changes, complicating time comparisons between them. One of the changes in work process has been the proliferation of voluntary and involuntary options for when a person should work. The sociologist Harriet Presser refers to this phenomenon as the "death of diurnal time" and speaks of the shift to a "24/7 economy." The proliferation of service jobs in areas such as recreation and health care drive the expansion of the workweek into the weekend and evening. Global production requires night shifts to maximize productivity. Making those diverse shifts work within a family requires management and compromise.[12] In professional work, changing work practices mean working across time zones, working longer days—9.6 hours and at least 50 hours a week.[13] Telecommuting, compressed workweeks, and flexible time add to the management burden of the household, for each shift must be anticipated and accommodated. The inevitable result is that other workers, too, must be available to deliver those services. One-quarter of all couples with at least one spouse employed have a spouse working nonstandard hours (nights, rotating shift work, weekends). That percentage increases to 30.6 percent for couples with children.[14]

Further complicating comparisons based just on time, families may also reveal intensified parental involvement in child care. Smaller family sizes, the reluctance of parents to permit unsupervised children's play, and preferences for structured, formalized children's activities require adults to transport and supervise their children. Many parents have also become more involved in their children's education and recreational activities, reflecting shifting norms of good parenting. These intensified activities lead to an increase in busyness, with little change in familiar measures of time on the job or with the family. Many examples in our book call attention to intensified parenting activities. The Schwartz parents used family vacations as teaching devices for their children, while the Tran parents brought their children along to maintain their catering truck as a means of building family bonds.

This intensification of activities or performance standards may extend beyond parenting. Family members often emphasized one aspect of their lives or another, trying to reach the highest standard of excellence, either as connoisseurs or performers. Arthur Schwartz, for example, did not just jog; he ran marathons. Alex Carlsberg did not simply consume; he found the very best bargains. Ethan Rodgers sang, performed in school theater, and participated in community service as part of his own personal enrichment agenda as a high-school student. This intensification of performance standards in turn drives busyness in many families.

Technology also looms large as a driver of busyness. As we shadowed family members and took notes on what they did, we found ourselves describing their interactions with various devices. Many of the people we were observing did at least some of their work using laptop computers perched on a convenient surface in the home, often after the children had gone to bed. Telephones, cellular or otherwise, generally were not discussed and had blended into the background, but they facilitated flows of information about jobs, organizations, projects, and regulations. Technology allowed work to *be*—rather than to *be taken*—everywhere.

Not only has the timing of work changed, but professional work has become more abstract in nature, requiring new skills and complex management. Contemporary accounting requires understanding software systems, multinational tax environments, and the specifics of organizational procedure and practice.

Worksites can be relocated and globally distributed,[15] but the effects of technology and abstraction were evident in homes and among family members. In fact, the same technologies, tasks, and skills associated with work were often part and parcel of running a household and being a responsible family member. We came to appreciate a new work of house holding that transcended the old "do-it-yourself" model. Understanding mortgages, individual retirement accounts, and the nuances of various insurance policies require an ability to track and manage information. Monitoring the cat's blood glucose data or a middle-aged woman's calcium intake also means handling data.

Devices and technological systems such as the Internet thus provide the conduits through which information flows, binding together workplace and home, jobs and family. While technology is not the only reason, it has certainly enabled the flow of tasks among different spheres of life. Seeing the effects in families was far more compelling than mere talk of keeping work and family separate, which was probably only necessary because the overlap was so obvious.

Despite the importance of technology, its effects hardly transform everything about daily life. People spoke of how parts of their lives were lived virtually, irrespective of the limits of time and space, but they were still subject to the constraints of Newtonian physics. As we describe in the next chapter, faith in the virtual is belied by the emphasis on creating routines, planning, and backup plans, all grounded in the constraints of space and time. Commuting, telecommuting, and distributed work, multiple school sites and after-school enrichment programs mean that people in working families must literally navigate topographies that can shape their choices. The geographer Helen Jarvis, writing about household coordination in London, argues that resolving the demands of employment and household involves moral dilemmas that are shaped by physical context.[16] She could have been describing the lives of families in Silicon Valley.

While local terrain constrains the busyness of families, global connections also penetrated many households. Information technology informed people about events elsewhere and involved them in dramas half a world away. The Australian Kent Hopkins began each day in his cubicle reading the online version of his hometown newspaper. He glanced at snippets throughout the day, and by day's end, he had read most of it. Much of this was simply keeping in touch with his Australian heritage, but it also allowed Kent to keep track of information that he and his wife, Peggy Johnson, could use to decide whether the time was right to relocate. Meanwhile, Peggy, who worked for a subsidiary of a Japanese corporation, tried to understand all things Japanese better. Even reporting events in the company newsletter provided opportunities for exploring the subtleties of cross-cultural communication.

Other families were similarly caught up in new global realities. Sophia Rodriguez, Bill Allen's wife, was very much at home in Silicon Valley, but her elderly father, who lived in Mexico, traveled annually to visit his daughter and receive medical care in the United States. Sophia had to arrange the logistics for his visits and help with the paperwork from two countries. The Mohans regularly visited their relatives in India. Binh Tran, on one of his recent trips to his native Vietnam, had sent back the elaborately carved rosewood furniture and the red and gold silk cushions that now dominated the family living room. Pat Carlsberg always struggled with how to allocate time to work and family; travel created special dilemmas for this mother of two boys. After our fieldwork ended, these dilemmas had been exacerbated by a new project that regularly required her to make lengthy trips to Italy.

Work, family, community, and even the ways Americans think of themselves in the world have all been affected by what has been called a "transnational revolution."[17] The effects of this revolution are varied and include the uncertainty and fear that distant events may affect local lives. For example, the hopes of the Tran family, for whom the American Dream was enshrined in their catering truck, were dashed when companies affected by an Asian economic crisis began laying off the workers who were their customers. The Trans' business collapsed, demonstrating a harsh reality of busyness in contemporary America: it is lived against a backdrop of uncertainty and even fear. We encountered people who were well aware that economic prosperity today could vanish tomorrow. Alex Carlsberg constantly upgraded his skills as protection against corporate capriciousness, just as his wife continued to work long hours to protect her job—and benefits—just in case. Bill Allen and his wife Sophia demonstrated a firm commitment to meeting their employers' needs and actively traded and sold real estate to build a hedge against the perils of living on moderate incomes in an expensive area. Humberto Mendoza turned financial management into a virtual part-time job, scrupulously watching and reallocating the family's resources. Suzanne, his wife, confirmed the wisdom of this strategy, for she had seen many in her profession of marketing earn substantial incomes but still live beyond their means.

Such concerns shaped decision-making in the families, often very explicitly. Individuals were well aware that mergers have reorganized the corporate landscape. Downsizing and the rise of contingent labor have led to new labor insecurity, even in the middle class. Corporate downsizing and reorganizations, outsourcing jobs to foreign locations, and new forms of corporate control may serve to remind people of the precariousness of jobs and intensify the demands on work life. The fear of "falling from grace" so eloquently described by Katherine Newman was palpable, even in boom times.[18]

Other drivers of busyness were revealed when we spent evenings with the families. "Family time," that presumed bedrock of domestic life, was often spent in articulating the lives of family members with other institutions. To be sure, families did spend considerable time helping family members in various ways or simply being with them. But much that was "family" was actually driven by other institutions, so that the family became a buffer between them and its members. Homework is an example. A familiar evening ritual was dinner, followed by completing any remaining homework. On the one hand, this secular ritual is quite unremarkable, and it is clearly focused on an activity that is nominally good for children and their futures. On the other hand, homework is a symbol of the government's power, an interloper into the private lives of families. It also serves to connect families to the school's increasingly complex set of requirements. Schools can use homework to communicate what is happening on campus, keeping parents "involved in the day-to-day experiences of their children's schooling."[19] Such communications may take on a moral tone when educators argue that parental involvement is the key to higher academic achievement. Homework thus shifts schoolwork to the family, which then must fit it into its routines. Doing so drives hidden work in time management and household organization. Family thus comes to serve as an extension of the classroom, with its discourse about success, skills, knowledge, and discipline.

Each family chose how to handle the burden of homework, yet this was only part of the decision-making process. More was going on than simply moving some activities out of institutions and into the household. For example, Suzanne Jones and Humberto Mendoza could have chosen to provide child care through their own efforts or those of family, but they carefully screened preschool after preschool to find the right private provider. They planned to engage in a similar process when the girls attended elementary school. Such school choice can translate into significant work for middle-class families in making and maintaining such choices. Wealthier parents can opt for private education, although as the Carlsberg family illustrates, this may mean significant "volunteer" work. Parents who cannot afford private education must make do with public schools and invest major portions of their time in getting the "right" school or the "right" teacher.[20]

Choosing among schools was only one aspect of a much broader trend toward deregulation that played out in the families. Collectively, the result is a proliferation of choices that "empower" us to make decisions, regardless of our desire or competency to do so. Banks that formerly offered ordinary customers just a handful of services and accounts now market aggressively and provide a bewildering variety of options. The variety of pension plans and investment options has likewise increased, providing us with both choices and obligations to educate ourselves about issues where the stakes are high. A wide variety of health insurance plans and providers are available, and the Internet allows us to become our own medical diagnosticians. Pharmaceutical ads on television instruct us what a reasonable person should ask of his or her doctor. Deregulated markets for utilities and airlines provide us more opportunities to choose, with the simultaneous necessity to "do it yourself."[21] The variety of educational institutions and programs has proliferated, but even here, our careers are largely our responsibilities, just something else to be managed. At the same time, we become partners in our children's education, often providing resources and instruction that are beyond the means of cash-strapped schools.

To make informed choices regarding these facets of our lives, a person needs expertise that requires information. The information available on any one topic is vast, and it is virtually impossible to acquire expertise in all of the topics that people need to deal with in their daily lives. But that is the responsibility placed on us with empowerment. No wonder many people express bewilderment at the choices they are constrained to make.

Deregulation has taken different forms in different industries, and it has undoubtedly resulted in instances of new services being offered or extended to new market segments and lower costs. Whether the proliferation of choices has resulted in a general increase in satisfaction is less clear.[22] What is certain is that responding to such imposed choices becomes a time-consuming activity.[23]

Ironically, deregulation is accompanied by a proliferation of rules and requirements to which families must adhere. The regulations may not be governmental, but are created by a variety of organizations. Private schools have their own rules to follow. When Ethan Rodgers took an early morning math class at a local community college, he did not realize that its rules would conflict with those of his Catholic high school. The latter granted dispensation for attending a religious retreat; the public college did not view that as a valid reason for missing class. Workplace policies abound in their variety and inconsistency. One spouse's workplace may provide insurance that covers foot surgery, but the other's does not. Who is covered, when, and by what?

Deregulation, with its hopes of unleashing individual initiative, is also associated with faith in community volunteerism. We listened as families that already had much to do volunteered to do more in order to build their local community, make themselves into good people, or otherwise get what they wanted. Sometimes "volunteering" was oxymoronic; it was required. Its scope was large, ranging from spontaneously helping out elderly neighbors or a friend in need, or just always being willing to lend a hand, to holding formal office in organizations. But the needs were great, and volunteering had a magnetic attraction for many people.

We also watched as families assembled relationships, things, and ideas into coherent lifestyles and their identities as families. To be a family was not simply given; it was the result of decisions about how to be a family and how to choose activities that enacted their vision.[24] We followed the Trans as they built a family identity based on the parents' upbringing in Vietnam, their experiences as immigrants, and their lives amid American communities and institutions. The Scotts also created a family identity, but one primarily constructed out of Roy's educational and professional successes. The Carlsbergs crafted themselves as the family that would volunteer when no one else would.

These then are some of the drivers of busyness we saw as we learned more and more about our fourteen families. We do not claim these are the only drivers of busyness and, in fact, we are sure that fieldwork among other families would reveal additional ones. We do claim, however, that they are very real in their effects on the families we came to know, and there are good reasons to believe that the experiences of these families are not exceptional. The drivers of busyness are not as discrete as the previous discussion might suggest, and their effects are complicated. They come together in idiosyncratic ways that drive the busyness of each family, as the following vignettes indicate.

Empowered Individuals?

ALEX CARLSBERG: THROUGH THE WHITEBOARD

Hands on hips, Alex gazed at the whiteboard attached to one wall of his office. Whiteboards are standard issue in high-tech cubicles and offices. More often than not they are covered with layers of partially erased boxes, arrows and labels, faded impressions of schemes that typically are indecipherable to outsiders. Alex's board contained no such diagrams, only a list of names, numbers and other words that reminded him of things to do. Although he carried a personal digital assistant, he was too busy to bother entering his "to do" lists in it. Instead, he preferred to gaze at his cryptic whiteboard.

Decoding the whiteboard uncovered the roots of Alex's busyness. "Alicia" and a phone number reminded him of an ongoing dispute with an insurance company regarding coverage of his wife Pat's chronic medical problem. The latter had been exacerbated by several traffic accidents, but the couple's medical insurance carrier would not pay the mounting bills until Alex and Pat agreed to settle a lawsuit regarding the accident. Alex was handling the case himself, because, he said, he feared an attorney would just say, "Sign the settlement, give me 50 percent, and get out of my office." The case was still unresolved after two years.

"Frances-David" and another phone number reminded him that he had to recover files from a co-worker who had been laid off. Alex had not been told that she was leaving, and data about all the projects she had been working on had been "dumped" onto a magnetic backup tape. Somehow, he had to find the tape and extract the relevant data.

"FSA" was his reminder that the Internal Revenue Service owed him money and the steps he had to take to get it back, while "Mac OS9 Turbo Tax" was a prompt to complete the paperwork for a rebate from Apple Computers.

"Kaiser Sacto" referred to a string of appointments he had to make with doctors in Sacramento in order to prepare for his father's surgery. Alex would need to rise early, drive his father to the distant hospital, and then return the same day. He anticipated several such day-long round trips. The next prompt also involved his parents. "Ralph" and a phone number directed him to increase the liability insurance on a rental house that he managed for them. He was unfamiliar with the agent, who had handled his parents' accounts, and Alex needed to call to find out the new premium.

Three names and numbers were scrawled on a corner of the board. The first called attention to a "technical issue" at work, which Alex needed to learn more about. The other two referred to items he had long forgotten. A bit removed from this was a cluster of three personal names, telephone numbers, and abbreviated company names. With a smile, he explained that these were related to the Internet company he dreamed of founding. He hoped that this would provide him with a way out if the company he worked for relocated to another city.

Next to these reminders were a few happy birthday wishes written by co-workers with dry-erase markers. Taped neatly to the whiteboard was a note printed carefully on a sheet torn from a newsprint tablet: "Daddy. Please ask your boss to let you come home early from work so you can play with me. I love you, Robert."

The whiteboard is almost too ordinary to notice and few of his co-workers bother to glance at it. Yet each message is a portal into a different sphere of Alex's life and the busyness that defines his days and weeks. Ask about one of them and stories emerge, comic, dramatic, or just frustrating. Each provides a glimpse into Alex's distinctive world, just as they remind us that he is not alone: millions of Americans live their lives in front of such portals that lead to the drivers of their own busyness.

ARTHUR SCHWARTZ: MIXING PROFESSION AND BUSINESS

Arthur Schwartz was a partner in a law firm that took on cases against insurance companies that refused to pay for attorney's fees. The legal issues ranged from sexual harassment cases that involved insurers to ones related to the Americans with Disabilities Act. Details, of course, mattered; after all, his clients were paying for him to have mastered them. The exact provisions of numerous policies and the legal decisions that surrounded each issue of litigation were daily fare. The environment was also one marked by stress and high stakes. Arthur quipped, "There is a hotline between insurance companies and God, so when people cancel insurance, horrible things happen."

Arthur was flooded with messages. As the secretary dropped more mail on his desk, he joked, "Incoming mail is like incoming missiles. I could die face down in an insurance book and my in-box would continue to fill up." Arthur constantly called clients, previous rounds of affiliated attorneys, and attorneys for the insurance companies. Because cases were negotiated, the information needs changed frequently, and he had to make sure he had access to the currently relevant data. Often he had to ask for documents from any given insurance company "about twelve times" just to resolve one case.

His wife Linda's work as an attorney focused on property issues within complex regulatory contexts. The American Disabilities Act, for example, specified kinds of construction that then had to be reconciled with various local codes. Protecting delicate electronic equipment used in manufacturing semiconductors required familiarity with still other regulations. Because Linda was often dealing with nonroutine decisions, discovering the relevant information could be a challenge. In addition, she had to understand how to interact effectively with people working within the different organizations and professions that were involved in particular cases.

One day, Linda looked forlornly at a stack of documents on construction and ownership. She picked up one and said, "It would be an interesting study about how we got from a handshake to documents like this! People complain lawyers cause problems, and they do cause some problems, but the reason for a document like this is people don't pay their bills." Law offices, said Linda, are built on "whole forests of paper." However, as those offices make the shift to electronic environments, attorneys' work practices change.

Over two decades, Arthur had also seen the flows of information through his office change. He had to sift through more information and handle more communications than before. He used an e-mail listserv where attorneys discussed how to frame particular cases and gleaned information pertinent to them. Tasks increasingly required expert knowledge, and so he had seen the support staff ratio decline from one staff member per attorney to one per three attorneys.

Arthur had bought a software program to help track his legal work, but it generated tasks of its own, such as the installation of a computerized accounting system. The program billed clients in fifteen-minute increments and included not only the attorneys' time, but that of the staff. A field allowed him to document what he said or did on behalf of the client, thereby maintaining a record that protected him against lawsuits. Still, the upgrade on this software program was filled with bugs. Arthur observed, "You would think if they were going to release a product to market, especially time slips for lawyers, they would be more careful." Apparently, the software company's web site contained angry messages from some of its customer attorneys. Arthur's firm had hired a consultant from the company to customize the legal library computer, but a redundant manual system remained in place for the times when the program failed.

Linda's ideas about the practice of law had also changed. As a student, she had not anticipated "client interaction irritation and the headaches of running a business." She had only thought about going to court and right-ing wrongs, and this was still important to her professional identity. As both her children often said, Linda "helps people." Linda joked that she was "a modern-day person on a horse with a jousting stick solving problems that they [the clients] cannot solve."

Linda also had to juggle the business of the practice, making sure that the office was functioning and staffed appropriately. Which was the worst day in Linda's life, so went the family joke: the day of her labor and Sonya's delivery or the bar exam? The answer was the bar exam. Birth traumas were over in a day, but her anxiety as a practicing attorney lived on. She was anxious about delivering value to her clients and treating them fairly. She worked hard to replace a legal secretary who had retired and a junior attorney who had been seduced away from the firm by stock options during the dot-com boom. Linda made sure that each calendar and billing system worked, and that redundant systems were in place should something go wrong, a point driven home forcefully when a new computer-based calendaring program failed to inform her of a court date. New technologies, regulations, and ways of practicing law drew her into a world quite different from the one she had dreamed about as a student.

Work often permeated the couple's thoughts at home, even though they strove to keep it separate. When they discussed troublesome cases, their daughter Sunny (Sonya), sensing their tension, would mutter softly, "the Neil case," referring to a particularly difficult case that had absorbed her father. When Arthur gave his trademark sigh of work frustration, Sunny and her sister Hettie teased him by calling it a "Neil sigh."

Arthur said his priority was "to make enough time for our family," but the challenge was to do "everything that we need to do in the time that's given to us." He downplayed his professional success, saying, "It's too wacky to get caught up in work. One of my partners who doesn't work a lot says there's no tombstone that says, 'Gee, I wish I had worked a few more hours.'" Still, he worked those hours, and his two daughters were well aware of the emotional cost of doing so. They once told him that he had been away from home too much, so he stayed home and left unused a prized ticket to a Rolling Stones concert. Sonya in turn canceled an outing with a friend so that she could spend time with him.

The saga of the Schwartzes' work life is quite ordinary, yet in it we can see the gradual changes that transform everyday life. They were professionals at heart and loved the practice of law, which they saw as making a contribution to society. Yet the context within which their practice existed was characterized by demands on them that they had never anticipated when they started their careers. They may have been "empowered," but they were required to deal with more complex and diverse regulations, and they were tethered to the peculiarities of software programs and the need to interact with various organizations. Although their empowerment did indeed allow them more decisions, coupled with their self-imposed effort to keep work out of their family and home life, it also brought new constraints.

D E B B I E   C A R S O N :   T H E   B U R D E N S   O F   E M P O W E R M E N T

While Martin Klein was juggling tasks as his workplace changed corporate hands, his wife Debbie Carson was awash in health-related choices managing her family's care. Debbie constantly weighed shifting ideas about what constituted appropriate health activities. Her range of medical responsibilities included herself, her sons, her parents, and even her aging and diabetic cat, Tristan. She lived within a web of diagnoses, the most problematic being multiple chemical sensitivities. She used a prominent HMO, vetting her biomedical diagnoses and therapies through a traditional Chinese medical naturopath who had earned her trust. She took up to a hundred pills a day, including homeopathic remedies, vitamins, Chinese herbs, and biomedical pharmaceuticals. Debbie's medical marketplace was complex and global. Martin helped her find particular Chinese medications while he traveled for work in Europe, although he did not share her confidence in alternative medicines.

Debbie could not easily go to any public space where people wore fragrances or where there were traces of cleaning chemicals. When, in her new career as a historical interpreter, her museum was remodeled, she had to quit, since the paint and glue fumes were unbearable to her. So Debbie monitored her environment closely and used special soaps and paints. She educated her family and friends to avoid scented products. She had become familiar with an array of suppliers where she could purchase unscented products, low-toxicity new materials that did not off-gas, and sealants, air filters, and masks that blocked organic vapors. Multiple chemical sensitivities is a diagnosis that receives little or no institutional support for disability management; it was Debbie's burden and a core feature of her busyness.

Her youngest son, Ethan Rodgers, was diagnosed with attention deficit hyperactivity disorder (ADHD/ADD), and Debbie monitored his behavior and managed his medications unremittingly. In addition, each year she requested the medical records for each family member, archived pharmaceutical containers, including over-the-counter medications, and documented every medical interaction. Each therapy was researched, documented, photocopied, and its effect noted. She investigated each prescription online and collected opinions of peers and various practitioners. These activities involved not just looking up the names of pharmaceuticals, but also critically examining each one. Debbie said, "I looked at the ADD support groups and I've got all of the material from CHADD—Children and Adults with ADD. CHADD is heavily funded by the pharmaceutical industry—about 80 percent funded by the people who make Ritalin. So, gee. Guess what their literature all touts? Ritalin!" A former high-tech purchaser, she had considerable market savvy to apply to her health consumption.

Debbie also acted as medical consultant for her parents. She provided the same services for them that she did for her household, with the added complication that they lived over a thousand miles from her. Her mother e-mailed, but Debbie did all online research for them on particular diagnoses or pharmaceuticals, printed it and faxed it to them. When their healthcare coverage changed, as happens to so many retirees, they increased their saving and stockpiled medications to buffer the blow of vastly increased expenses. Still, they needed more help. Debbie found out how to get medications from Canada, compiled all the necessary documentation, and did all the online ordering. Debbie had become the chief manager of a health-care system customized to meet the idiosyncratic needs of her family, which was quite different from that promised by managed care.

Choosing Within Constraints

THE SMITHS: THE BUSYNESS OF HEALTH CRISES

Because David and Janelle Smith had flexible work schedules, they had much time to spend with their two daughters. What they did not anticipate was that their time would be taken up with health issues and the busyness that followed from these. Their daughter Mardi was three, and her younger sister Mirella was only a few weeks old. Both had contracted acute illnesses, which Janelle attributed to living in the university dormitory. It is a "germ feast in this hall," she said. The baby came down with one cold after another. Whatever the causes may have been, the consequences were disruptive and time-consuming. Typical was what occurred on Father's Day. The Smiths spent it at an urgent care facility, where Mirella was treated for hives.

At first, the crisis that came to dominate Mardi's life and that of her family appeared insignificant: a bit of chronic constipation. Janelle tried home remedies, but these failed. After two months, Janelle took her to a doctor, who prescribed higher doses of juice and fiber. Mardi remained constipated, in part as a response to a painful bowel movement. She began to go eight days at a time without a bowel movement, and she continued like this for five months. Her parents became frantic with worry. Mardi's problem now had taken over their lives. In her bath, Mardi played that her dolly was having "poop issues so he is drinking tea." A co-worker told Janelle that Mardi appeared to need to "go," and Janelle replied, "This is our life."

During this stressful period, David made a career change that took the family to Los Angeles. The move required them to change their health insurance and providers. David and Janelle now found themselves spending hours studying health plans in an unfamiliar landscape of medical providers. One of their primary concerns was to determine which health plans could be used for Mardi's condition.

Meanwhile, Mardi's condition grew worse; she was severely impacted and no longer physically capable of pushing. The Smiths consulted a pediatric gastrointestinal specialist, who put Mardi on a severe six-day regimen of alternating enemas, laxatives, and purgatives. Janelle said she was annoyed that it had taken a year to be referred to the right specialist, since earlier intervention might have spared Mardi suffering.

During the intense moments of an immediate medical crisis, people obviously set aside other activities. When a crisis continues for months or more, it may come to dominate family life. The busyness of family members soars as they seek assistance for and relief from the crisis. The routines of daily life may be disrupted to such an extent that they never return to their previous state. That was what happened to the Smiths.

THE ALLEN / RODRIGUEZES: THE BUSYNESS OF ADOPTION

Sophia Rodriguez and Bill Allen brought busyness into their lives with their decision to adopt two boys. Adoption required them to deal with numerous policies and procedures that placed constraints on them and changed the organizational landscape in which they lived. Since Bill worked in an environment that was unresponsive to child-care exigencies, Sophia had to deal with the children. Fortunately, she could do this, because she worked in a place that gave her and other female employees considerable flexibility in rearranging their daily schedules to accommodate family needs. They routinely offered one another rides and information. Sophia said she was grateful to have a job with little responsibility or stress. She could leave work refreshed and ready to deal with her family's latest problem. She was a conscientious worker, widely admired for becoming an adoptive parent after raising her own daughters. There was thus a moral context to her busyness, and her co-workers were willing to be inconvenienced for her.

In contrast, Bill Allen's work group consisted exclusively of men. As a rule, they did not take on the responsibilities of adapting to the unexpected occurrences of daily life. If they were married, their spouses did this. Bill's brother-in-law was his supervisor, a fact kept secret from Bill's co-workers. To protect both of them from potential accusations of favoritism, Bill's brother-in-law gave him little slack to handle child-care responsibilities. Bill, a parts expediter, had to be at his workplace during normal business hours, since he responded to requests from engineers. He enhanced his reputation at work by being the de facto facilities manager, a role that also required his presence on site.

Work environments were not the only constraints that Bill and Sophia faced. Of particular concern was that they could not go off somewhere without first making sure that some relative was watching over the three disabled people in the household of Sophia's mother. Even the location of their house constrained their activities. Because it was in an industrial area with no grocery stores or gas stations nearby, they had to make sure their kitchen was well stocked and their cars were filled with gas.

On top of this, they added the constraints of adoption, especially those related to the supervision of children. To complicate matters, the schools that the boys attended had specific days when school was out early, and other "in service" days when classes were canceled. Someone had to pick up the boys at these odd hours. It was no surprise, then, that Bill and Sophia found themselves scrambling through the day and night to meet all of the obligations that now confronted them, with little or no margin for error.

Volunteering

THE CARLSBERGS: THE BUSYNESS OF VOLUNTEERING

For many of the families in our study, volunteering was important. Many people volunteered because they thought they would benefit personally by acquiring skills, forging relationships, or building obligations in that way. But they also volunteered in order to create a better community. In doing this, they added to their work, sometimes considerably. Volunteering became one more thing to coordinate in their daily lives, which meant that they increased the activities and management burdens of the family.

The Carlsberg family provides a stunning example of how volunteering can reverberate through the lives of family members and those who know them. Indeed, the centerpiece of Carlsberg family busyness was volunteering. It took on an importance as great as any other activity in this family, including employment. While many people benefited from these activities, the cost for the Carlsbergs was an enormous increase in the busyness and pressures of their daily life.

Robert, the youngest son, attended a private school. One of the conditions of enrolling him was that his parents provide the school with 40 hours a year of volunteer work. The Carlsbergs decided to try to get their older son James into the same school. Both boys wanted this, and besides, it would save on commuting time. To persuade school authorities to accept James, Pat and Alex volunteered 300 hours, hoping to be viewed as a valuable and desirable family. The strategy ultimately worked, and James was enrolled. Even after this, Pat and Alex continued to volunteer extensively.

Alex prepared hot lunches on alternate Fridays. Kitchen work exposed him to considerable gossip about the school, enabling him to learn how it really operated. But the work took several hours, broke up the day, and made it difficult for him to work on other projects, such as his incipient Internet business.

Although Alex's meal preparation far exceeded the minimum required hours, it was only one of the many tasks he performed for the school. Alex became an organizer of the annual school fund-raising auction and made an immediate impact on it. He applied his technical skills as a systems analyst to soliciting donations. First, he categorized the kinds of businesses that might be willing to donate prizes; then he performed online searches for them by geographic proximity. He searched for nearby restaurants, but also for theme parks hundreds of miles away. While sitting in front of one computer at work, he located phone numbers, called the businesses and asked if he could fax them a description of the auction, since sending unsolicited faxes was illegal. If they agreed, he sent the fax immediately through an adjacent computer. He solicited more donations in an hour than had been done in a day, and revenues jumped dramatically. He simultaneously solicited donations of supplies for the auction, thereby controlling costs, and the event was a stunning success.

Pat, too, volunteered extensively at the school. Both sons wanted her to be their room mother, but her own work did not give her the time to do this. Instead, she coordinated crafts projects that each class prepared for the auction, held annually in early March.

Pat introduced the practice of class projects for the auction, borrowing the idea from her sister. James's class decided to decorate a garden workbench with painted tiles. Pat would supply the design for the tiles and help the children paint them. A parent would bake the tiles in an oven to fix the paint. A lumberyard agreed to donate the bench. Another parent took on the task of priming the bench, and Alex offered to paint it green. Still another parent volunteered to set the tiles, after which Pat and Alex would grout them. Although Pat had never done a project like this, she anticipated no problems. In Robert's class, she volunteered to help the children paint wildflowers on patches of rice paper with watercolors. Then she would mount them on matte board to form a collage, top it with glass, and frame it.

Pat enjoyed her role as coordinator, because, by using her sick days for her school visits, she could be involved in her sons' classes in a way that fitted her work schedule. Through these projects, she did something good for the school and provided an outlet for her own artistic expression. Pat sewed, decorated, and did flower arranging, and her house displayed her creations.

Still, she had to fit her time-consuming volunteer activities around her work schedule. Pat and Alex found that tile setting was more difficult than they had expected, and the project fell behind schedule. In early February, the school sent them an e-mail asking why the project was not finished. Pat asked the teacher to find out if there was another parent who could set tiles.

In February, the school projects were scattered all over the Carlsberg house. A card table near the kitchen held the wildflower paintings that were ready to mount and frame. Pat had brought photographs of wildflowers and sheets of rice paper to the class, but the students had only twenty minutes in which to paint. She managed to get the children to write their names on their paintings, but there was no time to add the names of the flowers. She and Alex spent several hours matching the photographs and paintings so that she could write the correct name of the flower on each painting. Before mounting the collage, she tore shreds off the edges of each patch to "age" them while fitting them into the frame.

Pat had worked eleven straight days and was exhausted. She went to work at 1:30 PM Saturday and returned home at 2:00 AM Sunday. She went in again at 1:30 PM and did not come home until 10:00 PM. As soon as she completed one task, another arose; she found the pressure unbearable.

The garden bench, topped with its grouted tiles sat in the garage, unfinished. They had not had time to complete it. Alex stared at the bench and said, "They wanted it a darker green." He did not know who wanted this change. The bench accessories and decorations also had to be redone. A friend of one of the parents had set the tiles. Alex had borrowed this man's tools and had put in the grout. Because of the clamor about the bench, Alex hauled it to the school to show people that it was almost finished. The Carlsbergs had planned a weekend vacation, and Alex and Pat stayed up all night, worked on the bench, and delivered it to the school before they went on their trip.

But the bench still was not quite done. It had to be repainted and varnished. And someone insisted that Pat's painted ladybugs on the accessories be replaced with dragonflies. Primer failed to adhere to a galvanized metal watering can. The handles of the tools did not perfectly match in color and so had to be repainted.

At the auction, the bench sold for $1,200, more than any other item. James's teacher wanted to buy it and was upset that the bidding went higher than she could afford. Because Pat especially liked this teacher, she made a second bench. The entire class presented it to her as their end-of-year surprise.

The second bench proved to be as troublesome and time-consuming as the first: problems with structural stability, getting someone else to set the tiles, and delivering the bench on time. At 7:15 AM on the delivery day, the tile man brought the bench to Alex and Pat, and they took it to school later that morning. "None of us were sleeping," Pat said. Both she and Alex, exhausted by the ordeal, stayed home from work to ensure the delivery and then slept a few hours.

During this same period, Pat also had taken on the burden of decorating clear plastic wineglasses for the class's first communion. The school staff told her that they needed this done, saying, "You're so creative!" She responded to their flattery: She ordered 160 of the wine glasses, enough to be used in future years, but when she picked them up at the store she did not count them and was inadvertently shorted two boxes. "It just meant another trip down," she reflected. Pat agreed to paint the glasses for the children in Robert's class, but the hobby store did not have all the paints she needed. She wanted a specific gold calligraphy pen that was out of stock until Friday; the glasses had to be done by Thursday.

Because she was so busy at work, the cartons of glasses remained in the trunk of her car. Finally, she brought them into the house and worked on them for a week in the evenings, not going to bed until 3:00 AM. She produced 36 glasses for Robert's class, each decorated and customized with the child's name. She delivered them to the class and they were used once in a communion practice. Then the school decided not to use them any more. Pat was stunned, since the wineglasses had consumed so much of her time and had looked so beautiful. Alex said, "It's like the teachers sit around and think of what they can do to torture you." He continued, "I don't think they know what that did to her." When first communion arrived, Pat was exhausted and demoralized. She never had time to wrap the gifts for her female family members, nor was she able to make favors for the first communion: she made one for her mother, but had to give rain checks on the others. Alex said his wife was "deeply embarrassed about these things."

Alex's mother worked in her city's senior center. During its annual "volunteer appreciation day," Alex helped her by making place mats and programs on his computer. This year, his mother asked Alex and Pat to make a memento for each of the volunteers. They produced a pin and bookmark. During this same period, Alex was also preparing taxes for his family, his parents, and his mother-in-law. He was also a Cub Scout den leader and treasurer.

Since the mayor was attending the event, Alex and Pat were asked also to design and produce elaborate programs that would impress him. This took them an entire weekend on the computer. The program printed the names of the volunteers and some twenty or thirty of their activities, showing that the center did more than distribute meals.

Alex's mother thought that this was an easy task, since Alex simply did it on the computer. She had no idea of the laborious steps involved, the disruption that resulted from having to correct the names of some volunteers after the program had been completed, or the pressure making the corrections at the last moment put on Alex. On the day of the ceremony, Alex went to work early in the morning to print the programs himself. He cropped them by hand and delivered them just in time for the event. Pat commented about responding to the parents' requests, "This is worse than children."

For the Carlsbergs, volunteering was clearly a part of who they were as a family and as individuals. Despite their other burdens of work and family, they chose to be the people who would "do it" when no one else would. They saw themselves as good, helpful people; volunteering was as much a moral as a practical decision. It reflected their deeply held beliefs about what individuals should do and communities should be like, as well as the claims the volunteer could make on others. They expected others to accommodate to the constraints on their time because they were doing good, regardless of the constraints faced by those other people.

When the Carlsbergs volunteered, they were confronted with constraints imposed on them by other people and institutions. Volunteering was not a single act, but an opening onto a larger world of relationships and conditions that had to be met. Alex and Pat encountered this in the production of the garden bench and the first communion glasses. Even when such constraints were not imposed, the Carlsbergs' volunteer work brought with it numerous small tasks. In themselves, these were insignificant, but cumulatively, they could delay the completion of tasks and ultimately overwhelm them. The need to search for a special calligraphy pen or to make an extra trip downtown to retrieve missing wineglasses only added to the busyness of their lives.

The Carlsbergs' volunteering also exposed other people and institutions to the constraints of their busyness. Alex and Pat saw clearly how other people inconvenienced them and treated them unjustly, but they were probably less aware of the effects of their voluntary overcommitments on other people. Indeed, when we think about our own busyness, we often focus on what others could do to make things easier for us; we may overlook the question of what our busyness is doing to the lives of others.

Ultimately, Pat and Alex became ambivalent about volunteering. They wanted to do it on moral principle, but they came to question its value. Pat said that the biggest stress in their lives came not from work, but from volunteering. She wanted to have a "presence" in their school, but her children didn't want this. The time she spent benefited all the children and not just them. They wanted her to spend more time alone with them.

Pat and Alex concluded that volunteering had failed. People seldom thanked them for their many contributions, and they saw no benefits flowing to their boys. They said that volunteering was an intrusion into their family, one they found difficult to contain.

Creating Lifestyles

THE TENTORIS: FAMILY-RUN BIBLE CAMP

The Tentoris moved away from San Jose to find affordable housing and look for and develop their ideal community. They hoped to take advantage of the conveniences and benefits of middle-class life, while retaining the conservative religious values and practices that were the foundation of their family. They did not assume that their ideal community was simply out there waiting for them, but realized that they would have to take active steps to create it. The first step was to find people of similar views, reflected in their church affiliation. They would work with these people to create their ideal community. This entailed many time-consuming volunteer activities aimed at enhancing the spiritual development of both adults and children.

Soon after their arrival in the new town, Tom and Fran joined a small church. In addition to Sunday services, the church members held weekly evening Bible study sessions. This was a family affair that included a social hour, an adult study group, and a children's playgroup. Tom and Fran also sent Josh to Bible summer camp at a church in San Jose for a month. There Josh was thrust into an environment of Bible stories and teachings, religious singing and games, and group sports, along with instruction in proper deportment, which included respecting adults, as well as their fellow campers. These activities reinforced the values and teachings that Josh received at home.

Fran carried their religious teachings further. After Josh had completed Bible summer camp, she, along with several other mothers, organized and ran a five-day children's Bible day camp at the home of one of her friends. Here, in a more personal and intimate way, several parents proceeded to provide Bible instruction to their children in an atmosphere of family fun. The adults spent several hours a day preparing and then participating in this endeavor. Also attending was Adam, Josh's six-year-old friend and neighbor. Fran explained that she took a week of her vacation time to organize this volunteer activity because it would benefit Josh and the other children, as well as create closer ties among the adults who helped with it.

Fran and the other parents used prepared materials that they bought to use in running their Bible camp. These included stories, the items used for each session, instructions for crafts, games, songs, lists of foods to prepare for snacks, questions to ask the children, and biblical maps and pictures of biblical figures.

Fran instructed the younger children, including her son, reading and explaining biblical passages, doing crafts, and leading them in games that emphasized religious faith. In one of them, children put on a blindfold and followed the instructions of one adult to lead them around obstacles, while other adults called out false directions. The lesson was that just as they followed the true instructions of the one adult, ignoring the distractions of others, so too they should listen only to God. After her son successfully followed directions, Fran told him, "You've got to listen to God and blot out other voices."

After snacks, closing songs, and prayers, the adults gave the children little plastic surgical gloves. Inside were religious pendants of thick metal with fish or cross designs. The adults took several photos, and the group dispersed.

Fran was visibly tired, but exultant. The morning had required considerable effort and focus, but she had accomplished something for her son she could not have done as easily by herself at home: creating a learning situation for biblical history and values in an environment of fellowship and fun that brought together a community of people with similar social and religious values. This community was not merely found and joined; it was built through activities that took considerable planning and coordination.

RAJIV MOHAN: GLOBAL VIDEO GAME

On the way back from Hong Kong, Rajiv Mohan, a high-tech consultant from India who lived in the United States, bought his son Frank a well-known video game. Frank was so enamored of it that when Rajiv's nephew Surya invited the Mohans to visit India, Frank said he could not go because he would be without his high-tech toy. On his next trip to Hong Kong, Surya bought the video game and took it back to India. He then e-mailed the Mohans to tell them of his purchase and that Frank could play with it, so that he no longer had an excuse not to visit his relatives in India. Of course, Surya also bought this device for his own children.

This incident provides a glimpse on the provisioning of the globe with devices that enhance individual mobility. Surya bought the video game to encourage a visit by a distant relative. High-tech toys and Frank's relationships with those who use them became an integral part of his childhood experiences and socialization.

In the United States, Frank's friends kept in touch with each other to ensure that they did not buy the same toys. Different households had different toys, and Frank would go to these different places to use those toys. When Rajiv went on trips, he brought back many of Frank's toys. Each time Rajiv went to Japan and Hong Kong, he brought back pieces of a train set, down to individual sections of track.

When Frank's friends came over, they would play on each other's systems. Rajiv observed that the problem was "scheduling kids' events." Over the phone, they would try to find time to meet, only to find that someone objected to each suggestion; even those who lived in the same neighborhood could not synchronize their schedules. One neighbor could play with Frank, but his parents put him in day care all week and on Saturdays, so they had "time to shop and run errands and work around the house." Frank hardly ever saw this neighborhood friend. Play became a complicated exercise requiring considerable discussion between the boys and their parents. Describing this, Rajiv rolled his eyes. This was not the kind of growing up he remembered from his childhood in India.

CARSON / KLEIN / ROGERS: CREATING MULTIPLE LIFESTYLES

The extraordinary diversity of American families often goes unrecognized. As John R. Gillis notes, citing the work of the British sociologist Jon Bernardes, there is not one, narrow, ideal family form, but "as many as two hundred different arrangements that Europeans and Americans now regard as legitimate 'family.'"[25] In our study, the Carson/Klein/Rogers family reveals the complex relationships that develop, and the increase of busyness that follows, when parents divorce and marry new spouses. When divorced parents have different values and expectations for their children, the consequence can be a sharp increase in activities as parents try to exert influence on their children and the children respond to these pressures.

Debbie Carson married Jason Rogers, an electrical engineer, and they had two sons, Derek and Ethan who were in college and high school at the time of our study. When Debbie and Jason divorced, Debbie remained in their house with their sons. In her mid-forties, Debbie left her high-pressure, high-paying job of high-tech purchasing to pursue museum work and historical interpretation. She married Martin Klein, an information systems professional. Jason also remarried and bought a second house. The two sons had rooms in both houses, though Jason's second wife, Alys, refashioned their rooms into generic guest spaces.

In the first years after his separation from Debbie, Jason rarely attended the soccer games and performances of his sons, but later he began to do so, joining Debbie and Martin. These three adults had very different, often competing, expectations for the boys. In pushing what they desired for Derek and Ethan, they prompted the boys to pursue activities that pleased the adults. This substantially increased the busyness of everyone in the family. It also led the boys to consider a variety of lifestyle choices.

Debbie wanted her sons to be expressive and flamboyant; Jason Rogers expected them to become technically savvy, and scientific. Martin Klein was content that they learn how to handle finances. Debbie supported all theatrical activities; Jason, all scientific and academic endeavors; and Martin encouraged them to be fiscally responsible. As a consequence, the boys explored a variety of activities approved by one or other of the parents.

Ethan, prodded both by his mother and older brother, performed in a choir, three plays and a musical, and various Civil War reenactments. For several years, Ethan and his friends choreographed and performed skits for the high school talent show, and they also performed outside of school for their acting peer group, friends, and families. Ethan, echoing his mother's wishes, said that performing gave him skills that he would be able to use in management later in life.

But Ethan, influenced by Jason, also struggled to attend a dawn calculus class at a local community college, while still in his Catholic high school. He missed too many classes and was dropped from the class. He had mistakenly assumed that he had been excused to attend a religious retreat, as his high school allowed him to do.

After Ethan graduated from high school, his mother encouraged him to take a job. He worked at a large electronics store and used part of his money to buy his biological father computer games. Ethan figured that Jason wanted him to become an engineer, so Ethan applied for admission to an engineering university.

In contrast, Derek responded to his father by rejecting engineering. Derek, twenty years old, a student at a Catholic university, and a talented actor, pursued a theater major, writing, and graphic art, to the dismay of his conservative father. But Derek did not reject all that his father stood for. He thought highly of the six-figure salaries of his father and stepfather. Both Derek and Ethan picked up technological skills from their two "fathers" and mother. Derek's friends in the art community turned to him for technical support.

Derek also demonstrated his technical competence for his father, volunteering to burn compact disks for one of Jason's workmates and creating CD covers. Martin helped Derek set up the record player and the CD burning setup. In deference to his father, Derek took a college course called "Physics for Engineers." Debbie expressed skepticism that he could finish such a course, but his younger brother tutored him at night, and Derek passed the class.

While Debbie taught her boys some technical skills, she said that her primary task was to make sure that each of the men in her life, Derek, Ethan and Martin, developed social skills. She particularly worked on her sons' performances. Derek wanted his future to be creative, saying "I don't really know or care what I'm doing ten years from now as long as it's creative and expansive and it's not mind-numbing. I don't think I've met the right people at this school in order to do that, which is bad. But hopefully I've met enough people to bring me into larger circles that can get me to meet people who are doing weird, wild, and crazy things that nobody's really heard of. I can help do that and be involved in that."

Debbie, Martin, Alys, and Jason also attended the two sons' performances. Ethan drew on his mother's expertise and guidance in historical interpretation for his Civil War enactments. Debbie helped Derek with his monologues and his Shakespearean delivery. During Derek's performance of *The Winter's Tale*, Debbie attended all three nights, each time with different people. When Ethan had a role in *Crazy for You*, Jason, Alys, Derek and his theater friends, and Debbie and her friends attended. After the performance, they visited the greenroom and discussed the play.

The family can be a refuge from busyness, but as the Carson / Klein / Rogers family shows, it may in fact be a significant source of new busyness, additional activities, and uncertainty about the right courses of action.

Conclusions

The people we meet in these pages often spoke of busyness as a sort of force to which they had to adapt by balancing and juggling. They saw that as their responsibility. Indeed, they defined a responsible or skilled person as one who was able to manage everything he or she needed to do.

We have called attention to some of the drivers of busyness and have given some idea of the environment in which these individuals led their lives and exercised those skills. What emerges is the inescapable conclusion that busyness is not solely a matter of individual lives, nor is it a personal failing if people come to feel that things are out of control. We live in society and ours is a busy one.

To call a society busy is to say something more about it than that busy individuals populate it. Instead, it emphasizes the organization of important parts of society around busyness. A society of busyness may be reflected in material artifacts and the construction of places. Technological devices are central to busyness, and we have described the use of many throughout these pages. Space, too, may be configured around the demands of busy lives. We see this in airports, where only a few years ago laptop-toting business travelers stood out as they strung obstacle courses of power cords across aisles that tripped the unwary pedestrian. Today, airports have become just another workplace for the busy traveler and the means to connect are built into both devices and airport infrastructure. Other material elements are equally important, but largely out of sight, such as the computer server farms that make connectedness possible. Still other elements are visible, but their connection to busyness may be less than obvious.

Social relationships among people are also affected in a busy society. We live with products and services that are configured around busyness and that are designed, made, distributed, and sold. Services intended to ease the time burdens of others must be conceptualized, marketed, and delivered. There are thus markets for specific aspects of busyness that organize important parts of the economy, and the implications for the allocation of labor are enormous. Many services achieve their benefits by being made available to customers on demand, but doing so, of course, has repercussions for the individuals who provide those services (and for their families). Many of these people work nonstandard hours, including on weekends and in late afternoon shifts that take them away from their own children.

By creating markets for busyness-related services and goods, we see that its costs and benefits are unevenly distributed. Busyness is thus not simply a uniform "speeding up" of society; its effects are finer-grained. Being a busy society does not mean that everyone in it is busy in the same ways, or even that they describe themselves as busy. The effects of busyness are subtle, with ramifications in different parts of society and with different impacts on different segments of the population. Money and what it can buy matters and some people can simply buy their way out of some obligations, or more precisely, they are able to transform one set of obligations into another. The busy person's life then becomes linked to those of others, even if those linkages are circuitous and not obvious.

The social side of busyness also suggests there are several kinds of busyness that convey differential status. There is a value or prestige in being busy in some ways, and virtue can be demonstrated through managing heavy schedules. For example, we can use busyness to establish our willingness to sacrifice for others, as when we take on more obligations for the good of the kids, a partner, or even employer. Or we can exemplify devotion and caring by making sure the days of our children are properly filled with beneficial activities and that their movements from place to place are well coordinated. And if we are so "in demand" by others that not even our time is our own anymore, we may think we are establishing our own worth and status. Busyness may have a further texture in our society, one in which not all busyness is created equal. Some activities may convey prestige, status, and getting ahead, at least to some of the population, while other activities indicate low status, desperation, and falling behind. Busyness thus defines a metaphorical terrain in which social distinctions are produced and interpreted, with great consequences for a society, its people, and its future.

Finally, busyness may be reflected in the assumptions and values of a society. We take for granted the value of efficiency, often without subjecting its claims to close scrutiny. Whether a labor-saving device really saves labor may be less important than our faith that some combination of such devices will do so. The unexamined corollary, of course, is the expectation that users will suddenly discover that they have free time that will provide temporary relief from the pace of busy living. Seldom, however, do those minutes or hours seem to linger without being filled with new activities.

A related value is that of productivity, whereby activities situated in seemingly disparate domains may be subjected to the same logic. Accordingly, to speak of the productivity of our leisure time hardly seems oxymoronic, as evidenced by vacations that are less breaks from busyness than the transformation of one kind of busyness into another. Convenience, too, is both prized and often ill defined, but it becomes comprehensible in a larger worldview in which the necessity and desirability of taking on more is assumed. "Convenience" becomes the mantra of producers and consumers alike, suggesting that goods and services can be incorporated with minimal demands on time.

It is by engaging busyness through such tacit work that we fill our days and ourselves with the content that makes us who we are. While we might think of our "real" lives as being constituted by dinners, celebrations, and "quality time" with loved ones, our lives are equally constituted by the tacit work of busyness. Busyness, then, is not a cruel interruption of the real content of our lives; rather, it is part of that content. It is who we become. We are each constructions of particular cultural and historical moments, rooted in our time and our timing. One such condition is that we are busy, and this means much more than a measure of our tasks.

PART TWO

Coping

CHAPTER FOUR

The Hidden Work of Thinking Ahead

As we spent more and more time with busy families, a fundamental distinction emerged between two kinds of activities. Although the family members did not explicitly recognize this, it was nonetheless real. The first consisted of numerous activities that people felt they had to do in order to meet obligations. Regardless of why or how people were busy, they scripted their days tightly, and their unscheduled time was scarce. When it did occur, they often considered it "wasted" time. These were the activities that the members of our families spoke of when we asked them about being busy. They were the activities people had to do or wanted to do and that formed the content of their days and weeks.

The second set of activities, clearly noticeable to the three anthropologists who conducted the study, seldom warranted mention by the families. These were the practices people undertook to coordinate, manage, and otherwise fit together the complex sequences of activities that filled a day. They adopted these practices in order to cope with the sheer abundance of other activities. These management activities formed a hidden or tacit work that accompanied everything else that occurred each day.

We quickly saw that families developed routines to exert control over their everyday lives. This made their lives predictable and gave them a sense of their distinctive identity. Yet try as they might, people were sometimes unable to follow their routines, so they also formulated alternative plans and altered them as situations changed. Some of these plans were tightly connected to particular activities and hard to change without disrupting the lives of others, such as delivering a child to a scheduled sporting event or lesson. Family members also distinguished between rigid plans and mere guidelines that they could renegotiate or even ignore. Some people were more skilled at this than others, and indeed, some individuals spent considerable time and effort trying to make their own plans into moral constraints on others. Conversely, they sometimes tried to transform the ironclad constraints placed on them by others into mere preferences that they could choose to ignore.

Planning within families took place within a value system of mutual obligations and responsibilities. Some family members did not accept these values; they routinely contested specific plans, and even the right to plan. These actions took much time and effort. Families such as this might meet daily to confirm what obligations people were willing and able to accept. Other families did less planning than improvisation and, indeed, they often proclaimed that they planned nothing. For them, daily meetings were unnecessary and unwanted. Instead, they "touched base" via phones, pagers, and e-mail throughout the day, effortlessly adjusting their activities to one another's needs.

Planning was also accompanied by anticipation of things going wrong, and so coping was not just an activity visible to others but had a private, internal quality as well. Likewise, people facilitated planning and anticipation by seeking and obtaining timely and salient information, although they were not always sure that they had it. For some, seeking out and exchanging information that might affect coping was near continuous.

Herein lies the paradox of coping. It largely remains tacit background to daily life, hardly worth a comment, and yet it constitutes significant work that accompanies most everything we do. For the families in our study, it usually became noticeable only when it failed to provide the control over events that people relied on to get through their days.

Planning

Families vary widely in their approaches to planning, from those whose days are tightly scripted to those who respond to events as they arise. Eleanor and Jerry Flaherty make daily plans and amend them throughout the day to keep their strategy intact. Suzanne Jones and Humberto Mendoza do not have daily meetings, but Humberto constructs goals for the household that he views as having a strong moral authority. Sophia Allen is torn between her sisters, who dislike planning, and her husband, who depends on it. Planning works only if people cooperate. First, they must agree to make the plans; then they must allow them to continue, adjusting them when necessary. This social contract generates a management burden so large that it is sometimes hard to implement.

THE FLAHERTYS: A FAMILY THAT PLANS

The Flahertys viewed themselves as planners. Each morning, Jerry, Eleanor, and their children, Mary and Michael, would huddle in the kitchen to determine who would go where and at what time. The children did not plan, but they lobbied to get their requests on the agenda. Planning for them involved waiting at the right place for transportation, though they often called to alter the plans.

Once they came to agreement, Jerry and Eleanor proceeded throughout the day without contacting each other unless something upset their tightly coordinated plans. They needed to trust one another because they moved around and had crowded work schedules. They were free to do this because they had senior positions; if required, they could turn the work over to their subordinates and leave the office. Their subordinates did not have this luxury.

Because they put so much effort into making plans, Jerry and Eleanor were reluctant to admit that their plans might change. Jerry described a plan as a "social contract" that bound them to mutual obligations: to change a plan was to break the contract and interfere with the carefully laid plans of others.

In fact, their plans changed frequently. In one instance, Jerry forgot that Eleanor had called to tell him that he should not pick up their son Michael at a friend's house. When confronted with this example of a change in plan, at first, Jerry denied that there had been a change and then protested that this was an exception, Eleanor blurted out, "You did it to me yesterday! You were supposed to pick up the kids at 5:30 at Ray's, but you forgot about not being done with a dinner meeting until 6:30, so when you called, I drove over and got them."

Although the Flahertys claimed that they depended on plans to get them through the day, they really limited this to organizing the transportation and supervision of their children. Their other activities were not so tightly scripted or known to each other. In their planning discussions, they included other people who provided services for them. Ray Brody, their fictive grandfather, provided occasional after-school care for the children, so Eleanor reviewed the week's plans with him. Ray's important role in the Flaherty family is discussed in Chapter 9. On Tuesday, after school, Mary received a ride with a friend's mother and stayed at her friend's house until Eleanor picked her up. Meanwhile, Michael walked the half-mile to a train station and rode to the site where he volunteered. Jerry picked him up after work. On Wednesday, Mary went to a science fair at a convention center with a friend; Eleanor picked her up at 3:45 PM and took her to Ray's. Eleanor then went to an appointment with a hairdresser. At 3:30 PM, Jerry took Michael to an orthodontist's appointment and after that to Ray's before returning to work. Ray took both children home about 6:30 PM and ate dinner with the family. After dinner, he and Mary worked on invitations to a party celebrating the life of his deceased wife. On Thursday, Eleanor dropped Mary off at school. Because it was a short school day, Mary went to another friend's house, driven by the friend's mother. Eleanor picked up Mary after work. Ray picked up Michael at noon, brought him to his house, and then drove him to his volunteer job at 3:00 PM. Jerry picked him up at 5:30 PM and went home.

The children were constantly pushing to change this weekly plan. On Wednesday, Mary said she didn't want to go to Ray's, because she'd have to leave the science fair early. Instead, she pleaded to stay longer and then accompany Eleanor to the hairdresser. She did not get her wish. On the way home from Ray's, Mary said she wanted to go to a particular stationery store for pens. Michael asked to stay longer with another family at Lake Tahoe the upcoming weekend. He also asked permission to try snowboarding, saying that skiing was too "repetitious and boring." Hearing this, Mary asked if her friend could come along. On Thursday, Michael presented a new request: "I'd just like to come home early one day." He hoped to avoid going to Ray's or to his volunteer work.

The Flahertys' planning thus involved more than following a script; their plans made weeks in advance might change. Keeping track of them prompted modifications. Jerry discovered that he had overbooked himself: he had planned to use an afternoon to catch up on work, only to discover that he had filled that day with meetings, a fact hidden behind other data on his personal digital assistant. Another time, he was shocked to find he was in the wrong county just before he had to pick up his daughter. Again, the device he used to track his plans had concealed his commitment.

Sometimes, Jerry would make plans that he did not intend to keep. He occasionally scheduled two meetings at once. He might stay only a few minutes at one, or he might use his double scheduling to remind himself to send *someone* from his organization. Jerry knew that his plans were distributed among his own memory, electronic devices, paper records and the recollections of other people. When, at the end of the day, his PDA reminded him to collect his daughter at Ray's, he muttered, "This will be interesting. The PDA says Mary is at Ray's, but I remember that got changed and she is at Jenny's." Jerry used his plan as a starting point, but he altered it in light of new claims on his time and additional information. Certain aspects of his plan were more stable: meeting times, and above all his obligations to move his children from place to place.

The Flaherty family paid a price for managing their busyness. They spent time sharing information, reviewing, and reminding each other about their commitments. When plans changed or someone forgot an obligation, Jerry and Eleanor scrambled to pick up the pieces, adding to their time pressure.

THE ALLEN/RODRIGUEZES: PLANNING AND CONFLICTS WITH RELATIVES

Sophia Rodriguez and her husband Bill Allen depended on planning as a strategy, especially because they were trying to do so much each day. Both Bill and Sophia felt deeply obligated to help her relatives, but they also had to take care of their own children. As a result, they had to schedule their activities with little margin for error. On a typical workday, Sophia would drive Esteban, their oldest boy, to school, go to work, visit her elderly mother, her brother, and her uncle, all three of whom were disabled, and on top of that fit in additional errands. But Sophia's relatives did not appreciate what this took out of Sophia and Bill, and they frequently undermined efforts to coordinate wider family activities. Bill would become frustrated and annoyed. Sophia found herself in the uncomfortable position of refereeing between her husband and her relatives.

Spending time with the Allen/Rodriguez family opened a window on schedules planned and interrupted, frantic attempts to keep control of situations that threatened to get out of hand, and conflicts that erupted. Sophia and Esteban usually awakened while Bill was still asleep. Esteban prepared his own bowl of cereal while Sophia dressed. Then she drove him to the school bus stop a mile away. From there, Esteban caught the bus for his six-mile journey to middle school. Before leaving him, on this particular day, Sophia asked the boy whether he wanted her to pick him up after school, or take the afternoon bus and wait for her at the bus stop. She then drove eight miles down several freeways to her job as a data entry clerk, arriving by 7:30 AM. She put on her makeup, ate a breakfast brought from home, and settled into work. At midmorning, she and Bill e-mailed each other to discuss plans for the day and evening. Because she started early, Sophia left work early. By 4:30 PM, she was racing back to the bus stop to pick up Esteban and return home.

Making her daily connections was tight, and real havoc resulted when she had to make exceptions to her routine. Lunch hours were never leisurely. She used them to run errands or transport children. Her elderly mother, a brother, and an uncle shared a house a few miles from her workplace, and each had significant health problems. A sister who worked nearby at a part-time job sat with them most afternoons, but Sophia visited several times a week to chat, help with baths, or deliver prescriptions. On some days, Esteban attended a homework club after school and then took the bus home. On days when the club did not meet, Sophia raced to the boy's school, delivered him to her mother's house, hurried back to work for another couple of hours, returned to her mother's house to collect the boy, and then drove home. Once in a while, she took Esteban to her workplace, and then home or to her mother. Because Sophia and Bill were in the process of adopting

Esteban and his brother Ricardo, the boys spent many hours with health-care providers, counselors, and retailers. These necessary visits upset the family's routines and gave Bill and Sophia yet something else to remember.

Sophia told Bill that he had to pick up Esteban one day a week at school and take him wherever the boy needed to go. Two days a week, Esteban stayed at school for supervised tutoring, but on the other three days, Sophia and Bill had to arrange for Esteban's supervision. Bill used one lunch a week to pick up the boy at the bus stop, drive him the eight miles to Sophia's mother's house, and then return to work. After work, Sophia then picked up Esteban and brought him home.

Although it would add miles to her commute, Sophia considered enroll-ing her boy one day a week in a youth center program. "It will be great for long days," she said, "but I don't know if it's worth it the other days. They have a computer lab so he can do homework. It's still a good option and something I could work in." She shook her head as she described her time constraints, "Today, I will be leaving at 1:30 from here. Esteban has a 2:45 doctor appointment. That's my lunch."

This day was particularly trying. Sophia traded e-mails with Bill to find out if he was working late. If he were not, she would go Christmas shop-ping with her two sisters, Beatriz and Maria. He replied that he expected to be late, because he was doing an extra job of painting offices for his em-ployer, but he would cancel his plans and stay home with the boys if Sophia wanted to shop. Sophia insisted that he stay at work; she would get Jennifer, her adult daughter, to watch the boys. Sophia then e-mailed Jennifer, who agreed to baby-sit both the boys and Beatriz's two daughters. Sophia sighed, "And Beatriz might cancel after I've done all this. It's happened!"

Sophia then called and invited her mother to go on the shopping ex-cursion. Either her mother or her brother would go along, while the other remained with their disabled uncle. Sophia planned to pick up her mother so that, with a second passenger, she could drive in the carpool lane through the commuter gridlock to a shopping center about twenty miles away. Sophia worried that her mother might back out at the last minute, depriving her of the right to use the carpool lane. Because of this, Sophia and Maria discussed alternative shopping destinations.

Before noon Sophia took a quick break for lunch; an hour later, she left work for the day to transport Esteban to a medical appointment. Esteban ran to the car as Sophia neared the school and they headed off to the pet store to buy what they needed to house the boy's pet iguana. Sophia had forgotten that school was over early that day, and Esteban had been waiting for an hour. Sophia reached the pet store with insufficient time to buy everything for the iguana. She rushed Esteban to his appointment at a nearby county clinic, only to find that the clinic could not take him until 3:20. She left him at the clinic, returned to the pet store to complete her purchases, and then raced the six miles to Ricardo's school to pick him up. Bill usually did this, but he was painting that night. By the end of the day, Sophia was so exhausted from her errands that she collapsed into bed.

Clearly, Bill and Sophia had to rely on planning to get through their busy days. But Sophia's extended family saw no value in this and rarely kept to schedules. Bill expressed annoyance about Sophia's family being "constantly late, always changing plans. So I often tell Sophia, this is what *we're* doing." Since her relatives would not listen to him, conflicts erupted. One time, the family agreed to depart at a certain hour for Bill and Sophia's Sierra cabin. Bill left work early, packed, and was ready to go. One of Sophia's relatives then stopped to eat, delaying everyone else. During the Christmas season, Bill announced one day that he was going to buy a Christmas tree that morning and finish trimming it before dark. The family said they would go with him, but during breakfast, one daughter and Beatriz said they wanted to go shopping first. They asked Bill to wait for them. He refused, they argued for a while, and then all of them went off to buy the tree. Their fundamental disagreement remained unresolved.

THE MENDOZA/JONESES: WORK AFFECTS PLANNING

Unlike the Flahertys, the Mendoza/Jones family could not make daily plans, since Humberto's work in a local fire department pinned him down in discrete shifts and made his minute-to-minute activities unpredictable. However, Humberto did make long-term plans. Even if he could not forecast his day, he could map out the larger framework for his house, his family, and his career. He gave his own plans precedence and moral priority, leaving the daily life of Suzanne and the household to respond and be flexible. Suzanne was unable to stop this, despite her objections.

Morning planning meetings were not an option in the Mendoza/Jones household, given Humberto's work schedule. Instead, he and Suzanne exchanged information in passing and called each other once or twice a day. When asked, Suzanne laughed, saying, "There is no plan." They had chosen a strategy based on the idiosyncratic constraints on their daily lives. Humberto had a stable, predictable schedule of workdays, but variable work locations and no desk, because he substituted for others on vacation. He had little discretion at work and could not take care of family crises. If his replacement failed to arrive, he was not allowed to leave. He also stayed longer when responding to an emergency or completing paperwork. Suzanne did not expect him to arrive home at any particular time. Yet in an emergency, she could reach him easily through the fire department communications system.

Suzanne meanwhile was home four days a week, and with the girls in preschool on two of these days, she was able to respond to most family needs. Unlike her husband, Suzanne could do most of her work at home. As long as she completed it, she could rearrange her schedule to fit changing demands. Still, her ability to do so depended on her work conditions, which could change suddenly. She had had three supervisors in one year, each with different expectations and degrees of comfort with her job-sharing arrangement. Her new supervisor expected more regular hours and quicker turnaround in completing tasks.

Humberto and Suzanne could improvise because both of them were accessible at work and followed predictable routines. When Humberto was absent, Suzanne dealt with the inevitable small family crises and decisions of daily life as they arose. Other firefighters' spouses responded differently, and some phoned their partners five or six times a day to consult with them.

Although they improvised a lot, Suzanne and Humberto saw value in planning. "You have to think of your time and how you are going to use it," Humberto said. He frequently observed that the best uses of one's time came from careful planning. Suzanne described her husband as extremely responsible, as shown by his long-term planning. For example, the Mendoza/Jones family lived on a cul-de-sac adjacent to a hospital that would eventually be demolished. Humberto had begun to study what would happen at the site. He reasoned that if a high-density housing project were put in, the street would be connected, thereby increasing traffic, so he prepared an alternative proposal for a new library and park. He watched the city council meetings "religiously" on cable television and planned go before the council with his proposal.

Humberto also made plans for remodeling his house and yard. One morning, after returning home from a 24-hour shift, he sat at the kitchen table reviewing a design for backyard landscaping. He mentally moved the pool apparatus behind a screen to be built in a corner of the yard, thereby creating a play area for the girls. He planned to fence the pool and build a wider patio door that would open onto a rebuilt patio arbor. Because he would not tackle this work several years, Suzanne asked him, "Why do it now?" She was perplexed that he would put in this effort on a morning when he was so obviously tired. Humberto replied, "I want to know my costs."

His head was always full of plans. While thinking about laying new vinyl flooring in the newly remodeled kitchen, he described the *ultimate* remodeling of the room, with an island of cabinetry, window, reconfigured sink and refrigerator, and new dining area. "I was at a medical call and they had done the wall the way I would," he said, explaining where he got the idea. He had already installed all the rough plumbing for the remodeling and concealed it behind the drywall. He both planned and anticipated future remodeling.

Humberto exercised such planning every day on the job and in his career as well. While on duty one day as an arson investigator, he drove to another station to drop off some paperwork. Suddenly, the radio crackled with news of a fire and a request that Humberto stand by in case he was needed. He monitored the radio for a minute and then said he was responding, even though he had not yet been called to the site. He explained that he could tell just from the tone of the communications that this was going to be big enough to warrant his involvement, and that there were tremendous advantages to getting in quickly. "If I can get in there right away and knock it [i.e., the investigation] out, it makes a big difference." This would enable him to detect the cause of the fire before someone moved the evidence.

Humberto also made plans for his career. Many of his fellow firefighters avoided working Downtown at their department's administrative headquarters, but Humberto worked there as a fire inspector to develop a broader understanding of firefighting. Similarly, rather than serve in a single station, he roamed the city filling in for captains on vacation so that he could better understand the department and city. Rather than specialize narrowly, he had trained and was qualified to command a fire engine and the hazardous materials unit and to perform fire investigations. Although there was strong peer pressure to remain in a particular fire station, he insisted that this was "not necessarily what's best for you, your family or your estate." He sought out opportunities to develop and demonstrate managerial skills. He expected to pass the battalion chief's test and assume even more responsibilities. He took his current extra jobs as a private fire investigator and instructor to increase his Social Security credits and bolster his retirement income.

Suzanne both admired and was annoyed by Humberto's planning. On this particular day, they argued about his projects and their impact upon the family. Suzanne cancelled scheduled visits by tradespeople, objecting that Humberto had scheduled too many of these during a particularly busy and stressful period, and that his projects had driven her and the children from the house. "I've been on the road the past five weekends and it's hard," she said. The previous weekend, paint fumes had driven her from the house; she had spent a day driving around San Jose "falling asleep at the wheel." Suzanne pointed to the bathroom. The simple project of patching a three-inch hole in the wall had escalated into new wallpaper and a pedestal sink. Although Suzanne acknowledged that Humberto's remodeling had improved the house, she complained to him: "Your projects are all-consuming, and they consume the whole family."

Humberto vigorously disagreed. He insisted that the projects required careful planning and scheduling, which Suzanne neither saw nor appreciated. All she sees "is the doing," he explained. He was especially upset at the cancellations, because "When I schedule these guys, I'm scheduling so they fit into *my* schedule." As he saw it, this was not a matter of personal convenience but of the necessary sequencing of tasks.

This emotion-laden argument entailed more than paint fumes and inconvenience. For Humberto, projects rested on a moral vision of being a responsible person. Because these projects ultimately benefited the entire family, Humberto expected sacrifice and downplayed inconvenience. "How can I be doing too much?" he asked. "I'm just doing what I have to do. You don't rationalize it; you don't do it for convenience." He conceded, "I just like getting it done." But for Suzanne, there were other priorities besides remodeling projects.

Precisely because planning was hidden and seemingly ubiquitous, Humberto could invoke it to protect his activities from intrusions by others.

Once planned, his activity took on legitimacy. The unwritten rule was that others in the family should not tinker with it casually. When working on something that he had planned, Humberto spoke of "being in activity." It was a corollary to his principle that everyone should plan carefully, do just one thing at a time, and thus be insulated from interruptions that might reduce or impair productivity. Left unsaid was that Suzanne's work around the house and with the children was not formulated as a set of discrete, planned projects that justified the protection of her time. The contest was thus not merely over specific plans, but rather over access to planning as a way of controlling family members' time.

Humberto and Suzanne clearly managed, anticipated, and negotiated constantly, and this reflected far more than differences in temperament. The rhythms of their respective jobs affected the time Suzanne and Humberto could devote to household chores, especially their flexibility in doing so. Humberto's yearly work schedule as a full-time fire captain was posted on the refrigerator: three 24-hour days on duty (each shift separated by a day off), and then four days off. Since Suzanne worked three days a week as a job-sharing marketer for a high-tech company, the couple's schedules meshed to form distinctive weekly patterns, with further variations introduced if Humberto came home particularly exhausted from a demanding shift or Suzanne was facing a project deadline.

Suzanne had effectively given up her career when the couple began having children, and while they had both agreed to this, she still received offers from "headhunters" and occasionally toyed with pursuing a managerial position. When Humberto and Suzanne disagreed about how many hours a week her shared job demanded, they were really discussing each partner's relative contribution to the household economy. To make her case more forcefully, Suzanne prepared a chart of the "time allotted each month" to "household chores" and tallied the time contributed by each spouse. She listed chores, such as laundry, finances, grocery and household shopping, cooking, car maintenance, garbage, washing dishes, running errands, taking care of the dog, cleaning, and outdoor maintenance. She also included child care.

At this point, they ended up arguing. Humberto dismissed her claims about the legitimacy of her multitasking activities. In Suzanne's view, he refused to give proper credit to her for cooking and doing laundry while the children were napping. Because she counted her multitasking, Suzanne claimed that she contributed 73 percent of the time devoted to household chores.

A further complication was that they distinguished activities from responsibilities. Both of them recognized that this line of argument did not help them resolve other contentious issues of control: who had the right to perform particular chores and who had to accommodate the other's changing demands. Their disagreements brought to consciousness many aspects of their daily lives that they might not otherwise have recalled. Their attention to these details in turn generated further disputes about who was doing what and whose tasks really mattered.

The Flaherty, Allen/Rodriguez, and Mendoza/Jones families spent much of their time planning, reviewing, or coordinating their daily schedules. These internal mental activities became something more to do, thus increasing their sense of crowding in everyday life. They constantly fretted about what they and their family members should be doing and where they should be going. And in so doing, they contributed to their own growing busyness.

Anticipation

THE MENDOZA/JONESES: ANTICIPATION WITHIN CONSTRAINTS AND FLEXIBILITY

Suzanne Jones and Humberto Mendoza covered both work and family obligations by anticipating problems and bringing in other family members or fellow workers to help. Humberto's firefighting work was inflexible in some ways but not in others. Suzanne's job revealed a different environment of constraints and flexibility. The issue for them was how they could accommodate each other, weather family crises, and maintain the routines of their children without interruption. To do this, they had to utilize their work situations in various ways, and this in turn required them to anticipate possible adjustments in their routines.

Only rarely did Humberto or Suzanne travel for business, but when they did, they first made sure that these trips would not interfere with the continuity of child care. Sometimes, Suzanne asked Humberto to be available to pick up the children; at other times, her trips required more complicated scheduling. Humberto would take up the slack to ensure that Suzanne need not worry about their daughters, and Suzanne did the same for Humberto when he traveled.

One time, she went to Denver on a Wednesday afternoon and returned on a Saturday. Humberto was off work Wednesday and Thursday, but was scheduled to work Friday. To accommodate his wife, he traded shifts with another captain, enabling him to be at home with the girls until Suzanne returned. Another time, he left for a week-long professional conference in Dallas just when Suzanne was working full-time to "crunch a project, a *big* project." The couple brought Suzanne's mother from St. Louis to help while he was gone. Suzanne and Humberto paid her airfare. Humberto also completed his new home office, freeing up a guest bedroom for his mother-in-law. Because Suzanne was busy all day, she could not make the time to socialize with her mother, as she usually did on such visits. She took one day off to spend with her mother and made up the time by working evenings.

The couple displayed a distinctive relationship of flexibility and constraints in their lives. The starting point was the nature of Humberto's job. Firefighters had to be at a fire when it happened: they could not simply choose to leave and complete their work at home. There was no give in this aspect of the job. The stakes were high, and the firefighters revealed a strong commitment to community service. The job was embedded in a military-style hierarchy of control; evading the rules threatened a person's career.

In other ways, though, Humberto's job was flexible. While firefighters were required formally to request emergency leaves, they almost always received them, since almost everyone would need one sooner or later. Furthermore, Humberto and his fellow firefighters ran personal errands all day long. They could do so precisely because their command and control system kept them constantly in touch and ready to respond. The rotation system of three 24-hour shifts followed by four days off allowed them to have side jobs or businesses, and they could usually arrange for someone to cover a shift if necessary.

Humberto's predictable schedule allowed Suzanne to anticipate and plan her work activities, while her own flexibility usually allowed Humberto to avoid emergency leave. Other firefighters whose spouses worked in police or fire departments were under very different constraints. Their lives were so regimented that, unlike Humberto and Suzanne, they seldom saw each other.

Humberto Mendoza and Suzanne Jones illustrate the importance of paying close attention to one's work situation and how it affects other family members, to the family priorities one sets, and to accommodating to the needs and circumstances of other family members. To do this requires that one anticipate when routines might be interrupted and what to do about it. Because they do these things, and consciously think about them, Humberto and Suzanne have developed a successful solution to some of the challenges that might otherwise threaten the stability of their family life and what they stand for. Central to their solution is their recognition of the necessity and value of accommodating each other's needs, and the fact that they must take advantage of whatever flexibility they have in their everyday lives. They use flexibility to accommodate each other's needs and especially to maintain stability in the daily lives of their daughters. For them, flexibility goes beyond accommodation. It has become a stable and possibly permanent part of family roles.

THE FLAHERTYS: ANTICIPATING WITH CALENDARS

To manage his busy life, Jerry Flaherty maintained three calendars for different audiences. His home calendar contained information about his job commitments, so that family members knew when he was available for their activities. Similarly, his work calendar recorded family commitments, such as taking his son to school, that affected the scheduling of his work meetings. He also maintained a third calendar on which he entered information that he wanted no one to see, such as reminders to check out books from the library or drop off a pair of shoes for repair during work hours, even though "I don't ever take any breaks or don't ever take lunch." He used these calendars to encourage family members and co-workers to schedule his activities at times that were convenient to him. To do otherwise was to create a potential surprise that could send shock waves through his and their day.

Still, Jerry was not insulated from surprises. What was significant was how he turned them into assets. One time, he had a meeting scheduled in San Diego from 9:00 AM to 3:00 PM. He had stayed up until 1:00 AM the night before completing a report. After e-mailing the report to his secretary, he checked his ticket and fell asleep. A few hours later, he arose and left home at 7:15 AM for the short drive to the airport where he would catch his 8:15 flight. As he rushed to the gate, he looked at a monitor and saw there was no 8:15 departure and when he looked at his ticket he discovered it *arrived* in San Diego at 8:15. There were no more flights until 9:30 AM, so he could not get to his meeting until almost 11:30, three hours late. He called several colleagues in San Diego as they prepared for the meeting, briefed them on his presentation, and then called his secretary to tell her he was neither going to the meeting nor the office. He took the day off, wandering around stores thinking about Christmas shopping. He enjoyed the day so much that he programmed his PDA with a "PTO day" (Personal Time Off day) for every second Tuesday of December "for the rest of my life."

Jerry thus turned an unpleasant setback in his tightly scheduled work schedule into a holiday for himself. He would never simply have decided to take such a day off, but when it was thrust upon him, he seized it, and by the end of the day, he was no longer lamenting his poor use of the day but recognizing the virtues of an at least occasional unscheduled weekday.

Carpooling of schoolchildren is one of the ways in which parents try to share their burdens. It is also a way to anticipate crises that might prevent a parent from driving on a particular day. But carpooling adds another layer to families' busyness. Not only do people have to schedule rotations of drivers and times, but also they have to scramble when a driver suddenly cancels a turn.

Carpoolers generally assume that if the driver for that day has an emergency, others will find a way to get the children to school. These agreements in anticipation of crises are often informal and ambiguous. The people who assume them may lack accurate information and be unclear about what they have agreed to do. Jerry and Eleanor Flaherty found themselves in this situation.

They were part of a carpooling group in which parents took turns driving children to school. Their son Michael was one of the children. One Monday, Alice, the parent assigned to drive the children that day, asked Eleanor to take her place. Jerry and Eleanor had received favors from the other carpoolers. Now it was their turn. Jerry could not help, because he was about to leave on a business trip. He joked to Eleanor, "It's a long commute, but you can do it. Life is management." But Eleanor was disconcerted and had left her calendar at work. Jerry suggested a solution. Eleanor should first drop off their daughter Mary at her school and be finished with this by 7:40 AM. Then she could take the carpooling students to their school and still arrive at her own workplace on time. Eleanor doubted that this would work. Jerry asked if he should call Alice to confirm the new plan. Eleanor replied sharply, "Not unless you have something to say. I told her I would take care of it or call another parent." Jerry nodded, "Good orientation, good attitude."

Jerry intervened in Eleanor's carpool crisis because, even though he would be out of town, he was one of the carpool team. How Eleanor dealt with this crisis would affect not only her relationships with the other parents, but his as well. The other parents assumed that he or Eleanor could somehow pick up the slack when things went wrong, much as other parents had done at other times. Left unsaid was what this took out of them on a morning that became anything but routine.

Intelligence Gathering

The families we studied clearly managed busyness in different ways. But how did they create the circumstances that enabled them to follow their particular styles of management? They collected pertinent information, simplified, consolidated, broke tasks down into smaller units, and used technological devices. By doing these things, families gave themselves a better chance of succeeding with their plans.

For these busy families, information gathering was especially valuable. It allowed them to plan and improvise, to recognize surprises, and to know when conditions had changed in a way that might threaten order. They collected information regarding other people whose cooperation they needed for their plans to unfold as intended. They used information to recognize changes that could upset their plans or limit their capacity to improvise.

These families both received and gathered information. Since they were often unsure what would be useful, they constantly collected information. Any activity or encounter was a possible source of information, and the uncertainty about its usefulness made its collection, storage, and retrieval especially important. Most of the people in our study assumed that more information, more devices, and larger networks of people were helpful, especially since they were uncertain about where threats might arise.

Intelligence gathering came to characterize busyness, forming a tacit kind of work and requiring particular skills. Ironically, although intended to enhance order and control, it became something more to do, to worry about, and even to fail at. It raised questions for busy families, and they answered them in ways that reflected their own busyness. How could they ensure that their planning was good? How did they gather intelligence that allowed them both to plan and improvise, and to know when conditions had changed? What could they do to their activities and encounters to make them easier to control? How did they keep track of the information that allowed them to do all this? And what did all of this do to their lives?

JERRY FLAHERTY: AVOIDING LIFE'S ICEBERGS

For Jerry Flaherty, information gathering began at home. Its importance was that it enabled family members to plan and establish control over their lives. This is what he meant when he announced that extensive face-to face communication at home had "bandwidth" advantages. But sometimes the information was unreliable. On occasion, he and members of his family failed to meet expectations or communicate effectively. Even worse, on occasion, their failures were hidden or distorted. He observed that without accurate feedback, "you keep on going here without adjustment." He likened this to encountering drifting "icebergs," which could spell disaster in daily life. "When everybody does what's expected of them, things work out fairly well," Jerry said. "When anybody doesn't, it gets to be a very volatile situation, and if somebody's not honest about it, then it gets to be probably *very* problematic." He concluded: "To make things work, there has to be good communication. And the more things that interfere with that communication, the more independent your children's lives are and our own two lives are, the more difficult it is to cause those circles to intertwine at the right times and right places." In Jerry's view, as life became more complicated, it became more difficult to accumulate the necessary intelligence. Some necessary information was long-term, focusing on years rather than days.

Both Jerry and Eleanor spent much time and attention obtaining information on both long- and short-term issues. When Eleanor was required to volunteer at her son's high school during his sophomore year, she joined its accreditation task force, where she coordinated and analyzed a survey of parents. In this way, she learned more about the school, how her son could benefit from it in the future, and what might constrain his participation in its activities. She also created goodwill at the school, on which she hoped to be able to draw in the future.

PEGGY JOHNSON, SUZANNE JONES, AND HUMBERTO MENDOZA:
GATHERING INFORMATION AT WORK

The workplace is an obvious site for information gathering, and the stakes for collecting reliable information can be high. Yet jobs differ in how they facilitate learning. Three of the people in our study illustrate this.

Peggy Johnson used her full-time position at work to mine useful information. Her job ensuring International Organization for Standards (ISO) 9000 compliance gave her considerable knowledge about the company and how to find out about it.[1] She joked that when she asked for information, "few people say no to me. They just give it. Other people know this and then come to me." For Peggy, intelligence gathering was an effortless, almost inevitable accompaniment to her regular duties.

Because she job-shared, Suzanne Jones had to expend considerable effort to acquire the information that came easily to Peggy. Suzanne did not even know who her next supervisor would be. She shook her head and said, "I'm so out of it because I'm part-time. You walk in and find you're reorganized or something." She found this particularly demoralizing. Even though she was more qualified than many of her managers, she could not aspire to such a position due to her part-time status. When she was asked to develop a department newsletter, yet another task, she took it on eagerly, because it justified her chatting with co-workers about their activities, learning more about the workplace. She figured this would enhance her ability to make a greater contribution at work and to protect her job.

Humberto, Suzanne's husband, was continuously on the alert at work to find things he could use at home. His position as a fire investigator required him to interact with Downtown superiors. This gave him the opportunity to learn about changing job expectations and trends in firefighting. This information allowed him to plan his career step-by-step, confident that he was anticipating future department needs.

Humberto went to great lengths to ensure that the information he collected was trustworthy. He relied on people and situations he knew. He hired a painter for his house after watching him work on a city building. He hired firefighters to set tiles for him, which they did as a second job. He bought his used car from an automobile dealer whom he vouched for when the man ran into trouble with the law. Humberto's auto mechanic owned a garage that Humberto had inspected for fire hazards. By working with known providers, Humberto reduced uncertainty and guaranteed trustworthy information.

Enacting Rationality

THE HOPKINS / JOHNSONS: CONTROLLING SON WITH ROUTINES AND EMPLOYEES WITH CALENDARS

For Peggy Johnson and Kent Hopkins, establishing and preserving their son Sam's routines made them the kind of family they wanted to be. They viewed stable routines as the foundation of their family life, and they went to great lengths to maintain them for their two-and-a-half-year-old son, Sam, especially in the morning and at night, at the cost of substantial additional work for themselves.

Their own work lives were busy and hectic. In addition to their current jobs, each spent time trying to create separate new businesses. During the day, Sam was at preschool, so Kent and Peggy saw their morning and evening routines with Sam as essential to his well-being.

One morning, Sam was up and dressed by 7:10 AM, sitting on the sofa drinking milk and watching the black-and-white Frank Capra classic *Meet John Doe* (1941), starring Barbara Stanwyck and Gary Cooper. His parents were in the kitchen chatting about what each would do that day. Kent strapped on his pager, cellular phone, and company-provided radio.

At 7:15, Peggy reminded Sam that she would pick him up after work. She kissed him goodbye and left. Kent then asked Sam if he would like to watch a different movie. The boy nodded, and Kent lifted him up to a high shelf near the fireplace, where Sam selected a DVD of the movie *Stuart Little*. Kent put the boy down and helped Sam remove the disk from its case. The boy put it into the DVD player, located low in a stack of stereo components and carefully placed the case atop it. When the movie menu appeared, Kent clicked the remote on play. While Sam watched the movie, Kent performed a few final chores and told Sam that they would soon be leaving.

A few minutes later Kent put Sam's shoes on as they sat on the sofa. Since Sam was fidgeting, Kent asked him if he wanted the movie fast-forwarded. When Sam whined an answer Kent said, "Don't complain. Say, 'fast forward.'" He told him again that they needed to leave soon. Father and son sat together on the sofa, watching a couple in the movie head off for the local orphanage, where they passed up the opportunity to adopt one of the perfect children and instead chose a talking mouse.

At 7:28 AM, Kent said, "Come on, Sam. Time to go." Sam responded with groans and noes, and Kent replied, "Sam, you know it's time to go." He picked up the boy, carried him to the stereo and let him turn off the amplifier and the DVD player. When the boy wanted to do it again, Kent turned on the equipment and then the boy turned it off a second time. They went out to the pickup truck and Kent opened the door so Sam could climb into his car seat. Kent switched on the tape deck, and the sounds of the Australian ballad "Wild Colonial Boy" filled the cab. Kent urged Sam onward, "Come on, Sam. You can do it. Do you need help?" The boy methodically climbed into the car seat, turning himself around when Kent pointed out he was seated backward.

At the preschool, Kent opened the truck door and unlatched the seatbelt. "Come on Sam. Let's get down." After a brief struggle the boy made it to the pavement. They walked into the office, Kent signed the boy in and then they headed for the adjacent classroom, where an aide gave Sam a warm greeting. Kent lifted the boy and showed the woman that he was teething and warned her that he might chew on another child for relief. He put the boy down and asked for and received a hug and kiss. With a "Have a nice day, Sam," he then left.

At 4:45 PM, Peggy packed her briefcase and headed for the car. Suddenly, she remembered that she had forgotten Sam's regular treat, a pack of Sweet Tarts placed on the front seat of her van for the boy to find. She hurried to the vending machines in her employer's cafeteria and settled for a small package of cookies. At 5:00 PM, after a short drive of several miles on the freeway, Peggy arrived at the day care. She placed the cookies on the seat and found her son among a crowd of kids in a fenced play area. He was excited when he spotted her and ran to her when the aide opened the gate. Sam was all smiles as he ran to the room where his things were, struggling to pull open the door by himself. Peggy and Sam stopped briefly in the office to sign the boy out, and then they walked to the minivan. Sam climbed in the side and then leaned around the passenger seat and found the treat on the seat. He was pleased with himself, and Peggy asked if he wanted it opened. He nodded and then settled contentedly into his car seat, where Peggy secured the straps and then drove home. The departure took only eight minutes, but Peggy let the boy set his own pace, never admonishing him to hurry up. She commented, "I learned early on there's no sense in rushing. We take our time." By following this pattern as often as possible, she was able to rush Sam when it was necessary, because "he knows it's an exception."

Sam's mornings and evenings thus unfolded according to a set routine, one intended to provide him with fixed reference points, since he was out of his parents' care so much of the time. Kent usually took Sam to day care, and Peggy picked him up in the afternoon. When he was younger, she had taken pains to lessen his time at day care, working only between 7:00 AM and 4:00 PM. But she discovered that he enjoyed playing there. He was a very physical child and especially liked to play outside. She found herself rushing to pick him up at 4:00 PM, only to watch him play for another thirty minutes before he was ready to go, so now she simply worked longer and picked him up later.

Travel, either by Kent or Peggy, could upset their daily routine, but the couple tried to minimize its impact. When Kent traveled, Peggy followed his schedule, spending time with the boy in the living room, dropping him at day care, and not arriving at work until 8:00 AM. She did this because the morning routine was "pretty much set." Then she picked him up a little later, much as Kent did when Peggy traveled. As long as she got her work done, Peggy was able to arrange her own schedule, so she could handle the child-care duties.

Sam's evening routine was long and complicated. It began around 7:15–7:30 PM, when he started to get ready for bed. He feared the dark and wanted one of his parents in the room until he fell asleep around 9:30 PM.

They sat in the adjacent room and read, but this still limited their ability to work at home. Furthermore, the house was small, making it difficult to separate Sam from the devices and spaces they needed to work. Because of this, they tried to complete their work at the office. Despite Sam's nightly routine, he slept fretfully and awakened four or five times each night. In describing her own daily routines, Peggy commented, "We're both operating off significant sleep deprivation." Peggy used to awaken at 5:00 AM to work out, but she changed her routine; arising between 6:00 and 6:30 AM instead, she exercised in her employer's gym during a break.

Both Kent and Peggy were committed to protecting Sam's routines, and they did so by adjusting their own everyday lives. Peggy pursued a graduate degree largely in her cubicle at work to minimize the impact on the house, which was set aside for Sam's important routines. She and Kent both worked as much as they could on their own start-ups while at work, again to protect Sam's routines and ability to roam the house. Even his evening routine was buffered from the couple's weekly routine. Peggy spent Monday nights at a local university campus taking classes toward a second graduate degree in business, and Kent spent Tuesdays in medieval combat exercises. While the one was away, the other stayed with Sam. They seldom planned Wednesday through Friday, but evenings were typically taken up by Sam's bedtime routine. Usually, he took a bath, played, brushed his teeth, and then listened as one parent or the other read four or five books to him.

PEGGY JOHNSON'S MEETING CONTROL

At work, some people put their efforts into controlling meetings. But Peggy Johnson, the reluctantly self-described "ISO 9000 lady," feared that meetings might easily swallow up all of her time. She decided instead to use her calendar to control her time, thereby creating space to be productive.

She installed her weekly schedule in the program that scheduled meetings on all employee computers. This allowed others to view her availability and schedule Peggy into their meetings. Peggy filled in her calendar on Mondays to protect the day so that she could complete essential tasks and get the week off to a good start. Otherwise, she would be overwhelmed by meetings early in the week and would fail to meet her commitments by Friday.

Peggy had to be careful in protecting her time. If she filled her calendar with dubious commitments, she would be unresponsive to her customers' needs, a heinous fault in her company. Likewise, she needed to be able to schedule the time of co-workers, and she did not want a reputation as someone who cared only for her own convenience. Peggy exercised control in a world where others were doing the same thing and where finding the correct mix of discretion and constraint was critical.

THE FLAHERTYS: SIMPLIFYING THROUGH CONSOLIDATION

The Flahertys consolidated their activities and relationships to reduce time spent in transit. Eleanor Flaherty did this when she enrolled her daughter Mary in the same theater camp that Mary's friend Heather attended. This was a consciously conceived strategy that developed when Eleanor tried to figure out how to manage transportation during the summer. "I have to have some carpooling," she muttered to herself.

Eleanor had enrolled Mary in a summer theater program. She knew that Heather was in the same program, but possibly in a different town. Both locations were equally inconvenient for Eleanor, but Heather's mother was her good friend, and Eleanor wanted to enroll them in the same location so that they could take turns driving the children. Eleanor called a staff member at the theater program and asked, "How do I handle this? I need Mary and Heather together." The staff person offered to help. Eleanor said, "Let's get Mary moved over to the other location and I'll tell Heather's mother." Eleanor then called Heather's mother, saying, "I talked to the theater program and they moved Mary. There's plenty of room there for Heather, but they haven't gotten her material yet, so you might want to check with them." They arranged to carpool, thus freeing Eleanor from driving her daughter every day.

The Flaherty's son Michael had a close circle of friends who all came from the same neighborhood and elementary school, but he attended a high school different from that of his friends and far from his neighborhood. Michael was initially unable to make close friendships in his new school. Since these students lived far from one another and Michael was too young to drive, they rarely saw one another except in class. Michael's friends remained his old elementary school buddies. He did not choose this situation, but rather responded to his transportation constraints.

THE CARLSBERGS: TRANSPORTATION TRICKS

Because of deep departmental layoffs and a seemingly solitary workweek, Alex Carlsberg had no need to protect his hours from interruptions. But he did protect family time from sudden intrusions by work-related travel. On numerous occasions, his employer asked him to delay a planned family vacation. As a result, he began buying nonrefundable airline tickets, so that if the company asked him to delay, they had to reimburse him for the tickets. This usually protected his scheduled vacation.

His wife's efforts at control, on the other hand, focused on daily transportation and the need to be able to respond quickly to a crisis. Once a week, Pat drove to her job with a co-worker. Although she enjoyed his company, agreed with carpooling in principle, and appreciated getting into the carpool lane and speeding past all those single-occupant cars stuck in traffic, she disliked losing control of her transportation. When she was driving, she had to consider another person's needs; when she was the passenger, she might be stuck without a ride, far from home, husband, and schools. Pat liked to be in control of her transportation just in case of a crisis, especially a sick or injured son at school.

THE CARLSBERGS: A NINE-DAY, 8O-HOUR SCHEDULE

Like many working parents, including several in our study, the Carlsbergs faced a particularly pressing logistical nightmare in the summer when their children were on vacation from school. The tactics the Carlsbergs had developed for the school year did not work during the summer. They had to manipulate their work schedules to meet both family and work obligations.

The Carlsbergs' solution was also used by the Tentoris. First, they relied on friends, grandparents, summer school, and various summer camps. When that did not work, they used a vacation day each week to provide summer care for their boys. Alex Carlsberg used his company's "9-80 schedule," in which he worked eight nine-hour days and one eight-hour day during two weeks, and so had every other Friday off. That alternate Friday was the critical buffer that allowed him to catch up on tasks that he had delayed when his plans changed. Ideally, it would include a nap to make up for the previous weeks of inadequate sleep.

Conclusions

We spent much of our time watching families prepare for their days and following them as those days unfolded. We discussed what they thought about their decisions when plans made earlier in the day had to be changed because of unforeseen developments. As our fieldwork progressed, our very presence educated people in the families to offer explanations for their actions before we asked. "You're probably wondering why I did that" became a common refrain.

Coordinating the events of the day was, for the most part, uninteresting to the families. Their focus was on their activities, for that is what they saw as the real content of their days, whether that content inspired or depressed them or was simply tolerated as necessary. The content was about doing their jobs, paying a bill or two, or having lunch with a former co-worker. But they did not count coordinating those activities as itself an activity, even through it was necessary, a tacit form of work, and in fact quite time-consuming for them. The families had little to say about coordination and in fact were often puzzled by our growing interest in it. For the most part, they were oblivious to the enormity of this tacit work in their lives. For example, a lawyer was keenly interested in the law and his or her cases, just as a fireman was passionate and articulate about saving lives and the nuances of hazardous materials. As far as they were concerned, the task of coordinating their activities with family members and friends was just the backdrop to the real stuff that filled their lives. That we three professors should be paid to study what to them was an unavoidable, humdrum part of life seemed mildly bizarre.

Yet life is largely lived in the humdrum minutiae of everyday existence. It is highly significant that individuals talked so little and so inarticulately about their coping but spent so much time doing it. This ubiquitous coordinating was clearly a high-stakes game, because days and weeks could fall apart if an appointment was overlooked or if someone else failed to be precisely where and when they had said they would.

Why do we claim that this tacit work of control is so important to our families when they didn't think so? Simply put, individuals had much to do. They were correct that they were burdened, or "empowered," with many obligations and tasks. Still, there was much more going on with their busyness, and being busy was not just a matter of working hard. Busyness, our families were teaching us, is grounded in realities of modernity that confront us with a question seldom asked in traditional societies: How shall I live my life? In modern societies, how people come to identify themselves is not merely handed down across the generations; it is adopted through countless small and large decisions: what to wear and eat, how to act, who to be with, and when.[2]

At the heart of individualism in modern societies is the creation of a lifestyle. Despite its associations with marketing and connotations of superficiality, lifestyle choices are central to our self-identities and daily activities. Lifestyles consist of practices we adopt for utilitarian purposes, as well as to give form to the stories we create about who we are and what we aspire to be. There is always effort, then, in creating a lifestyle, choosing and seeking out the activities that will allow us to actually live a particular way.

Families are preeminent sites where lifestyles intersect. They are where individuals with possibly divergent lifestyles come together, and where an all-encompassing family lifestyle might be negotiated. Lifestyles are not just found and embraced. They are actively assembled, and the work of doing this can be prodigious. There are a proliferation of choices about how to live and few firm guideposts about how to choose. The activities that come to constitute a lifestyle can be dispersed across space and time, so that we must be in certain places at certain times with certain people. Furthermore, knowledge is always provisional, so that even our trust in respected, reliable authorities is limited: we are always awaiting additional information that will modify what we have been told is true. Finally, media technologies expand the scope of information that is suddenly (and somehow) relevant to us.

The result is that lifestyles are a major cultural production. The planning, routines, improvisation, anticipation, and intelligence gathering recounted in this chapter are not just about efficiently getting through the day, but also about enacting our lifestyles. It is not surprising, then, that coping looms large in daily life. What is more surprising is that we often ignore the larger context of our coping. The latter is hardly trite or banal. It is at the crux of who we are and who we will be.

CHAPTER FIVE

Making Manageable Worlds

If Suzanne's monthly team meeting in Los Angeles began and ended just right, she could say goodbye to her girls in the morning, catch a flight south, and still be back for a late dinner. She had "educated" her teammates about her priorities, and usually they were able to accommodate her requests. In a small way, Suzanne was trying to make the world around her more amenable to her obligations. Often, she and the other members of the fourteen families had to demonstrate their flexibility by conforming to the constraints imposed on them by other people. But sometimes they could ask those around them to adjust, and sometimes the latter were willing to do so. Our protagonists were not revolutionaries who were rebelling against the pace of life or the obligations imposed on them. They harbored no illusions of stopping the world and getting off; rather, they tinkered with their busyness. They addressed specific issues that mattered to them, and where they thought they just might succeed. However few their victories, they reveal another facet of coping: creative, proactive efforts to make a world that supports people in their busyness.

In this chapter, we explore two practices we saw families adopt that in principle should result in more manageable everyday lives. First, people spoke frequently of the need to simplify their lives. When they were buried in their hectic daily schedules, they had little time for reflection, and they realized this. Often, this took the form of a broad lament, uttered on particularly difficult days, and little was done about it. Yet to varying degrees and in different ways, people did simplify: individuals and families eliminated what they decided was unnecessary. Ironically, this necessitated another kind of tacit work. People had to negotiate the criteria for deciding what was necessary and then decide whether something in particular should be retained or jettisoned.

A second practice was that of breaking down larger activities into several smaller ones that people could recombine in an opportunistic way. Such modules or chunks provided flexibility. Ideally, they were relatively self-contained, not interdependent with others, and could be easily combined in order to achieve larger goals. Again, we watched as the tacit work of breaking down activities played out. People had to keep track of the fragments they had created and prioritize what to do with them.

Simplifying

THE CARLSBERGS: CONSOLIDATING DENTISTS

Sometimes simplification was limited in focus, intended to control a particularly troublesome feature of a family's routine. The Carlsbergs visited three dentists, whose offices were located in several cities. While they liked each, there were logistical headaches when visits were necessary. And so they consolidated by choosing to patronize a single practice that was not necessarily anyone's favorite: It was far from home, school, and work, but it was near where their daily commutes intersected.

THE MENDOZA/JONESES: SIMPLICITY AS A GUIDING PRINCIPLE

Simplification could also organize whole households and the lives of the people who lived in them. When Suzanne Jones said, "We're trying to simplify our lives," she was expressing the grand principle of life in her family. To achieve this, she and her husband, Humberto Mendoza, lived well beneath their means and carefully scrutinized every purchase and relationship that entered their home. According to Suzanne, Humberto "cannot imagine any trash left in our house. He's a neat freak." The house was indeed well organized and sparsely furnished; it lacked the clutter of many homes with children. The living room contained a sofa facing a media console, separated in winter by a white area rug. Pictures hung on opposite walls. Every few months, Humberto scoured the house, disposing of clothes, books, and other items. Suzanne commented on a neighbor's mound of rubbish awaiting curbside pickup. She and Humberto would never create such a heap: the moment they decided something was unwanted, they threw it in the garbage, donated it to charity, or drove it to the dump. Suzanne followed the same principle at work. She gave away her gifts and promotional items of Waterford crystal, bottles of wine, and chocolates. She dismissed them as "stuff," useless clutter.

For Suzanne and Humberto, simplicity involved more than giving things away and restricting new acquisitions. It entailed thinking about the choices they made, which Suzanne said many people did not do. But for Suzanne, this was central to her life. "To me this is simplifying because I'm choosing what I'm going to focus on. I'm choosing that family happiness is most important to me." Her choices were to pursue less expensive, intrinsically rewarding activities. "I want to do more of those kinds of things that are very simple but very enjoyable," she said. "Going for hikes, things that don't cost money. I had a blast when Angela and I had a picnic out in the front yard, and we sat there, and we talked. And those are the kind of things I really want to do, the simple stuff."

Suzanne and Humberto both grew up in low-income families, and this experience influenced their worldview. Their commitment to simplicity was based on their belief that they should act responsibly through sound financial management. They kept every receipt and lived within a budget that was well below what they could afford.

Suzanne's co-workers talked constantly about money, cars, vacations, and expensive restaurants, but Suzanne was unimpressed. "If I asked them if they had savings they'd say no, or at least not commensurate with their incomes." She said that many of them believed that they were very important and so deserved significant rewards, but Humberto and Suzanne laughed at this. When Humberto and Suzanne received an unexpected tax bill, they immediately put off some planned purchases. To buy some gifts and children's clothes, Suzanne cashed in an unused airline ticket, and she brought her own lunch to work. They took these small sacrifices for granted as part of their money management strategy.

Simplification for this couple was based on larger assumptions and values. "I don't want to be so caught up with the outside world," Humberto proclaimed, "that when you leave the house you just get so bombarded and you get pulled into this superficial world and forget what is really important." In that superficial world, "you need the cell phone to be in contact with someone. You need to have this latest, greatest toy because this is going to make you more efficient and more effective. I find that it's a fallacy." What truly mattered to him was time, and these devices diminished his freedom to do what truly mattered: "You can't do more with less time," Humberto said. He traced this sense of personal responsibility and importance to his parents' Central American cultural influence: "It communicated that there was a value of commonness, that it's not what you possess, it's what you are as a person; it's not the material things that bring you value, it's the integrity of who you are."

The Mendoza/Jones family had to work at simplification. Tracking assets and liabilities consumed time and effort. It was a kind of work that they took on in order ultimately to have less to do. Suzanne's greatest simplification, job sharing so that she would have more time with her family, led to power conflicts within the family. Now that she no longer worked full-time, she and her husband argued about their relative contributions to the family. A full-time job would legitimize her economic contribution to the household, but it would also reduce her time with the children.

Chunking

THE CARLSBERGS: FRAGMENTING MEETINGS AND ITS CONSEQUENCES

To manage their lives, the Carlsbergs not only consolidated certain activities but also fragmented others into smaller chunks, breaking up what previously they had considered a single task. When they had the time, they worked on these fragments, but they interspersed them with other activities over longer periods. Pat Carlsberg in particular developed "chunking" into a conscious strategy for getting things done, but in doing so, she created more to manage, which in turn gave her a heightened sense of busyness when she shifted from one activity to another.

Both in her volunteer activities and at the office, Pat learned to work on tasks in shorter and shorter time periods, seizing opportunities to work, not as originally planned, but at the last minute, with renegotiated deadlines. She complained that she could finish tasks at work if only she could work on them uninterrupted. But the myriad demands on her time prevented her from doing so. Even her meetings were broken up into fragments and held piecemeal. Each week she was supposed to meet for an hour with a supervisor. He put it off until the end of the day, just when she was ready to leave to pick up her children. He was unmarried, without her complex obligations, and did not need to leave work on time, but he also refused to accommodate to Pat's time pressures. While Pat wanted to have a full hour to meet, she knew that would not happen. Pat's solution was to fragment the meeting into pieces. She prepared the meeting agenda in advance and met with him for thirty minutes to deal with the major items. The rest of the week, she met with her supervisor on the run: at the water cooler, coffee machine, or at other meetings. By the end of the week, she had covered an hour of meeting time.

By contrast, Pat's husband, Alex, found working in time fragments to be alien, frustrating, and inhibiting. He needed long blocks of time to think about and develop his business plan. Since he lacked long time periods, Pat expressed doubts that he would be able to bring his business plan to fruition.

Pat Carlsberg claimed that she lost nothing in adopting her chunking strategy, but there was a hidden consequence. Pat had to work at boundary management. She had to recognize the larger activity and then decompose it into pieces that were optimal for doing the job, without always knowing what was optimal. Pat had to keep track of what she was doing, remembering the status of each item and how far she had proceeded. Here, too, she was often unsure, because she no longer had a single agenda. She never knew for certain that what had been discussed was actually resolved. She admitted that things did "fall between the cracks."

Chunking allows Peggy Johnson to help her husband, Kent Hopkins, develop his business plan and to work on her own employability. Breaking apart their tasks is essential, since their son Sam's routines and their cramped living quarters require Peggy and Kent to work wherever and whenever they can.

Peggy Johnson was able to control her time at work. Unlike Pat Carlsberg, she regularly attended lengthy formal meetings. When she had a three-hour project, Peggy could schedule the time to work on it, and this was possible because people did not constantly interrupt her. Furthermore, her job ensuring International Organization for Standards compliance allowed her to interrupt others and schedule meetings, since her assistance was crucial to many department heads.

Like Alex Carlsberg, Kent Hopkins was developing a business plan, but unlike Alex, he did so in the chunks that Alex found difficult to master. Peggy offered suggestions on a draft of the plan, and Kent rewrote sections of it at the office. He brought it home for her to review and asked, "Is this what you mean?" Gradually, the plan developed in small pieces, which he then revised and assembled into the complete document. Peggy, too, worked in chunks on the plans for her and Kent's businesses. She also did this with her own graduate education. She stored this material in readily identifiable blue folders in case of a layoff. Meanwhile, she worked on it intermittently. Kent and Peggy did not prefer to work like this. They did it to preserve longer periods of time for their son Sam and his routines.

Suzanne Jones and Humberto Mendoza consciously thought about the fragments in their life that they had to manage, and they reorganized them opportunistically. For example, Suzanne divided up tasks both to deal with the minutiae of everyday life and to accomplish a grander goal: job sharing. Suzanne and another woman were allowed to divide their shared job in various ways. One option was to work jointly on all projects for all distributors. Her partner liked this, but Suzanne preferred to divide up the distributors and then separately service those each had chosen. Suzanne insisted on this to protect herself in case her partner failed to complete her share of the work or did it poorly. In effect, Suzanne took a larger job and divided it into two autonomous chunks.

Some jobs thus supported or prepared people to work in fragments, while others did not. Alex Carlsberg's work as a systems analyst required him to trace extensive webs of relationships, where he needed long periods of focused attention. His job required concentration and reflection that simply was not amenable to chunking. In contrast, Humberto Mendoza's work as a fireman was consistent with living life in chunks. One night, a firefighter was about to pay for a cassette at a video rental store when a medical call came. He dropped the cassette on the counter and ran to the truck where Humberto and the rest of the crew waited. With sirens blaring and lights flashing, they raced several miles to a house, rushed inside, and found an unconscious cancer patient. They administered first aid until the ambulance crew arrived to take him to the hospital. As soon as he was gone, the firemen asked where they could find the nearest video rental store. This was typical of their nights, shifting back and forth between life-threatening emergencies, personal errands, gossip, and renting movies to watch back at the station. While these abrupt shifts appeared to occur effortlessly, Humberto observed that in fact they caused many of his colleagues to suffer from stress-related diseases, and to avoid these, he maintained a rigorous exercise regimen.

Tracking and Prioritizing

The busyness of everyday life and its simplification also required people to be able to communicate with one another and to track people, activities, and even ideas. Technological devices were critical here. Family members used lists, calendars, and PDAs (personal digital assistants) both to organize information and to avoid a catastrophic lapse of memory, such as forgetting to pick up a child or attend a meeting. Keeping track involved a complex bundle of activities. Sometimes, people focused on their activities and deadlines, fearing that the sheer number and frequency of these might overwhelm their ability to remember and organize. At other times, people concentrated on keeping track of themselves. Whatever direction this took in various families, keeping track constituted an important category of work provoked by busyness. People kept track of their activities in order to do them efficiently and avoid failure, but the consequence, again, was that this gave them something additional to do.

ALEX CARLSBERG: TRACKING WITH PDAS

Alex Carlsberg was equipped with the high-tech means of keeping track, a PDA, but his busy schedule overwhelmed his ability to use its "efficient" functions. Instead, a variety of high-tech and low-tech devices, and even walls, became aids to keeping track.

Alex's office, containing a refrigerator, a large collection of compact discs, and an espresso machine, had a comfortable, homey look, but it also housed a laptop and three desktop computers, whose screens glowed in the dim morning light. While he worked on the computers, he used low-tech devices to keep him on track. As mentioned in Chapter 3, his whiteboard displayed ten cryptic reminders of what he needed to do.

The PDA contained the addresses and phone numbers of family members and people at work. He could have sorted and clustered them electronically but said he didn't have the time. If he had, he would have pared down the list, since he had forgotten many of the people. He did enter items on the "to do list" of his PDA, but he seldom checked anything off as completed. Some items were ongoing reminders, but others were large and complex. If he completed only part of an item, it remained on the PDA. Alex could have divided the larger items into smaller chunks, but since that also took time and thought, he preferred to use his whiteboard reminders, "so at least I'd see them."

On occasion, Alex would call his home telephone to leave a message reminding himself of something to do. His wife Pat remarked that she served as his personal reminder. She also had a PDA, but she never used it, preferring instead a tiny, crumpled address book stuffed with business cards. "I would die without this," she said. She also kept a daily calendar in her purse. Pat described herself as a "list person" who was not "that electronically facile." She stuck Post-Its all over her car and by the phone at home.

SUZANNE JONES: THE "TO DO" LIST

Tracking involves more than the mechanical process of defining, identifying, and noting the individual pieces of a life. It also requires people to assign meaning and value. Should a "to do" list include only pragmatic requirements, or also goals and objectives that serve a higher purpose in the family?

Suzanne struggled with balancing efficiency, doing what is minimally necessary, with that which is desirable, building community and developing a sense of mission within the family. Her struggle involved negotiation and communication with Humberto, her day-care providers, and her children's friends. Of particular significance is that these activities, devoted to building an infrastructure that enabled Suzanne to manage her life, led to piling on another layer of invisible work.

The daily lists of Suzanne Jones revealed her assumptions about the nature of her activities and how she hoped to organize her time. Suzanne created them "so I do the things I have to do instead of what I want to do." This approach annoyed her husband, Humberto, who argued that she should only list what must be done each day. But Suzanne insisted on including things she liked to do, interspersed with her obligatory chores. She neither checked off all the items on a daily list nor ignored them. Rather, she used the items to reflect her larger assumptions about time and its organization and as a resource for navigating a particular day. "I can see what'll give me the most bang for the bucks. It's like the 80/20 rule" (accomplishing 80 percent of her goals by completing 20 percent of her items). But she also made her day easier by including chores that were enjoyable, even if they accomplished less. On some days, she was deliberately "inefficient," arguing, "I don't mind it: it's my break."

Suzanne found that prioritizing a day's activities was often difficult and only remotely connected to action. She described a day's list of twenty-one chores. They were typically heterogeneous. She undertook them knowing that she would not complete all of them.

> I had to do a written letter to the day care this morning telling them how Nicole's gastroenterologist appointment went yesterday because I'm a little concerned that this is the ninth week and I don't want the day care to do anything drastic like say, "Oh, we can't take her because you can't figure this out." I needed to go to the bank; I did that. I need to pick up a particular

test that they want to do for Nicole from the laboratory. I need to get an oil change. I've got to get gas in the car. I gotta get chlorine for the pool. I need to order some fruit for the party, for Angela's birthday party. I need to go get some high-fiber foods for Nicole because we're going to try that with her, and then I need to write a thank-you note to someone who gave us a gift the other day. Pick up some photography. See, it's a lot of little stuff, and Humberto just doesn't do all that little stuff, and not all of it needs to be done.

Suzanne shifted her lists from scraps of paper to her PDA, which consolidated items and allowed her to "grade" their priority. On this day, she gave an A grade only to nine top-priority items. "B means, after I get the A's done the B's come. And then the C's could probably never be done and it wouldn't faze anybody." Yet Suzanne expected to tackle some B chores if she could do them while completing the A's. The C chores were merely "nice things that I'd like to do," as well as important chores that she knew her husband would do. "Humberto can take care of those things tomorrow while I'm at work. I'm gonna put some of the C's down here at the bottom: They're things he can do." Her list thus revealed her expectations about what each partner could and should do. "He's not going to call the ten people that are coming to Angela's birthday party," said Suzanne, "It's just not something that he's going to do. He's not into the party planning, social thing. It's not that he can't do it, he's not gonna do it. Anything that has to do with her birthday party on Saturday I'm going to do. He'll help me when it comes time to go pick up the cake and get it loaded into the car that morning and make sure we've got everything we need."

By creating an infrastructure of devices to keep track, Suzanne ironically created the work of keeping track of how that infrastructure was used. She kept track of people and activities using a paper annual calendar posted on the refrigerator, a thick paper date book that she carried to work, and a PDA that contained her daily list. She transferred information from the PDA to a slip of paper to use while running errands, and she also used scraps of paper and Post-Its to record notes that she later entered in one of her formal calendars. Suzanne wanted to consolidate lists and calendars but said this would be difficult. She shared the refrigerator calendar with Humberto; its very conspicuousness guaranteed that she would not overlook a critical deadline or event. While the PDA consolidated her "to do" list with other information, such as a calendar and address book, it did not allow her to view how an event fitted into longer units of time, such as weeks or months, thus making it difficult for her to plan. She found the PDA cumbersome to use while dashing between errands; that was why she kept the paper version perched on the dashboard. Because she job shared and divided her week between paid employment and family-related activities, Suzanne also manipulated lists and calendars to differentiate and integrate those domains of her life. For example, she kept extensive work-related information on the PDA, which she filtered from the "to do" lists of family-related errands: "I don't want that invading what my primary goal is."

Suzanne's busyness thus provoked her to find numerous ways to keep track of information relevant to her everyday life. In doing this, she altered her life in subtle ways. Keeping track became a sort of tacit work, with tasks as diverse as shopping for the optimal record-keeping device, thinking about how activities and people could best be organized for easy recall, and locating herself in space and time to be efficient, and on occasion, deliberately inefficient. She drew other people into this activity as prompters and recorders who helped her think about how her life was situated in space and time.

At this level of self-reflection, Suzanne could elaborate and compare her management strategies with those of others and share and imitate the best ones. In doing this, she produced an inscription of everyday life that was both a normative vision of what constituted daily life and a description of how she lived it. She inscribed movements and destinations and the actors who entered and departed as their trajectories intersected with hers. Her feelings of accomplishment and failure were shaped by the relationship between the exigencies of daily life and the inscriptions she used to keep track. As she modified and reinterpreted them, her life became a co-production of the lived and inscribed.

Suzanne's language of keeping track thus conveyed a practical, matter-of-fact sense of daily life. Suzanne took for granted these people and activities. But keeping track also rendered these very activities problematic. While the inscriptions accounted for the stuff of daily life, they also constituted it. Suzanne's lists, for example, were extensive and included itemized mission statements for her and her family, as well as lists of her values. She used these to provide a direction to her life and to keep track of her progress in achieving her mission or enacting her values. She kept paper and digital versions of the lists, thereby externalizing information about her sense of self and family through technology: what might be considered deeply intimate glowed on a small screen and could be sent as an e-mail attachment to other people.

Suzanne said she reflected upon her lists and in doing so enacted them in her life. For example, her mission statement identified her as a keen listener, someone "with great negotiation and persuasion skills." "I can attest to this," she said. "I've repeated this to myself and I actually became this. I didn't start out being a great negotiator and a persuader, but I have become that. Because if you're reading it to yourself twice a day, you go to sleep with it in your head and then you wake up and when a situation comes in which you have to be a great negotiator, you'll hop in and try it, because you've told yourself you are it. And it works." Her list thus did more than describe the tasks of everyday life. It also helped to constitute her as a particular kind of person. Not only did it help her keep track of a day, it also helped her to keep track of the direction to her life and thus made her who she had become.

Information gathering pervades our daily activities, made critical by busyness. What we collect enables us to react to a fast-changing world and to anticipate what we can and should do. While intelligence gathering yields information about the world, it also creates a parallel universe of data that must be managed. Advertisers are fond of persuading us to keep in touch with people in an increasingly connected world. Although less often discussed, keeping track is equally important.

Information gathering also matters because of what it tells us about the world in which people are busy. Often, our focus is on what we can do to improve our daily activities or manage them more efficiently. But at a deeper level, we seek intelligence about what we should be thinking about or doing. Information gathering involves more than finding information that we think is missing. We also use it to discover what might affect our lives in ways we can barely contemplate. It is about making sense of the world as much as collecting facts.

Conclusions

People hope that simplification will enable them to cope with the world more easily, but paradoxically it sometimes creates additional tasks. An enduring dream is that if only we could eliminate artifice and distractions, we could live better, more meaningful lives. But it is one thing to lead a simple life in a traditional society where everyone's life is relatively simple and quite another to do it in the context of a modern one. In the latter, simplification is a choice, and realizing it takes effort, such as the simplifying work of Suzanne and Humberto. Simplification opens up a space for meaning in one's life, but the latter is not just a given; it involves creative work. When all those distractions are stripped away, no excuses remain for meaninglessness. In effect, simplification opens the door to the possibility of meaning making, but it is just that, a possibility. The real work remains to be done. The result is not the solace of living in simpler times, but the responsibility to make a life that is meaningful in a world abuzz with possibilities. Simplification, ironically, is not simple, and it reveals the fundamental question lurking behind busyness: What would we do if we did have more time?

Chunking is also a form of simplification. It involves creating modules of activity in everyday life, and doing so is consistent with modernity in general and the American worldview in particular. John Blair claims that modularization is a distinctly American approach to living in modern society, and whether it is furniture, a university curriculum, or assembly line manufacturing, it is all accomplished through modules.[1] Blair explains that modularity shifts the emphasis from wholes of various kinds to interchangeable, individual components. In effect, we perform the work to create unities or wholes, which are not intrinsically in the parts but in how we arrange and rearrange them. Modularity effectively diminishes the integrity of the whole, for the modules selected may be varied, leading to different configurations or unities. This is as true of modular furniture as it is of everyday life. Living with modules implies a responsibility to be willing and able to rearrange parts into new wholes, even if we never actually do so. Life is lived against a backdrop of possibility and, necessarily, of things not done.

Modularity provides an openness that leads to creativity and innovation, but its very flexibility leads to a sort of shortsightedness, in which everything can be "repurposed." Long-term goals, beyond those of maintaining the system, are difficult to define, and there is a sense of reshuffling the deck chairs. What is often missing in the modular view is a vision of the hand or agent that puts it all together, that performs the innovation, and that creates unities.

What may vanish are the larger rituals that organize human experience in most societies.[2] They do so by enacting cultural models that people think with. Information can be decomposed into pieces, but meaning cannot. Meaning is essentially about assimilating new information and experiencing it vis-à-vis what we already believe we know. The making of meaning is not only solitary but also social, and it takes time to coalesce. The modular vision focuses attention on flexibility, contingency, transience, and the superficial. It does not eliminate meaning making, but it reaffirms the proposition that there is a work of making possible the everyday and the taken for granted. For the families, that work took the form of coping in ways that created continuity among the building blocks of their days.

CHAPTER SIX

When Things Go Wrong

Pat Carlsberg admitted that she could carpool with a co-worker. Doing so would reduce the cost of her long commute and, even more important, save time because a second rider would allow her into the carpool lane. Still, she rode alone. Her great fear was that something might happen that would upset her plans and that she would need to be able to travel quickly—and alone. The possible needs of her mother and Alex's parents or of her two boys loomed large in her daily thoughts.

Although people devised inventive and ubiquitous coping practices to control daily life, they often encountered surprises. Good coping sometimes seemed less a matter of imposing control in an uncooperative world than dealing with the impact of a surprise, such as a change in someone else's carefully laid plans.

A person who coped successfully with surprises typically could do so because of his or her ability to anticipate alternative courses of action. But coping took more than this, for anticipation without the ability to muster the necessary resources usually led to failure and frustration. How people coped with surprises revealed not only personal abilities and temperaments but one's place in a larger web of technologies and people. The *real* surprises, of course, could not be anticipated, and dealing with them took more than flexibility. While small surprises were annoying, bigger ones could change lives. They could be "fateful moments," those junctures in life that threaten the "protective cocoons" in which we wrap our lives and identities. Decisions made in response can have an irreversible quality.[1] How they were interpreted and what people did about them went far beyond what an individual might desire or could tolerate: they changed webs of connections among people.

Ordinary Surprises

Despite the plans and routines that people establish, coping with surprises becomes a part of daily life. Families are buffers against most surprises; their ability to adapt to changing circumstances is critical. Parents may well work hard to minimize the impact of the unforeseen on their children. Many parents do this by trying to make the world predictable for their children. Meanwhile, other family members may be scurrying to make sure the day unfolds as expected.

THE FLAHERTYS: WHICH SUSAN?

The busyness of family is thrown into high relief when things go wrong. People divide up tasks at home as they do at work. Eleanor Flaherty knew her commute routine so well that she followed it automatically. Her husband, Jerry, knew a different part of the family's busyness, which he followed without thinking about it. What neither of them realized was that they did not know the details of the other's routine. Ordinarily, this did not matter, but when they faced an unexpected change in their routines, they found themselves unprepared to take over from the other family member. The consequence was a spiking of anxiety and hurried added activities.

Mary Flaherty often visited her friend Susan after school, and on those days, Eleanor Flaherty usually drove to pick up her daughter. One time, however, Eleanor asked Jerry to do this. After work, he raced to Susan's house, pulled into the driveway and knocked on the door. When no one answered, he wondered if he had misunderstood the message. Mary also had other friends named Sue and Susie, so perhaps Eleanor had told him to go to one of their houses.

Since Mary was not his usual responsibility, Jerry did not carry the phone numbers of her friends either in his PDA or his head. Panicked, he raced across town in rush hour traffic to Sue's house. Sue's mother looked at him quizzically and told him that his daughter was at Susan's. Jerry headed back to Susan's, worrying that his late arrival would inconvenience Susan's mother. He called home on his mobile phone and asked his son Michael to look up Susan's phone number in the school directory. While the boy was searching, Jerry's phone batteries died. A few seconds later, his pager sounded and revealed an unfamiliar phone number: Michael had paged him with Susan's phone number. Jerry found a pay phone and called Susan's mother to say he would arrive soon. He casually confirmed the address. Upon arrival, he realized that he had previously gone to the wrong house. Mary and Susan had been playing next door all along.

THE MENDOZA / JONESES: THE BUSYNESS OF CAR BREAKDOWNS

Despite carefully laid plans and robust routines, unexpected events may cause families to scramble to get through the day. Often, these unforeseen occurrences are neither large nor dramatic; their very ordinariness belies their consequences, near and far. They reveal the complex and often hidden interdependencies of people's lives: a small crisis in one place can have far-reaching effects, especially if it disrupts a particularly critical connection. Such events may reveal the hidden infrastructure that a family uses to cope with a minor crisis. Particularly noteworthy are the numbers of people who can become drawn into such dramas.

Late one afternoon, Suzanne Jones discovered that her car's engine would not turn over. Humberto was not expected back from work until the following morning. Suzanne had spent the day running errands and had just picked up her daughter Nicole from day care. She called for a tow truck and was told it would take 30 to 45 minutes. She called her mechanic, but it was after 5:00 PM, and no one answered. Suzanne vowed that in the future she would keep his personal cell phone number. Then she realized that she had to pick up Angela, her other daughter, at another day-care provider and did not have that telephone number with her either. Both day-care providers belonged to the same support network, so Suzanne got the number and called to tell the other provider that she would be late. She assumed that she would be charged an extra $20 for this, but the provider offered to drive Angela to the broken car. Happy and grateful, Suzanne left a message with her supervisor that she would not be at work the following day and changed her voice-mail greeting to that effect.

When the tow truck arrived, the driver discovered that his vehicle could not transport the car and called for another truck. Before leaving, he told Suzanne that after towing the car to the garage, he would put the key under the floor mat if there was no drop box. Angela arrived, and Nicole's day-care provider drove Suzanne and her daughters home. Suzanne called Humberto. He was so concerned about the keys that he requested a leave from work and drove to the garage to retrieve them. The car had not arrived. He instructed Suzanne to cancel the tow truck and have the keys left at Nicole's day care; then he returned to duty.

The next day after his shift, Humberto headed directly to the abandoned car. Surprisingly, the car started, and he drove it to the garage. The mechanic drove him back to his own car, which he drove home, arriving around 10:00 AM. He was late to pick up his mother, who had just undergone surgery at a local hospital, and Suzanne called to delay her checkout time until 11:30 AM. Humberto then drove his mother to her nursing home in the Central Valley, a four-hour drive, after which he began the drive back. During this time, Suzanne stayed home with her girls. Late in the afternoon, the mechanic arrived with the car and announced he could find nothing wrong with it. Humberto finally arrived home at 1:30 AM; he slept briefly and then left for his 7:00 AM shift.

Suzanne resumed her routine; she dropped the girls at their day-care providers and spent the day catching up at work, but when she departed at 5:00 PM, the car again failed to start. She headed back to her office to call a taxi, but this time, her supervisor offered to drive her to retrieve the girls. After finally arriving home at 6:30 PM, Suzanne called Humberto at work to inform him. Increasingly frustrated, she also called her mother in St. Louis for moral support.

The next morning, after taking the girls to day care, Humberto and Suzanne visited the broken car. Humberto put the key in the ignition and it started, so once again he drove it to the garage. The car needed a new starter. Although this was a simple repair, the two days of disruption and stress had taken their toll. The couple argued about retrieving the car from the mechanic. Suzanne did not go to work the following day, and a few days later she remarked, "I was wrung out like a wet towel. I could barely function. I had to replenish. I am *still* recovering."

Suzanne's inopportune car breakdown disrupted this family's days, suggesting that carefully laid-out routines and plans may be little more than a sort of hope or faith in their power to impose order. This tale of chaos was an unremarkable snippet from the Mendoza/Joneses lives that would soon be forgotten, to be replaced by other unexpected surprises. The breakdown was significant, not in itself, but rather because it occurred in the context of busy lives structured around chains of contingencies that could suddenly unravel.

Consider the ripple effects that occurred when Suzanne's car stopped. This machine linked the lives of Suzanne, her husband and children, day-care providers and their families, co-workers, and clients. When it broke, it sent a shock wave through a network of lives that revealed layers of relationships, assumptions, and values. The most immediate effects of the disruption were seen when Suzanne dealt with her children, who expected to head for home. She feared the reaction of Angela's day-care provider but was pleasantly surprised when the latter volunteered to bring the little girl to Suzanne. Similarly, she warmed to her supervisor when she offered to drive and her children home.

The automobile breakdown also provoked a management response. Troubleshooting and repairing the car reconnected Suzanne and Humberto with a mechanic. Because of their lengthy relationship, he gave their car crisis special attention. Suzanne called this man for his recommendations, and he alerted her to that model's problematic starters.

The mothers of Humberto and Suzanne also became part of the drama. Humberto was delayed in picking up his mother from the hospital and returning her to her nursing home, disrupting his routine. The breakdown revealed more than a technical problem; it provoked emotions that wreaked havoc for days afterward. Retrieving the car from the garage became a workshop for effective planning and individual responsibility, with claims and counterclaims. Suzanne's mother provided moral support, both for the brute fact of a frustrating day and for her son-in-law's manner in dealing with it. Humberto's home remodeling projects and even the couple's readiness for a third child entered the debate. And days later, even after hurt feelings were assuaged, Suzanne still felt the logistical, managerial, and emotional impact of the defective car starter. Having fallen behind in her work, she had to catch up.

In the Mendoza/Jones family, car crises sometimes involved more than breakdowns. Suzanne and Humberto misunderstood where they had put a car seat. In so doing, they failed to communicate an important link in the coordination of their family activities, temporarily disrupting their social contract. The absence of a simple material object interrupted the whole family routine.

Humberto moved easily from firehouse to firehouse, toting diskettes of his activity logs and drafts of fire investigation reports. Regardless of situation, he could be reached through the fire department's communication system. Yet the powerful constraints of simple objects caused surprises in his life. At 5:20 PM, Humberto walked into his daughter Angela's day care and greeted her. When he asked for the car seat that his wife was to have left, the staff members responded with blank stares. The seat was not there, and they knew nothing about it. Humberto called his other daughter's day-care provider to find out if Suzanne had arrived to pick up the girl. She had not, and although he had the preschool's phone number on a card in his wallet, he could not remember Suzanne's work telephone number. He finally got it from the day-care files and called Suzanne; she was not there. He then called home and left terse messages at each number instructing her to bring the car seat immediately. A few minutes later, his pager buzzed. He returned the call and found that his wife had just arrived at Nicole's day-care facility. She thought she was supposed to leave the car seat at their house. Humberto objected that that made no sense. When Suzanne suggested that he drive the mile home and get it, he told her to bring it to him because it would be too disruptive for him to leave his daughter right after saying hello. Humberto and Angela waited in the front yard of the day-care facility, and twenty minutes later, Suzanne arrived with the seat. Humberto placed the girl in her mother's car, and both cars then headed home. Humberto said nothing about this incident to Suzanne. He didn't have to. He noted, "She will know I am angry." But he also agreed with Suzanne that another car seat would be a good investment.

THE TRANS: MISUNDERSTANDINGS AND PLANS DEFLECTED

Binh and Sheila Tran had strong networks of relatives and friends, who helped them weather their economic and social crises. But these refugees from Vietnam were far less successful in figuring out how some American organizations worked and how to use them to get needed resources. Binh successfully figured out how to prepare for and pass the state construction contractor's license exam, but he and Sheila encountered difficulties with the schools their children attended. Part of the problem was that these working parents had no time to attend school functions; more important, they did not understand why they should attend them or what was expected of them as parents.

This was not for lack of interest in their children's education. In fact, they had big plans for Ron and Ginny, their eldest and youngest children (the middle child, Paul, had Down Syndrome). Ron and Ginny were expected to attend college, earn professional degrees, and eventually get high-paying, prestigious jobs. Binh and Sheila expected to help them with homework and prod them in what they saw as the right direction. In this, they were doing what many Vietnamese refugees have done to succeed in America. The ingredients for their success were hard work, adaptability in facing new challenges, a willingness to undergo personal sacrifices, and an extremely high motivation to provide economic security for their families in America, and, for some, for their relatives in Vietnam too. Above all, they held the educated in awe. Education would be the path to success. It was in the details of their plan that things went wrong. Similarly, the schoolteachers who expected parental involvement from the Trans failed to grasp why they did not show up.

With a worried frown, Mrs. Taylor, Paul's middle school special education teacher, complained that Paul's parents did not participate much at school.

She said she knew very little about this family and was especially puzzled that Paul did not do his homework. She wondered about Paul's cleanliness, and whether or not he took frequent baths or showers. He wet himself on occasion, and they kept extra clothes for him at school. She was worried about what would happen in the future to this disabled boy. She wanted to know if he received support or help at home to do homework and in other aspects of his life.

Mrs. Taylor was unaware of the Trans' strong family values and that they did many things together—attending church, visiting relatives, martial arts, camping out, chores at home—and that Paul was specifically included in all of these activities. Paul's parents expected to take full care of him when he became an adult. He did take frequent showers, and his family emphasized cleanliness. He would wet himself because of his condition, and because of this, he wore a diaper. Every night, someone in the family sat down at the kitchen table to help Paul do his homework. Mostly it was his mother, but his older brother and younger sister also helped out. Although he received a lot of help and encouragement, however, he simply did not understand the assignments.

One evening after dinner, Paul was working on multiplication tables at the kitchen table and asked his father if his answers to the problems were correct. Binh looked at the paper and said harshly, "Why do you say you don't need help? It is all wrong." He crossed through each solution and handed the paper back to Paul, who was crestfallen. Silently, Paul took the paper and carefully erased each answer.

"The school assigns these complicated problems but he never can do it," Binh explained. "My wife stayed up with him until 11:00 PM and he still couldn't do them. I don't see why the teacher continues to give him such difficult problems and so many of them. He's got to do them. This is homework for tomorrow, and when he does it, they send it back. He didn't do it right. Then he has to do it over again."

Binh drilled Paul on his multiplication tables. He sat across the table. "How come you cover that one?" he said to his son. "You haven't finished that one yet." Paul struggled with the math problems. Sheila came out of her room and looked at Paul's work. She sat next to Paul to help him, and Binh left. Sheila instructed Paul in Vietnamese. As she helped him, he erased his mistakes. He received verbal practice in Vietnamese: "One times nine is more than . . ." The instruction lasted until 11:00, and Paul had still neither mastered nor completed his homework.

Binh and Sheila Tran had no idea that Mrs. Taylor was genuinely concerned about their son. In turn, she had no idea that they strongly valued education and had a deep commitment to taking care of their disabled child. Although they had lived in the United States for over fifteen years, Binh and Sheila Tran retained attitudes and assumptions typical of people in Vietnam that inhibited their wider participation in American schools.

Parents in Vietnam assume that teachers are experts. A teacher who solicits the opinions of parents is considered incompetent, while a parent who interferes with a teacher's task is out of line. New arrivals in the United States, and even those who have been here for several years, often are shy about meeting teachers and school personnel. Their comprehension of English may be insufficient to follow what a teacher says. They have no idea how to approach teachers and are unaware of the implicit assumptions and routine behaviors that teachers take for granted. Jobs may interfere with their participation. This was the situation of Binh and Sheila, who worked full-time on their catering truck, preventing them from attending parent-teacher conferences.

In many refugee households, the parents encourage their children to do well in school, but their own levels of education and command of English limit the amount of specific help they can give in particular subjects. This is what Ron, a junior in high school, meant when he commented: "I was stupid. My younger sister, I talk with her in English, so she is smarter and gets good grades. I didn't have anyone, just Mom. If you have brothers and sisters, you always talk English to them but always speak Vietnamese to parents. Mom could help me in math and Dad could help me in English, but it was easier for Ginny. I helped her on English and all subjects."

Ron and Ginny, born in the United States, clearly had a different outlook from their parents. They understood, at least in part, what teachers expected, but they often had a difficult time conveying this to their parents. For example, Ron was accepted at a summer engineering internship program at a local university. Working as interns under the supervision of an engineering professor, students both learned and earned money in the program. Ron was required to get his parent's signature on a form and return it to the university. He explained to his mother in Vietnamese that this project was both work and study (*vua di lam, vua di hoc*), but she hesitated to sign a form she did not understand. "Wait 'til your father gets home," she said.

Ron replied, exasperated, "No, sign it, sign it, Ma." She refused. She wanted Binh to explain it, but he was away working. The deadline was the coming Wednesday, and it was already Sunday afternoon, so Ron was agitated.

Finally, Sheila relented. There were two forms: one was for the parent to give permission for the student to participate. The other was for the student to complete. Sheila started to sign the wrong form. Ron, raising his voice, said, "No, Mom, not that one. This one. Now look, you're signing mine." He pulled it away and gave the other one to her.

Usually, Sheila, the authority, was in control and would order Ron to do this or that. Here, she was intimidated, hesitant, and tentative. She didn't understand the form or what the job was at the university. Was it work or school? She did not grasp that it combined both. Ron now was in control and dominated. Sheila signed, with some reluctance, since she was unsure about what she was signing. She looked uncomfortable. She wanted to help her son, and would sacrifice time, money, and effort to pave his way to higher education and a good job. But she had no idea how to help him negotiate the educational system. Ron had found out about this summer internship on his own at his high school and taken the initiative to apply for it.

For Ron, this was the beginning of his journey through a world utterly unfamiliar to his parents. Ron went on to complete high school, attend a branch of the University of California, graduate with a degree in business administration, not in engineering, as his parents had expected, and get a job in the business office of a major publishing firm. To celebrate their son's success, Binh and Sheila hosted an all-day celebration and feast, including a whole roasted pig, at the new home to which they had moved.

The Trans' story of organizational misunderstanding of American institutions is, of course, grounded in their upbringings in Vietnam. The surprises that they encountered might have derailed their grand plans. Native-born Americans can perhaps empathize with the elder Trans and similar families by asking themselves how *they* would fare after being transplanted to a new country, or how, as the son or daughter of immigrants, they would learn how to deal with an unfamiliar bureaucracy. We can also use the Trans' difficulties to better see the tacit work that is routinely performed in order to interact successfully with organizations in order to obtain needed goods and services. We should not assume that people automatically know how to use or gain access to the resources of organizations. Their inability to deal with them is more likely to lead to unexpected results. The magnitude of the challenge is only exacerbated when we consider how we string organizations together in ways that facilitate our everyday lives and enable us to pursue our grander dreams and those of our children.

If difficulties in gaining access to organizational resources can complicate daily life and visions of family betterment, the ability to tap them can make a profound difference in the quality of everyday life and the ability to get ahead. In fact, equality and inequality in America is to a large and growing extent a matter of access to particular organizations, along with the capacity to utilize and direct their resources.[2] With Ron's success, the Trans have made a significant first step. To be sure, such a capacity is only partially a matter of individual skill and knowledge. It also reflects the nature of the organizations to which someone is attached and their positions and roles within them. Organizations thus differ in the resources they offer people, who in turn may have different abilities to use them.

Many of the family members we studied were able to use organizational resources to facilitate their adaptation to busyness. In effect, people were able to colonize organizations—that is, employ them for their own purposes—by channeling or simply using their resources to ease the burdens of busyness in ways that allowed them to better pursue their long-term goals. But even these people often encountered surprises in the pursuit of their goals.

Preparing for the Unknown

HUMBERTO MENDOZA: PREPARING FOR THE UNKNOWN WITH THE FIRE DEPARTMENT'S INCIDENT COMMAND SYSTEM

Humberto Mendoza drew upon training at work to make himself into someone who could adapt quickly to new situations. He viewed himself as a self-made man, designed for maximum efficiency and productivity. More important, by becoming flexible, he also prepared himself to face the unknown.

The ultimate tool of Humberto's flexibility was the Incident Command System, or ICS, adopted by his fire department. "ICS is my tool box," he said. "You can use this flow chart for anything." When a fire company responded to an incident and was "first in," its captain assumed command of all functions of firefighting. If additional alarms were called, there had to be a predictable way of shifting command to higher administrative levels to ensure that all functions were implemented to form a coordinated response. The ICS identified the basic functions of operations, planning, logistics, and finance that were mobilized during an incident, and how these functions were allocated to personnel on site. It thus defined both the basic processes that firefighters had to think through when confronting an incident, and it provided a way to shift between organizational levels as an incident expanded in magnitude and response.

For Humberto, the ICS was not merely a set of organizational procedures, but a way to organize his "skills, knowledge, and abilities," whether as a firefighter, engine driver, inspector, investigator, or captain. Humberto internalized this written document, meant as a guideline for firefighters, and used it literally to improve himself. "This is how I think on duty," he reflected. When he interviewed for the position of captain, he used the seven minutes to describe who he was in terms of the ICS, literally connecting the four support functions to himself as an incident commander. For example, the finance function represented that "I am rewarded for my efforts. At the same time, I'm fiscally responsible to make sure I'm judicious, because I'm using city property. That represents my relationship with the community."

The ICS was thus Humberto's seemingly universal tool for flexibly responding to situations, be they at work or elsewhere. He successfully introduced it to a firefighters' professional association as a way to organize their annual conference. He even used it at home, because "ICS helps organize your tactics and strategies." As an example, he used it to organize his ubiquitous home remodeling projects. "Today I've got to paint. This is a paint day." He lumped together all the painting to be done in all rooms and did nothing that day but paint. Another day was "electrical day." Sometimes, he organized his efforts by dedicating days to a specific room. No matter how he did this, he thought through the projects by using the four functions of operations, planning, logistics, and finance. Humberto assimilated the

ICS, importing it from his workplace and profession into how he thought about himself acting in the world. He argued that it provided a stability that enhanced his capacity to respond to surprises, whether they were life-threatening incidents or arose in the course of regularly scheduled events or projects around the house.

Humberto's self-creation around the ICS also demonstrates how flexibility can be variously constructed. Although he was inflexible in many ways, he was in fact a planner par excellence. The ICS itself was a rigid template for acting, not a basis for improvisation. When Humberto spoke of flexibility, he referred to his ability to assimilate new experiences and to respond constructively, but he seldom abandoned his plans. His flexibility was thus selective and constructed in a personal way.

Indeed, flexibility always operates under particular conditions and is defined in specific ways. Ironically, it may constrain how other people can act, thereby restricting *their* flexibility. In this way, it is not merely a property of individuals but a social production that contains elements of morality play, good theater, and hard bargaining.

Humberto's practices exemplified one of the most basic approaches to protection. He anticipated problems and attempted to forestall them through preventative maintenance. He assumed that things would inevitably go wrong and tried to minimize the probability of this happening and ensure a timely response if it did. His training as a firefighter was relevant here.

Humberto carefully maintained their cars to avoid precisely what happened to Suzanne in the parking lot. Indeed, he generally tried to minimize surprises in a variety of ways. He insisted that the mail be collected when it was delivered to prevent curbside theft, and he used a shredder to avoid identity theft. He told Suzanne to keep only one pocketbook and to avoid the popular backpack purses, because they were easy to slit open and rob. Humberto and Suzanne were scrupulous regarding household cleanliness; they vacuumed thoroughly and scrubbed surfaces. To minimize the likelihood of a back injury in his physically demanding job as firefighter, Humberto regularly visited a chiropractor to "be aligned" and did systematic stretching exercises.

Many of the families we studied expended considerable effort trying to avoid unexpected events and then controlling or limiting their effects once they inevitably occurred. Once they had set up plans and routines, they tried to protect them, but as with the Mendoza/Jones family, their strategies sometimes had only limited success.

Like many Americans, the Tentoris had uprooted themselves from their familiar surroundings and set out to build a better life elsewhere. They knew what they were looking for: less expensive housing and a community bound together by its Christian faith. Things did not turn out exactly as they had planned, though, and their long commute and the fractious politics of the local school district increased their busyness. They persevered, certain about what was ultimately worth striving for, drawing upon the resources of a larger community in the process. When mundane means failed to ensure predictability, Tom and Fran Tentori typically turned to their religious faith to influence the wider world in which they lived.

Shortly after they had moved to the new town, they joined a storefront church. One of its attractions was that its members had several children who were the same age as their son Josh. The church, which was expanding, had submitted a proposal for the construction of a church building, but was concerned that the town's planning commission might reject it. Several church members decided to help the process along with a prayer vigil.

On a Saturday evening in November, Fran went to the prayer vigil. Tom, exhausted from a full day of refereeing three high school football games, did not accompany her. The one-hour prayer vigil took place at the mobile-home park residence of John and Barbara. Another couple, David and Dolores, also joined them. The group sat around a table in the dining room. Barbara served cookies and soft drinks.

This prayer vigil group had been meeting for four months, usually involving three or four couples, and a few single people. Once a month, they shared a meal. They rotated their meeting places, and in this way, they came to know one another.

The participants began with a list of prayer requests for people who were ill or suffering from some problem. After this, they prayed for the people of the church. Then they prayed for success in getting the planning commission to grant them a permit to construct their church building.

They referred to biblical passages, including Philippians 4:11: "I have learned, in whatever state I am, therewith to be content." John discussed this further. "Be content with whatever the circumstances bring," he said. "We want to build a church building, but we are content with whatever the future brings. We assumed that the storefront church we have now is temporary. But what if it is not? Be content."

Then Dolores quoted another passage and asked the group to pray for people who were ill, who owed rent they could not pay, who had cancer, and who were divorced. Then she prayed that the planning commission would give the church permission to construct its building, and that the meeting to decide this would be peaceful. She also prayed for a Christian film festival that was in town.

Fran prayed for the planning commission and the commissioner, as well as for the church. John then said, "It is hard to be content, but that is what He looks for, contentment. The church sold the building [it used to have]. Now it has a temporary place. Maybe that is God's will now." Then he prayed to Jesus: "Whatever happens at Wednesday's planning meeting is Your will. I can endure the problems that come my way because it is temporary. Life is temporary, and then I will be saved and get eternal life. Thank you Lord for giving me this. I can deal with life's troubles because of the eternal reward that follows."

Fran then said: "I pray for contentment. I pray that you work on the hearts of the planning commissioners. Please make the hearts of the planning commission open. Agricultural land will remain open [the land where the church hoped to construct its building was agricultural]. Your will, if agricultural land is needed, you will provide that and the churches, too." After several more prayers, the vigil concluded.

This prayer vigil is another example of the interplay of choice and constraint in busyness. The Tentories were not simply buffeted by forces beyond their control, for they had thought long and hard about their situation and ultimately acted to create their ideal community. Their pursuit of that dream occurred in a social environment that clearly affected the outcomes of their moves quite independently of their intentions. Their story also reveals the connections between their moral visions of community and the good life, long-term concerns about uncertain futures, and short-term busyness.

FERN LE: CONSULTING A FORTUNE-TELLER

Coping with busyness is not just about rational planning and efficiently lived lives. If uncertainty and the threat of doubt are ubiquitous, so too are the practices that people use when the plans they rely on fail. Unlike Fran Tentori, who drew upon her group of fellow Christians, Fern Le, a high-tech employee and Vietnamese refugee, sought certainty by consulting fortune-tellers to alleviate her anxieties about a world that she viewed as uncertain. As in the situation of her son's Vietnamese preschool, Fern's turn to fortune-tellers is indicative of a world in which the traditional and the modern had become inextricably entangled. These activities also led to increased busyness when Fern endeavored to carry out the directions she received from her trusted fortune-teller.

Fern Le's favorite fortune-teller was a man who used a computer to come up with forecasts based on traditional Vietnamese beliefs. Fern said that he was, "so amazing. He entered into the computer a couple of things, my name and address. Then he printed a statement about me. He could tell things about me that I did not tell him. He said I was married but separated [she had just separated from Dan], and that I had three children [one from her first marriage and two with Dan]. He said that I would meet another man. He is very accurate about my past."

The fortune-teller's printed forecast both portended the future and prompted a self-fulfilling prophecy: Fern was given a direction, which she then might follow, confirming the prophetic powers of the fortune-teller, while justifying Fern's own choices and behaviors.

Fern not only depended on fortune-tellers for guidance, but also used them to provide certainty in an uncertain world and to justify major changes in her life. Fern's life involved major turnings in which the outcomes were often unpredictable and even life threatening. As a child, she had lived in a Vietnamese village in the middle of a war zone. Her younger sister had drowned in the Mekong River, an event that scarred both Fern and her mother. Fern was separated for eleven years from her father, who was sent off to a Communist reeducation camp, where he was subjected to forced labor and starvation. She did not see him again until he escaped and made his way to America. By that time, Fern, her mother, and brother had made their own perilous fourteen-day escape by boat from Vietnam, landing in a refugee camp, and subsequently being resettled in the United States. Fern had to learn to cope with a new culture and the losses of the past.

Fern rebelled against her mother's strict rules and discipline, a moral framework emphasizing that proper behavior for women consisted of dependence and submissiveness to males, self-sacrifice for the family, and compliance with strict rules of etiquette. Fern said, "She would correct me, 'Eat right, don't slurp your soup, don't click your chopsticks against the bowl. Only the lower class do that.' Even when I was grown up and married, she interfered in my life. Since I was the oldest, I was supposed to be responsible for everything that any younger brother or sister did. It's my fault if they didn't behave." The unspoken criticism was that it was Fern's fault that her sister drowned. Fern continued: "She criticizes me on how I should rear the children, how I cook, what foods I eat, too much fat, or too little vegetables, or many things. And I get angry."

Fern married her first husband "to get away from home. My mother was in the middle of everything. My first husband treated me badly. I refused to take it. My husband called my mother and complained about my behavior. My mother did not side with me but with him, even though she knew how he mistreated me. She called me and told me to obey my husband. That is the proper thing to do if you are a Vietnamese woman."

Instead of obeying, Fern took an uncertain path. "I would not put up with him. I left him and my daughter and went home, where I lived with my mother. I took nothing with me. He kept everything. Instead of encouraging me, my mother told me how I had ruined my life; who would marry me now? Finally, I could no longer take the constant criticism and I left her home."

Each subsequent turn in Fern's life thrust her into unpredictable situations: moving to a new city alone, divorcing Dan, her second husband, and leaving their two sons with him (he subsequently remarried), changing both employment and professions in a volatile job market, starting new business projects, embarking on new personal relationships, and marrying for a third time. Her new husband was of European descent. For Fern, the fortune-teller provided an anchor and a predictable direction for a person whose life had been tumultuous and whose major life-course choices had led to uncertain outcomes.

Faith need not be religious or spiritual. It can show up as confidence in expertise. One of the most worrisome uncertainties confronting Americans is how to rear their children. All sorts of experts dispense advice designed to produce children with particular values or social skills. Americans place great faith in experts who can give informed opinions. But the variety they offer increases rather than minimizes uncertainty.

Like many parents, Michelle Scott worried whether or not she was rearing her children properly.[3] What bothered her deeply was that she and her two sisters had different parenting styles. Michelle's older sister, a professor in the South, had allowed her twin sons to sleep in her bed and scribble in crayon on the walls of their bedroom. By contrast, Michelle's other sister had raised her kids quite differently. Now that her nieces and nephews from these two families were teenagers, she detected no differences, and this troubled her.

In her quest to improve her parenting skills, she read books about child rearing and often questioned her own parenting decisions. As a result of reading John Saul's book *Second Child*,[4] Michelle came to recognize that she gave Crystal more attention than April. Her husband, Roy, a second child, observed that they read to Crystal far more than to April, in part because Crystal often interfered with April's reading sessions.

When Michelle read one of Ellen Galinsky's books on work and family, she was struck by the idea that children imitated parental attitudes about work. Michelle said, "You come home and you bitch about work, and then your kids pick up the vibes that work isn't a cool thing to do. And you know what? That is so true." Michelle and Roy therefore made positive remarks about work to their children and spoke in code to prevent their children from overhearing their complaints and frustrations about work.

The worldview of American parents has long been characterized by uncertainty about how to prepare children for the future and what constitutes "good parenting."[5] Michelle and Roy's concerns are thus not new, but uneasiness about what lies ahead and what is likely to lead to a good future increases the sense of urgency. As this couple works on its family future, the very range of alternative child-rearing practices and the belief that the stakes are high for both child and parent add to their busyness, their stress, and their continuing uncertainty about what to do.

Uncertainty means that we live against a backdrop of anticipation as well as stress. Surprises erupt, even when we have done what we can to establish order and control. Some surprises are immediately disruptive, as when people on whom we depend fail to come through. Less obvious, but more consequential, are the grand uncertainties of modern life. These include events that are difficult for most of us to predict, such as stock market and corporate scandals or terrorist attacks. They also include the gradual processes that can transform our jobs and communities, such as changing global markets, outsourcing jobs, or new technologies. These uncertainties prompt us to raise fundamental questions about what we should want, what we should do for ourselves and our families, and what it means to better ourselves. The real danger is not a disrupted day but a disrupted life. Dealing with obvious, everyday busyness may distract our attention from these larger issues, the harder-to-see processes that are transforming the world in which we are busy.

Rearranging Households

THE SMITHS: MOVING ON

Contemplating her family's impending relocation to Los Angeles, Janelle Smith remarked that she truly hated moving. The burden would be lessened by the help of volunteers, including university students, whose "community service" would consist of lugging cartons. It had not been so long ago that everything fitted in the back of her mother's car, but that was before marriage, two children, and the accumulations of a household. Already, she and her husband, David, had moved several times within Michigan, then to San Jose; now they were moving to southern California. And their journey would not end there. They planned to live off David's income and save Janelle's, so that they could make at least one more move to an affordable housing market, such as Sacramento.

David and Janelle had been successful in the Bay Area, had enjoyed jobs that gave them emotional and professional satisfaction, and their children had enjoyed the attention of adoring adults. Still, the high cost of living in Silicon Valley made owning a home there impossible, and their jobs did not offer immediate prospects for promotion. Janelle's father's family was located in southern California and her half-siblings lived there, although she did not know them well. The cost of living was less, and there was the promise of different jobs. Furthermore, southern California offered a multi-cultural social milieu that they felt would be compatible with their values.

The couple were well aware that the move would not simply be to a different city, but to very different living arrangements. Since David was residence director of a university dormitory, with an office 100 feet from his two-bedroom apartment, his job inevitably brought together family and work. From 8:00 AM to 2:00 AM, he and Janelle, a speech pathologist, juggled child care and work on an hour-to-hour basis. Their daughter Mardi had become integrated into the rhythms of her parents' work. She would ride her father's shoulders as he did his nightly rounds of dormitory halls and watch as he distributed blue raffle tickets to students doing their homework. Their younger daughter, Mirella, was often at her mother's side when Janelle was called to emergency after-school meetings with her clients' parents.

As the only toddler in a world of college students and other adults, Mardi received constant attention. Students populated her world, and she bene-fited from small indulgences. When dorm residents had a "Return to Child-hood" night, for example, David was asked if he would like to take home the excess Play-Doh. Mardi got so many presents from students and co-workers at Christmas that her parents stored some until her birthday in May.

Space in their campus home, however, was limited. Once, Janelle wanted to bring home her new suitcase-sized phonics kit from work to check it out, but she decided it was too big. She also wanted to work at home on some of the many reports she was required to prepare, but she could not do so. The county had switched to new forms, but her home computer used an incompatible operating system. While she owned a compatible computer, a daughter's dresser was now in its place. David had promised her a work-station in his office, but it, too, was overcrowded.

When Janelle thought about moving, it was in the context of what was best for her husband and children. Such considerations were central to who she was. She had cut back on work hours to be the parent she and David valued. She loosened her attachments to particular activities and discovered that the schedules that had worked with one child had to be adjusted when there was a second. She enrolled in a class to improve her Spanish, but found herself overextended. Janelle waited for a break during class and departed, never to return. Later, she asked David, "Have you ever had a chorus going in your head?" Then she sang, "Something's got to change." Janelle explained: "See, we all have that little subconscious that says, 'Oh, this isn't quite right.' Nothing is quite right, and if I want it to be right, something has to give and I have to be flexible." Being "flexible" meant accommodating to the needs of her family and trying to organize time so that both she and David had time for their own activities. This enabled her to "refocus on the things that are important—the girls being happy and adjusted. I really try to keep my harriedness away from them."

David maintained two careers, one as a professional in student life development at the university and the other as an athlete on the cusp of the National Basketball Association. These careers affected the family's mobility, with universities acting as magnets that attracted them. Basketball added another complication. "We almost ended up in Turkey in August [for David to play professional basketball,]" Janelle remarked. David was recuperating from an injured knee and still worked on his professional career. His workout regimen was demanding and finding competition was a challenge. He would hold back when playing on campus so as to not make his teammates feel bad, while at the same time trying to build his strength and stamina. Janelle's flexibility took the form of making sure he had the time needed to stay in top shape.

David's other career involved a constantly shifting panoply of tasks and relationships. He handled incident reports, such as when a student was accused of pulling a knife, or another of stalking. He sometimes had to evict residents for violating university policies or laws. Although his days involved completing forms, writing memos, letters, and reports, and keeping up with the information needed to do his job, he also had to patrol the residence halls. His days were filled with give-and-take banter with students and staff, as well as serious discussions about careers and staffing. Once, after such an intense conversation, he helped two women get the candy they had bought from a misbehaving vending machine by giving it a firm whack. David dryly attributed his success to his problem-solving perspective and to having a master's degree. Above all, he was a constant role model to students.

Janelle's flexibility helped this career, too. When David and Janelle first moved to San Jose, Janelle had worked as a full-time school speech patholo-gist from 8:00 AM to 3:30 PM. David had watched Mardi three days a week, and they had hired a babysitter for the other two days. This had made it dif-ficult for him to interact with university personnel during regular business hours, affecting his career. After Mirella was born, Janelle worked half-time, allowing David to hold meetings.

Janelle also took being a parent seriously, and her parenting was informed by her work as a professional educator. When she saw a little boy playing on the computer, navigating around the screen and clicking on things, she concluded, "He's smarter than my kid." Soon she was in a large discount store buying software and discovered: "Kids, if they're exposed to it, they just figure it out. And she [Mardi] did!" Janelle helped the girl get started with most games and worked with her if she was playing a higher-level one, but Mardi usually played independently. David and Janelle accumulated a collection of educational media intended to develop the girls' abilities.

Mardi's room was filled with educational toys. She turned her squeaky Sesame Street blocks into mock chocolate chip cookies and manipulated her puppets like oven mitts. Paper became flour, and she cracked pretend eggs, then poured imaginary tea and milk into cups to accompany the cookies, which she presented to her mother. She played with each of her electronic toys, including an animal sounds game, a Winnie the Pooh identify-the-body-parts toy, an alphabet board, a phone, and a musical keyboard. After playing, she put her electronic toys into a crate, with the large puzzles under-neath. Janelle showed Mardi how to organize her toys and tried to make sure that she did so each week. She placed her food toys in the toy oven or in a tray on top of it and put her animal toys and dolls into another crate.

Janelle's priority was her husband and children, but her work as a speech pathologist also filled her days. She worked in different schools, and classes could be lively indeed. Yet working in the classroom with children was only part of her demanding job. She assessed children with possible speech pa-thologies, prepared reports, and attended meetings. The stakes in such meet-ings could be high for school, child and parents, and successfully navigating them required working within a team of colleagues. For example, one such meeting was attended by a program specialist who was just one of five in a district of over fifty schools, the school nurse and the school psychologist, a special education teacher, an outside contractor to the district, an advocate from a disability center, the child's parents, and Janelle. She commented, "I spend more time doing paperwork, and I would like to spend more time with the kids!" Paperwork was the obstacle between her and the children. It was, she commented, "a sign of the times: do paperwork, cover yourself."

David confidently began searching for a new job. Well qualified, with an MA degree and two years' experience, he had a good track record of getting job offers. He attended the National Student Life Conference, applied for jobs, and was interviewed for positions in several states. He was tentatively offered the residence directorship at a large public university in southern California, which paid $50,000 a year and included free housing. It offered him opportunities in sports and provided the multicultural environment he and Janelle sought. He let his employer in San Jose know that he was expecting to resign, but Janelle remained in her job until David had been hired.

After two months, they still didn't know. David was just about to rescind his resignation when the university in Los Angeles told him they might offer him a *different* job, but a formal offer could not be made until the housing director returned from vacation. Meanwhile, other staff people at this university continued to interview him on the phone.

Janelle and David were ambivalent about the move. David was disenchanted with the job offer, and Janelle worried because she did not know whether they would stay or move, and she was unsure what she would do in Los Angeles. David could not make up his mind. The new university had more resources, slightly better housing, more varied on-campus activities and residents, and a better campus sports program, but the position did not include greater responsibility. His current employer was willing to redefine his job around his unique talents; the new employer made no such promise.

In the end, he accepted the job offer, although he was not convinced that it was the right thing to do. Still, he felt that the job was better, and he would continue to work as a residence director at a university, which he found satisfying.

Janelle and David rented an apartment and prepared to move. Janelle anticipated seeing the sites of southern California and Mexico and doubted they would return often to northern California. A trusted medical specialist in San Jose provided referrals to former teachers and classmates so that her child's health condition would be effectively treated after the move. A friend knew a speech pathologist in Los Angeles who was going on maternity leave and Janelle could temporarily take over her practice with independent clients and at a school for hospitalized children, thus easing her transition into the new region.

David, too, prepared to depart San Jose, already thinking ahead. When a former supervisor called to tell him of a job in the Midwest, he politely declined. He had already made a commitment and explained, "It doesn't do to burn bridges" by not living up to them. He reaffirmed his desire to keep in touch. He also thought it might be easier to move to another job within the state university system by already being employed at a campus. As he packed, he found old GRE scores and remarked that he was thinking about pursuing a doctorate at his new campus. He mused that Los Angeles might be home for a few years and then it might be time for the move to Sacramento.

The move to southern California did not turn out as the Smiths had hoped or expected. Mardi, four years old, developed difficulties in her preschool. While she related well to individuals, she did not know how to behave as a member of a group in the classroom. Janelle had an explanation for this. Because she and her husband had integrated their work and family lives so closely, Mardi had spent all her life around adults: co-workers, college students, and friends. Mardi had not had the experience of being with groups of children her own age, which she was now doing at school. Because of Mardi's troubles, Janelle reorganized her schedule to include volunteering in the classroom several days a week. Janelle hoped that this would help ease Mardi into her new environment.

Janelle also began her work with independent clients, but she had to work around David's schedule and Mardi's preschool hours. This required her to be constantly on the road, which was uncompensated time. Her work life improved when, through a friend, she found a temporary position at a school for children with autism. Now she had a predictable schedule, and, unlike with her previous school-based speech pathology work, she was able to chart the progress of her individual clients.

Child care remained an issue, however. David said: "Well, I want to make sure that I am meeting the responsibilities of the new job but then also meeting the responsibilities of a father, too, and trying to be flexible for Janelle. Coming here, it was tough at first, because we didn't have any babysitters." David took care of Mirella and Mardi while Janelle left for interviews or work, and on occasion, Janelle's sister would look after them for about a half an hour. David continued: "Now we have students here, it's great, because I can always use them as sitters, or I'll keep Mirella with me sometimes. But it was hard, really hard, at first, and knowing that I need to be in the office, but then I also have my kids, but I don't want my supervisor to come by and see me having the kids running all over the place and make it seem like I'm not working, but I am working, you know."

A year later, David was running a summer camp for a professional basketball team, a job he continued in the following years. He loved being "in the game." Then he left his university employment to work for a dot-com that did small business support software. He and Janelle bought a fifty-year old house, whose previous owner had made many idiosyncratic renovations. A Spanish-speaking caretaker helped with house chores and children. David then left that job because he decided that the company was selling a service to businesses that could not afford it. He took a job as a recruiter for information technology professionals in the entertainment industry. During an economic downturn, he found another residence director position at a different university, also in southern California. By then, they had to sell the house. Meanwhile, Mardi was enrolled in a private school on the opposite side of greater Los Angeles and appeared to be happy there. On weekdays, Janelle and the girls lived with Janelle's father; they visited David's two-bedroom apartment on the weekend.

The Smiths' relocation was part of a grander strategy, but the move was not simple and the outcome was unclear. It is a reminder that our lives are embedded in the resources of a region, often in ways that are hidden from us. A move, by severing one set of ties and compelling us to develop new ones, reveals them and creates tasks for which we may not be prepared.

THE JACKSONS: BECOMING HOMEOWNERS

When Americans buy things or a service, they make a statement about who they are, who they want to become, and how they want others to see them.

In this context, consumption has become an integral part of the American experience. It is also one of the most powerful arenas in which busyness is expressed. What we buy and where we shop speaks of the kind of family we want to be.

Few purchases are more identified with aspirations to middle-class living than buying a house. For the Jacksons, acquiring a house of their own became a dominating concern. To buy a house was no mean feat in the superheated housing market of Silicon Valley in the late 1990s. They figured, however, that with a house of their own, they would be able to exert some control over their financial lives and improve their standard of living. Buying a house was not simply a financial transaction but a statement about the future that they hoped to achieve.

What they failed to anticipate were unexpected and unwelcome changes in their life that accompanied the acquisition of their new house. This included an eruption of busyness, both self-generated and caused by events outside the family, which took them far beyond anything they had anticipated. Not so hidden was a pervasive concern that periodically became a cause for near panic. Working in high-technology jobs, with their many rewards, came with a risk. Layoffs were an ever-present possibility and could, in an instant, derail their dreams for the future. Vic and Karen exemplified the fragility of the American middle class.[6]

Since both were fully employed professionals, Vic and Karen could easily afford to buy a house if they moved to one of the poorer sections of town. Their problem was that they aspired to live in a middle-class neighborhood, in a house with three bedrooms, two baths, and a large fenced backyard where their daughter would have room to play. Houses like that listed right at the upper limit of what they could afford, with prices rising as much as 15–20 percent a year.

When their daughter, Tina, was born, they were renting a house. To save a bit of money and to have a family member take care of their child, they brought Sarah, Karen's mother, from Colorado to live with them. All three adults worked, and they rotated child-care duties. Tensions soon arose over cramped space. Vic complained that there was not enough room for the possessions that Sarah had brought with her. Both Vic and Karen often did some of their company work at home, but there was no quiet place. Their computers took up a corner of the family room, right next to the kitchen and to the sliding doors that led to the back patio.

Conflicts also surfaced over lifestyle differences, including child-rearing practices. Sarah, an independent, twice divorced woman in her mid fifties, was a high-energy person who expressed strong moral values concerning work, responsibility, and child care. Sarah tended to smother Tina with affection and dominate child care. When Tina woke up late at night, Sarah would rush to her, pushing aside Vic, who expected to take care of his daughter. Vic said he resented this, because it prevented him from bonding with his daughter at a crucial time in her life. Sarah would continuously tidy the house, picking up Tina's clothes and toys, indirectly expressing her disapproval of their housekeeping and their child care. One weekday, both Vic and Karen stayed at home, but each focused on their paid work. Tina watched them hunched over their computers. That day, recalled Sarah, "Tina acted up. She was crying and fussing all day. Karen asked me, 'Mom, what's wrong with Tina?' I said, 'It's you and Vic. You are here but you are not paying attention to her. That's why she is so disturbed. You cannot be here and not pay attention to her.'"

But it was not that easy for Vic and Karen to just turn off their jobs to focus on their daughter. Although he was allowed flexible hours, Vic, an electrical engineer whose job was testing integrated circuits, had to be physically present at his company office for long hours, especially when projects were nearing completion.

Meanwhile, Karen, a health care applications specialist at a medical technology company, was troubleshooting a software system used by hospitals all over North America. Through e-mail, an 800 phone number, and sometimes her personal pager, she was linked to eighty-nine different sites in different time zones. She worked from 5:30 or 6:00 AM until 3:00 PM, after which she returned home to take care of Tina. She took calls for help ranked by their seriousness, the most urgent being the crash of the whole system, which might wipe out hospital records and endanger the lives of patients. One day a week, she was on call at home from 4:00 PM to 5:00 AM. She used a dedicated computer supplied by her company. At these times, her daughter might be in the same room, but during serious calls, Karen could not devote her time to Tina. If Karen left the house during on-call times, she was required to contact the office every twenty minutes by laptop or phone. If emergencies arose, hospitals paged her.

Karen's mother Sarah also worked long hours, first with Tina's child care in the mornings, sometimes sharing these duties with Vic. After Karen returned from her job, Sarah went to work as a gardening department manager in a large retail store. She was on the go from 7:00 AM to 10:00 PM or later. Sarah's job did not involve life-and-death issues, huge financial risks of failure, or periodic threats of layoff like the jobs of Vic and Karen, but she had stresses nonetheless. She trained and monitored employees in her department, which had a frequent turnover of workers, and she had to make sure that the records and receipts had been entered correctly each day.

The Jacksons thus organized their working hours around child care for Tina. But on occasion, their ordinary routine was upset, most often when Vic's schedule varied because of deadlines on his projects. This forced Karen and Sarah to rearrange their work schedules. Sometimes Karen's work schedule changed or she traveled out-of-state on company business, forcing the others to change. When both Vic and Karen required schedule changes, they negotiated who went to work and who stayed home, based on whose project was most pressing. If both had to be at work, Sarah remained with Tina.

Even more stressful than keeping track of each other's work schedules were the tasks of becoming homeowners. The Jacksons were desperate, fearing that they would be unable to achieve their middle-class dream. The topic of house buying dominated their discussions, and this spilled over to their workplaces. At lunch, Vic and his colleagues would discuss how his house search had progressed, and they would give him tips on lenders, neighborhoods to buy into, and what to look for. Similarly, the Jacksons' house-buying efforts dominated the lunchtime conversation of Karen and her fellow employees. Throughout the day, either Karen or Vic would hear from their realtor about another hot prospect, telling them about asking prices and what they should offer. Then Karen and Vic would phone one another, discuss the deal, and decide whether to look at the house and bid on it. At this time, the housing market was so tight that a slight delay often doomed a prospective buyer's chances of bidding before the house sold.

Karen recalled the frenzy of that time. "Buying a house was stressful, the whole game of prequalifying, how much you prequalify for. And then the realtors tried to prequalify us for more than we want to prequalify, and that turned out to be stressful. We didn't want to be financially *strapped* with a house payment."

Sometimes Karen would look at a house and tell Vic, who would then decide whether to look at it or not. He was distracted by the pressures of work, coping with his mother-in law in the same house, and looking for a house. Finally, after weeks of searching, the right house came on the market and the couple made an offer. Vic's distractions persisted, and he found himself driving through a red light. The resulting accident only increased his stress, and he told Karen that if they did not get the house, "he didn't want to look for any others right now." Ultimately, the realtor was forty minutes late, but they got the house "as is." On Monday, Vic remained at home, but he called Karen at work, still worrying about the accident.

The Jacksons were now homeowners, but far from alleviating the stress they felt, this created a whole new series of crises. The first occurred while moving. Karen recalled: "It was stressful because my mom had come to live with us, and I wasn't visualizing how much stuff we all had together, cumulatively, so I misestimated the size of the truck, and that turned out to be many more loads than I had imagined."

Once they moved in, Vic immediately started remodeling. Confident in his skills, he covered the garage floor with a sealant. Then he removed pipes that had been used for solar heating because they were located in the place where he wanted to build his office. The main shutoff for their water line was broken, an ominous portent of catastrophe. Vic worked with a friend to clear things so that a plumber could come in and make some changes in the bathroom adjacent to the garage. The problems began when they discovered a small leak around the toilet. It didn't look like much to repair, but when they pulled the toilet, they discovered the extent of the leak and serious damage to the drywall. Meanwhile, they could not turn off the valve to the toilet, and, because the main valve to the house didn't function, the leak continued. Vic then took apart the bathroom, starting with the sink and the walls damaged by the leak.

The Jacksons had bought the house "as is," so there was no point in calling the realtor. Vic was handy, but he did not have the time to make the repairs. When the bathroom crisis mushroomed, a major product at work had failed to pass its tests, so Vic and his team had to spend long hours desperately trying to fix that problem. Then Vic called in a plumber who came highly recommended by a friend. However, this workman failed to correct the problem and actually made it worse. Vic fired him. The bathroom remained gutted and unused.

Meanwhile, Karen said, Vic was going through "sticker shock" at the new monthly payments for their house. They were so high that the family had to economize in numerous ways. They could not afford to pay for child care other than Karen's mom. When Karen was assigned on-call duty, the situation became "almost impossible," since Karen had to provide child care while working online, which interfered with the effectiveness of her work. She found this highly stressful. Because of their economic straits, the Jacksons could not add another phone line for a few months. They had only one phone line, in their bedroom. This created further problems, because phone calls came in at all hours, keeping them awake. With only one line, customers trying to contact Karen were kept waiting, adding to their frustration and anger when they finally reached her. Vic changed his schedule to help take care of Tina, and he traded off times with Karen's mom. He told Karen that he could do this indefinitely, but she did not believe this. "He has said this before, and it didn't last," she said.

Adding to the household tension was the growing conflict between Vic and Sarah, who were unable to accommodate to one another. Sarah moved out, thereby creating the immediate further problem of finding child care for Tina. After interviewing several candidates, Vic and Karen selected a woman who provided child care in her own house. But this also increased their obligations and stresses, since Vic and Karen now had to conform to the caregiver's rules for delivery and pickup of their child, and handle day care themselves when Tina became ill. The crisis of child care escalated further when this caregiver became seriously ill and stopped providing day-care services.

The stress did not end there. Throughout the house buying, house repairs, conflicts with Grandmother Sarah, and uncertainties of child care, both Vic and Karen weathered several extensive layoffs and reorganizations in their companies, which utterly demoralized their work groups. Both Vic and Karen endured several mandatory unpaid "work furloughs." Vic's entire work section was relocated to other work sites, then disbanded, and most of his colleagues were laid off. When her company was sold, Karen scrambled to learn new tasks, and, like her husband, she was one of the few employees who survived the cuts that followed. They lived their life under the Damoclean sword of instant economic ruin and the sudden disappearance of friends laid off at work.

Not surprisingly, the looming threats of layoffs pervaded even the happiest of occasions at home. Tina's first birthday party took place the week before an impending work furlough for Karen. Twenty-five people had gathered, including friends, in-laws, and Tina's godparents, Pastor Baldwin and his wife. Vic had barbecued, and Karen and her mother had prepared salads and side dishes, along with an elaborate birthday cake. Brightly wrapped gifts were piled on the covered patio, next to the tables with birthday tablecloths and festive decorations. In between singing birthday songs, cutting and distributing the cake, and helping Tina open her gifts, the adults discussed the economic downturn in Silicon Valley, layoffs, horror stories about friends who had lost employment, and what to do if that happened to them.

Reflecting on the events that had befallen his family, and those that might still occur, Vic remarked with rueful irony, and not a little uneasiness, "We're seeing what we can do to raise the stress level for the purposes of social science research." Of course, his situation was not unique, but simply a reflection of the rising financial risks faced by middle-class American families in the twenty-first century.

Conclusions

Many of us have experienced the minor crises of a potentially ill child or a critical meeting that we inadvertently omitted from a calendar. We plan and build our routines with the knowledge that things can go wrong. Dealing with the unexpected is part of the human experience. Most Americans today arguably encounter fewer cataclysmic surprises than did people a few generations ago. Actually, when a surprise disrupts our daily routine and we cannot cope with it, we may discover that the results are not as catastrophic as we feared. Much busyness has this quality of investing banal activities with disproportionately large sentiments. There is a sort of hubris of the busy person who feels that his or her need to get through the day is paramount and the stakes are inordinately high. They may sweep others into their busyness, persuading or making them take on new obligations or demonstrating "flexibility" by letting go of their own plans. Some people immersed in their busyness are completely taken up with the importance of their own priorities. Others adopt a more detached, reflective perspective regarding themselves, in which they acknowledge the absurdity of their stressful, frenetic activities. Both face the specter of their inability to cope with uncertainty and surprises. Clearly, some surprises can be wrenching in their consequences, such as the birth of a child with a disability, the loss of a job, or a divorce. They may constitute a rupture in the continuity of a life, compelling a dramatic change in lifestyle.

Such surprises, regardless of their consequences, are played out against the backdrop of a risk society.[7] Risk is not quite the same as danger. Danger, according to Mary Douglas, can be statistically measured and so correlated with the realities of a particular way of life. Humans have always confronted dangers, and their potential to disrupt is real. Risk, she argues, is different. It is as much about how we see the world as what is in it. Risk is constructed by the societies in which it is experienced, both in the sense of how members assess it and in the complex systems we have created and in which we live our lives. Those systems have created so many interdependencies that it is impossible to track or measure them all. Danger is based on tangible threats, and the resulting emotions are palpable. By contrast, risk is generalized and nebulous. Risk reflects the fact that our lives can be irrevocably altered by distant events of which we may be blissfully ignorant. Pervasive media bring them to our attention. We may not even fathom the interdependencies that make us vulnerable until an unexpected event reveals them, just as we cannot fully enumerate risks, but we know they are there. That they are unseen and ill defined only exacerbates the edginess and sense of vulnerability of daily life, even when no specific dangers have been identified.

In addition to the risks posed by a world of complex interdependencies, other factors intensify the sense of risk. Increasingly, we are responsible for protecting ourselves. We may receive assistance in doing so, but as governments cut back on services, we may feel that we are on our own. Surprises in such a world remind us not only of how unforgiving our own days might be, but also of the limits to control in general. If we cannot control the mundane, how can we ever hope to handle life-threatening risks?

Even our knowledge is not always comforting. We have created systems of expertise that are constantly being revised, so our knowledge is necessarily contingent. The more knowledge that is created, the more our own relative ignorance increases: we simply cannot be expert in everything. Certainty is eroded, and knowing how to prepare for the future is problematic.

By placing surprise in the context of a risk society, we do not wish to imply that our families constantly feared the unknown, and that everyday life was unduly precarious to them. But we do claim that the idea of a risk society helps explain the urgency people may feel in their coping and their anxiety regarding surprises that may challenge their capacity to create an acceptable future for themselves.

If coping is primarily done by individuals and is limited in its success, then surprises remind us again that busyness is not just a matter of individual responsibility. We are thrust into a society of other people who also are coping and who know that their efforts to do so are precarious. Surprises, real and imagined, therefore underlie the need to build an infrastructure of buffers that aid us as we cope. This infrastructure ideally is enduring and can be shared with others. In this way, controlling our busyness is as much social and public as it is a personal, private burden.

PART THREE

Building Buffers

CHAPTER SEVEN

Using Things

A distinct characteristic of ethnography is that it takes time, and this study shows why duration matters. As days with the families became weeks and months, patterns that were invisible in the short term revealed themselves. When we watched people for days or weeks, we saw them doing certain things, but such snapshots could be misleading. What we saw today could easily be extrapolated into the future; coping practices could appear permanent, when in fact they were not. Such observations focused attention on individuals, since it was they whom we shadowed. The passage of time allowed us to see both the limits of individual coping and the enduring infrastructure they created. We call these infrastructures buffers of busyness and refer to their creation and use as buffering practices.

Buffers came about as a result of the interplay between intentional design and seizing opportunities. Regardless, they constituted resources that allowed some individuals and families to make coping look effortless, while by their own admission, others struggled through their everyday lives. How a family coped could have as much to do with its buffering practices as with the obligations and activities that drove its busyness.

In this chapter, we introduce a set of practices that provision the world with a material infrastructure that might make coping easier. It is about places that are configured around busyness and objects, especially the technological devices that form communication systems. Some high-tech devices hold the promise of tracking things, people, and data in order to create efficient days. Yet like coping practices, there is a tacit work of creating these buffers and then living with their consequences.

Places

KAREN JACKSON: A VOLUNTEER SITE FOR COMPANY WORK

Confronted with the obligation to do her company's work at home, Karen devised a novel response that enabled her to work while volunteering at her church. To do this required her to use the resources of the church and to draw on the participation of her entire family. She devised this complicated arrangement because she really loved her volunteer work, to such a degree that, by her own admission, she overextended herself. "I prefer working at the church," she said wistfully. "If I could, I'd quit my job and spend my time at the church." Karen was deeply involved in volunteering before she married Vic, and she continued to be afterward, despite Vic's efforts to rein her in. Vic's concern was that her church work intruded on their family life and time together.

Karen's response to Vic was to adapt her work and family time to her church activities. Wednesday evenings were the time for the church's weekly contemplation service, choir practices, and volunteer construction of the church nursery. But it was also the day each week that her company required her to be on call from 4:00 PM to 5:00 AM and, if away from home or office, to contact the office every twenty minutes by laptop or phone. On this Wednesday, Karen answered work calls while at home with Tina, her six-month-old daughter. Late in the afternoon, Karen drove to the church with Tina. This was her second trip to the church that day. Earlier, she had organized the brunch at a morning jazz service. In the afternoon, between taking work calls in Pastor Baldwin's office, Karen organized the church's donation records and filled out permit applications for starting a day-care center. Around 4:00 PM, Karen's mother Sarah arrived in her pickup. Sarah looked after Tina, while Karen continued to take work calls. Around 5:30 PM, five other people, including Pastor Baldwin, arrived, bringing salad, lasagna, fruit, and cookies. Over the next hour, they ate and socialized, and Karen joined them in the kitchen and adjoining rooms when she was not being paged.

At 7:00 PM, they moved to the church, where Pastor Baldwin conducted a prayer service with interludes of contemplation. The worshippers sang, and the pastor read a religious passage. Baby Tina remained silent, seemingly interested in the reverberations of song and spoken word.

Around 7:15, Vic arrived, just as the silent contemplation began; he held his baby daughter, while his wife and mother-in-law sat in front of him. Because his work projects required him to spend long hours at the office, often late into the evening, Vic did not do much volunteer work. He described himself "as an enabler. I take care of Tina while Karen is doing her volunteer work."

By 7:30, each worshipper had gone to the front of the altar, where Pastor Baldwin blessed them, after giving them some juice and a cracker, the blood and body of Christ. With this, the prayer session was over. Karen brought Tina to the service because she wanted her daughter to have a religious upbringing.

The Jackson family and a couple of other volunteers walked over to the nursery, which was under construction. The walls were painted bright celery green, and furniture was stashed in the middle of the room. Five-gallon paint cans and paint cloths were strewn everywhere. Vic helped Karen fit a colored paper covering on the curtain rod, while Sarah held Tina. Then, after some wrangling about placement, they pressed several pink, blue, and green flat cloth animals and trees on the wall.

Karen told Vic that she had had to take a work call at the church.

Vic asked, "Did you solve it?"

"No."

"Why not? You need to get on this. You cannot let it wait while you're doing work here at the church."

Karen replied: "It can wait. It's not a critical serious service call. If it were, I'd be on it right away. I told them I'd get back to them later. I'll tell them to check with someone tomorrow."

Vic, Karen, and Sarah had each come to the church in their own vehicles, and now they left separately. Tina went with Karen.

Karen's church volunteer activities were connected to her compelling desire to find and be part of a community. She chose a particular Protestant church because of its pastor. Karen explained: "Pastor Baldwin pulled us in. I liked him. He and his wife had us in their house and introduced us to other new young couples. Although he's Catholic, Vic chose to join because he was very impressed with Pastor Baldwin."

Pastor Baldwin considered all the children he baptized to be his godchildren, but the Jacksons developed a special bond with him. They visited his house at least once a month so that Tina could be with him and his wife. Karen said that they were like Tina's grandparents, and Pastor Baldwin said that Tina was like his daughter. Church activities, intertwined with Karen's work, became an extension of family activities, socialization, and the inculcation of values held dear by Vic and Karen.

Since Karen's employer controlled a portion of Karen's home space, family time, and routines, Karen responded by making this situation work for her. The very portability of her job enabled her to perform it at the locations of her choice, in this case, her church. She used the resources of her church so that she could complete her work there, while engaging in the volunteer activities she relished, and she recruited her family to help her. Work, family, and volunteering merged for Karen's benefit, as well as the church, but not without costs both for the family that supported her and the church whose resources she colonized.

Examining the organizational context of busyness reveals how it is created or driven by the ordinary transactions of everyday life. Those transactions occur with organizations to such an extent that we often take for granted the necessary skills and knowledge that make those transactions seem commonplace and effortless. Even small difficulties with organizations can absorb our time and stymie the most resourceful among us. We often think about organizations only when such difficulties occur, but it is a mistake to view them only as impediments to our pursuit of happiness. People often conceptualize workplaces as adversaries of families, although they are also sources of ideas and practices that people export to their homes. Just as jobs can make us busy, so too they can provide resources that aid us in our busyness.

THE TENTORIS: THE AUTOMOBILE AS A SOCIAL CENTER

In 1998, Tom and Fran Tentori moved far away from their work sites in San Jose so that they could buy a larger house for a smaller price. Additionally, they went in search of a community that would be of their liking, preferably centering on a conservative Protestant church group comprised of families with children around their son's age. The consequences of this move reverberated through their lives, and the lives of others who knew them, often in unexpected ways, with surprising new turns of busyness and new uses for familiar things and places. One of these was the automobile.

When they lived in San Jose, Tom and Fran lived close to their places of work. In their new location, they separately had to face long and tiring daily commutes, coordinated so that they could arrange day care for their son Josh before and after school. Tom and Fran staggered their work hours so that one parent could be with Josh in the morning and the other in the afternoon. They had to adjust to new neighbors and look for and join a new church group. They had to find day care for Josh, which over several weeks involved interviewing and checking out over forty applicants. Josh had to cope with a new school environment. Within a year, Tom and Fran, with several other parents, became dissatisfied with the turmoil and policies of the public school system, so they placed Josh in a private religious school, but not before the change disrupted their routines, absorbed a great deal of their time, and for several months contributed mightily to increased stress in their lives.

In San Jose, Tom and Fran had an active social life that centered on Tom's wide circle of relatives, neighbors in their condominium complex, and members of their church group. In their new location, much of their potential leisure time was swallowed up by their commute and the scramble for child care. Their solution was to adapt their commutes to double as locations for leisure. Tom listened to a Christian radio station on his way to work. Fran turned her commute into a social arena for car-poolers. The car became, not simply a means of transportation, but a place both to form a community and maintain it.

Each morning, Tom awakened about 4:00 AM, dressed, ate, and was out of the house and on the road by 4:30. He commuted alone, listening to his favorite station, usually arriving at his place of work by 5:45. He would relax for a few minutes, listen to the radio and then start work at 6:00. At lunch-time, he would return to his car to catch other religious programs.

Fran would rise at 6:00 AM, have toast and coffee, and awaken her son at 6:30. After Josh dressed, Fran would take him to Carol's house, right opposite the school. Carol, the mother of two sons, six and two, provided day care for Josh. She gave him breakfast, and he remained there until school opened at 8:00. After school, Josh, a second grader, would walk back to Carol's with her oldest son, Mike, who was in first grade. The two children played in the house or went to the school playground, visible from Carol's house. Josh remained at Carol's until his father arrived to take him home, usually around 4:00 PM. At home, Josh played, read, sometimes did a little homework, and watched television. His favorite program was *Pokemon*, and he had a collection of Pokemon cards. Since Fran would not return home until 6:30 or 7:00, Tom cooked dinner.

After dropping off Josh at Carol's, Fran picked up her carpool passenger, Evelyn, a friendly and voluble woman who lived in an older section of town. Fran found Evelyn when someone mentioned to her that a woman living in the same town also commuted to San Jose. Fran said, "At first, both of us were really skeptical. We wanted our freedom and didn't really want to carpool. She'd had bad experiences previously. But both of us work the same hours at offices that are close to one another." Then a friend told Fran about a web site that matched prospective car-poolers, listing names, phone numbers, residences, and work sites. Through this, Fran added two more car-poolers. Barbara lived in a town halfway along the commute route. Candace lived in a town several miles from Highway 101. She would drive to a crossroads off the highway, where they would pick her up. They rotated cars. When it was the turn of Barbara or Candace, Fran and Evelyn, whose commutes were longest, drove part of the way, parked, and transferred to one of the others' cars.

On this particular day, only Fran and Evelyn were commuting. Both worked in San Jose, Evelyn in one of the courts and Fran in a government law office. Evelyn was married with two children. Her husband worked as a nurse at the local hospital. Most of Evelyn's relatives had migrated to the United States from the Philippines. While Evelyn and her husband were at work, Evelyn's in-laws helped with childcare. Evelyn said that without the help of her in-laws, it would not have been possible for both parents to be working. Tom's parents, who lived in San Jose, also served as backup child-care providers during summers and emergencies.

On the trip back and forth to San Jose, the two women talked about family and listened to a radio station that broadcast Christian music and toned-down news. Both women belonged to Bible study groups, and when just the two of them commuted, they discussed the Bible. Evelyn had a vast knowledge, based on her education in the Philippines. Fran described what she learned from these discussions. "It's one thing just to read the Bible, but it's another to have somebody there to talk about it with you. As a woman she can understand what I'm feeling."

Fran and Tom, who commuted separately, did not use cellular phones. As a result, they sometimes lost track of one another. Fran recalled one of those times. "Evelyn and I were driving on our commute on Highway 101 and we saw Tom on the side of the road. His old 1987 car had broken down. He had been standing there from 5:30 AM until we came by around 7:00 and rescued him."

Because of this and other incidents, Fran, Tom, and Evelyn developed emergency procedures. Fran explained, "If my son Josh has an emergency and needs help, Tom is unreachable at work. I can leave my office, but Evelyn cannot easily leave her work, which is in court. I go home. She takes the train to a town about halfway to where we live and I come back and pick her up at 5:30. If Evelyn has to go back to one or both of her daughters, I just take off and go with her."

On occasion they ran into difficulties when one of the other car-poolers did not show up. Fran recalled that one time, "I waited in the rain at her car, but Candace never showed up. Evelyn was waiting at her stop. I don't have a cell phone. I walked over to her [i.e., Candace's] office. She was frantically trying to get eighteen overnight expresses out the door, and she had no way to contact me to say she wasn't going to make it. Candace gave me her keys and I ran over and picked up Evelyn, and we came back and picked up Candace."

Once in a while, the car-poolers ran into traffic backups on the freeway. They learned how to take back roads. Fran remarked, "The offices are cognizant of our long commutes and they make allowances for occasional delays in our arrival."

When Tom and Fran moved away from San Jose, they had to rearrange their own lives, and in doing so they affected the lives of many others, starting with their son, who went to day care at Carol's house. Fran could no longer remain at home and take care of Josh, since she had to work to pay for her new house. She spoke of this with regret. Fran's office made allowances for her occasional commute delays and other surprises. Tom's parents were on call in case of emergencies, as was Carol. An additional busyness was integrating their routines with Fran's three car-poolers, especially Evelyn, who used her husband's in-laws for childcare.

Fran discovered a mobile form of community in a car pool that had become much more than a means of transportation. But at least for a while, it created constraints on her time, vulnerability to events beyond her control, and led to increased activities. Significantly, neither Tom nor Fran accepted this state of affairs as inevitable. They put up with it for a period of about three years, during which they sought ways to reduce the burdens they had created. First Tom and then Fran moved their employment to offices near their home, eliminating their long commutes, the tight schedules, the complicated dance of people who were affected when things went wrong, and the nagging underlying fear that something might go wrong, even when it didn't.

Devices

THE MENDOZA/JONESES: PRESCHOOL SURVEILLANCE

The routines of the Mendoza/Jones daughters are the result of parenting, a deliberate, self-conscious set of values and activities designed to mold children. In the American cultural framework, apparently trivial choices take on a special significance. What is the implication of taking children to McDonalds, letting them play video games, or sending them to a particular day care? Parenting issues may seem trivial, but they can suddenly confront us with larger moral dilemmas.

One day when Suzanne Jones dropped her daughter off at preschool, Alice, the preschool owner, approached her with a mildly panicked look. Her husband had proposed installing a video camera so that the parents could enter a password while sitting at their office computers and see their child at the preschool. Alice was uncomfortable with this intrusion into her workplace—parents looking over her shoulder from afar—but she felt compelled to ask them if they wanted the service.

To Alice's great relief, Suzanne explained that she objected to it. She had interviewed at many preschools and visited others. The decision to leave her child in Alice's care was based on her extensive research and it reflected her trust in the staff's judgment. Simply *looking* at images of her child would violate that sense of trust, and so she encouraged Alice to resist the intrusion of technology into her place.

Later, Suzanne explained that she placed Alice's inquiry into larger issues of technological surveillance, to which she strongly objected. She and her husband, Humberto, were protective of their children, and they welcomed information about them. They tried to surround the girls with trustworthy adults, and surveillance undermined that larger commitment.

Parents are bombarded with new devices that promise easier, faster, and more intrusive communication with their children. Often these come associated with moral messages about the need to protect children, with the not-so-hidden threat that not to use this device is to reveal bad or neglectful parenting. In this case, the video camera was proposed to cope with presumed parental fears of mistreatment of children at preschool. The device would enable parents to have the best of both worlds. It would protect their children at a distance while they attended to work and other matters. Humberto and Suzanne didn't buy this argument. Instead, they remind us that there may be compelling reasons to reject the use of such devices, once we realize their hidden cost, and the moral consequences that follow.

THE FLAHERTYS: ZIPPERED BAGS

Jerry Flaherty created time buffers within his workday. While at the office, he would never stop to eat lunch; he would eat on the run and use his lunch hour to do errands, catch up on paperwork, or respond to messages. Lunch hour was his self-proclaimed "safety valve," which allowed him to be productive even on days when other unexpected events left him with insufficient time to complete planned tasks.

Jerry also created physical buffers that saved him time when he was especially harried. At Christmas, Jerry raced from store to store filling a zippered bag with small gifts for Eleanor. To deal with small emergencies, the Flahertys kept such zippered bags in each family car containing a penlight, a universal combination tool, a small eyeglass repair kit, and packages of breath mints, along with a collection of energy bars, quarters for parking meters, 40 one-dollar bills and other emergency items. In effect, Jerry had created a time-saving protection against emergencies.

Such protections or buffers are varied and include both things and people. Often, the aim is to best manage the use of time. Buffering is an accompaniment to daily life, and some people are better at it than others or simply have access to more resources.

RAJIV MOHAN: GLOBALLY CONNECTED

Personal digital assistants, cellular phones, e-mail, and pagers are among the accoutrements of modern busyness. While they can indeed help people cope with busyness, they also create additional tasks, as well as demands of their own. These include comparison shopping, learning to use them, and maintaining them. Rajiv Mohan, a highly mobile worker, gladly took on the burden of using the latest communications technologies to organize and manage his complex social network. Rajiv's use of technologies connected him globally, whether he was dealing with the health problems of a relative in India, his international business interests, or his wife when she visited her relatives in India.

One day, Rajiv telephoned a cardiologist in southern California. Rajiv's mother had long ago told him and his brothers to treat this doctor as their sister. Now, Rajiv's brother in India was showing symptoms of a blocked artery, and Rajiv asked what to do. The cardiologist urged Rajiv's brother to visit a doctor for an angiogram. He refused until Rajiv called him several times and sent him e-mails. The doctors in India discounted the symptoms, but Rajiv and the cardiologist were adamant that they perform the procedure. The damage was extensive. The doctors gave the data to Rajiv's nephew in India, who scanned and transmitted it to the cardiologist in southern California, who was a member of the medical team. She concurred that an angioplasty was warranted. She said she would be "in" the Indian operating room via conference call, participating in the procedure from her

American office. If anything went wrong, Rajiv and the cardiologist's husband, also a cardiologist, would fly to India immediately. Rajiv said that between work and family, he had a lot going on, but "you sometimes have to step in and do this."

Rajiv's tale of family obligation was made possible by modern technologies that transformed his relationships to space and time. Through telecommunications, he both learned about a family problem half a world away and was able to set in motion the steps that led to diagnosis. The same technologies allowed a cardiologist to be a virtual member of the operating team, and the taken for granted miracle of the passenger airplane allowed virtual membership to become physical presence within hours.

Rajiv also had business interests in Europe and Asia, where he traveled regularly. Each day he kept in touch with family members, investors, clients, and co-workers using a high-tech network he had put together. Most people reached Rajiv by calling his office phone, which had voice-mail capabilities he could use when busy. In addition, he could remotely set the phone to forward calls to the cellular phone that was always at his side. That phone also had a direct number, known only to family members, friends, and close associates, and those calls registered as direct ones on the cellular phone. He tried to answer the direct calls, but accepted the forwarded ones only when convenient. He kept an international cellular phone in Hong Kong for use only there. Since this created difficulty when he traveled to other places, he used another cellular phone with a local area code and universal number that had international capabilities. Anyone dialing this phone number would reach Rajiv anywhere in the world, provided that place had cellular service. Due to the high cost of service and the potential for incoming calls twenty-four hours a day, he gave the number only to family members and a few co-workers. He used this phone for emergencies and still carried his domestic cellular phone. The new phone also allowed him to send and receive cost-free e-mail messages anywhere in the world, but because its screen was small, the messages had to be simple, such as "Call me within 12 hours."

Rajiv sometimes used his wife's cellular phone to solve domestic communication problems. For example, when Nita visited India, he gave her phone to their son Frank, who was attending a summer course in California. "That becomes the security connection for him and for me," Rajiv said. Father and son spoke to Nita every few days, but she initiated most of the calls, since she was on the move. She had a local cellular phone in India that she had borrowed from one of Rajiv's brothers, although she made her international calls from hotels or his brother's house. "She has very good infrastructure there," Rajiv observed.

Rajiv also was in touch through a mobile phone with conference-calling capabilities when he was in his car. He preferred to use this phone when driving, for safety reasons, and only called out on it. In addition to the phones, Rajiv communicated via e-mail through his laptop, which had a wireless modem. He received about seventy e-mails a day, but only responded to about ten of these. The rest were just for his information. Finally, he used a PDA to receive and send "extremely critical" e-mail. "I have my whole life on it," he said, referring to its calendar and address functions.

Rajiv's technological infrastructure was both complex—reflecting a life lived on several continents—and familiar, built from a system of widely available devices strung together to meet his needs. As with other such systems, Ravij had not designed it from the top down but assembled it piecemeal, adding and deleting components to serve new functions and meet emerging needs. The people he contacted and the relationships he maintained were even more important, needless to say, than the "cool" high-tech devices he used. They were the ones who sent those appropriately simple e-mail messages and responded to requests for action when Rajiv was halfway around the world. The system itself was a social production: co-workers and friends exchanged information about the right device to purchase to enhance the system's capabilities. Rajiv used the high-tech infrastructure, but it continued to grow because of his social networks.

Rajiv's technological infrastructure allowed him to "be in touch," but even here there was more than met the eye. Sometimes being in touch meant communicating with people without actually moving to be physically co-present. At other times, "touch" was achieved through physical co-presence; the challenge was to coordinate the movements that made it possible. The virtual and global reach of Rajiv's infrastructure, while awesome, was also firmly grounded in the demands of local logistics, such as chatting on the cellular phone about fruits and vegetables for dinner while sauntering through the produce section. The material properties of buttons, screens, and bandwidth, too, exerted powerful constraints on the infrastructure, reminding Rajiv that he remained tethered to a mundane physical world that technology did not transcend. Indeed, a fundamental component of Rajiv's communications infrastructure was the luxury sedan that he used to move from place to place. His car was so commonplace for Rajiv, as it would be for many people, that he never mentioned it as a device for "being in touch."

"Being in touch" also referred to access to devices themselves. Although part of Rajiv's technological infrastructure—laptop, PDA, cellular phones—traveled with him, other components were distributed around the world. A second cellular phone awaited him in Hong Kong, and he accessed it by flying there. Nita did not carry her infrastructure to India but while there used devices provided by friends, relatives, and companies. Rajiv and Nita thus lived in a world where infrastructure was both owned and parts could be casually borrowed. They in turn provided such infrastructure for people who visited them.

Rajiv's communications infrastructure shows us how devices and services can permeate everyday life. Boundaries between family, work, recreation, community, and other familiar domains of life were routinely penetrated. The challenge was less that of connecting than of being overwhelmed by interruptions, potentially, twenty-four hours a day. Rajiv highlighted a particular kind of challenge: how to gain access to the people he needed while simultaneously controlling others' access to him. Meanwhile, others were pursuing their own strategies for connection and disconnection, and his access interrupted them. He filtered accessibility by using different devices and codes, which involved calculations of costs and benefits, the emotional and relational propinquity of people, the time sensitivity of messages, and bargaining with others for mutual access. To be successful, he knew about the lives and desires of other people regarding his specific communications. Like them, how he succeeded partially reflected his idiosyncratic assumptions and values. He performed tacit work that was essentially political and moral in nature and that underlay his efforts to contain busyness. Even paying for the various phones and services was part of a moral calculus of "what I can live with," Rajiv laughed, shaking his head. He had his different phones billed to different companies, but who owned what was complex and overlapping, making it difficult even to determine who should pay for what.

Rajiv created technological infrastructures in part hoping that they would at least partially solve the problem of busyness. Perhaps they helped, but their impact on the individuals and families affected was not straightforward.

Rajiv's technological infrastructure created new work for those who used it, especially those who had to support or accommodate to its constraints. Enhancing connections might have made daily life more efficient in some ways, but they also threatened to overwhelm users and provoked apparent inefficiencies.

THE CARLSBERGS: DEVICES IN THE BUSYNESS OF CHILDREN

Robert and James Carlsberg provide an elaborate example of how children embody and challenge busyness, and the devices that are part of their world. Day care is followed by class time. After school, day care provides nurturing "unstructured time" from the adult point of view, and unending boredom from the boys' perspective. The boys live in a web of activities tailored around their parents' busyness. However, the boys have their own dreams to pursue, and they comprehend the world of work in their own fashion, often combining entrepreneurial daydreams with skepticism about the emotional rewards of work. What emerges from the story of Robert and James Carlsberg is a critique of busyness and the devices that perpetuate it.

Robert and James Carlsberg ate their breakfasts from television trays pushed to the edge of the kitchen's vinyl flooring, safely off the white carpeting in the family room, where food was prohibited. Across the room, a large screen television glowed with the cartoons that seized the boys' attention. It was 6:00 AM and the start of another school day. Pat and Alex bustled around the spacious kitchen preparing the boys' lunches, quizzing them about the readiness of their book bags and confirming each other's respective plans for the day. Since both parents had early meetings at work, they dropped off the boys at their school's day care by 6:30 AM. Pat referred to this as an "easy day." The boys were content because early arrival allowed them to be first in line for a ten-minute slot at the Nintendo station, their favorite activity. With luck, they could complete their play in time to sign up for a second or third turn.

Pat directed the boys into the car. Ten minutes later, they arrived at day care. She signed in her boys for the day and, after a hug and "I love you" for each, headed to work.

The room contained two computers dedicated to games, tables for art and craft projects, several game tables (e.g., foosball), and a television for playing videocassettes chosen from the facility's library. The room was neat and tidy and contained items donated by parents. On the walls hung a few photographs of group activities and posters. Noticeably absent were posters of contemporary pop-culture icons or athletes. A hand-made poster listed the day-care rules:

1. Show respect in language and actions
2. Stop, look and listen
3. End of day: Everyone helps clean up
4. No means no
5. Hands to yourself
6. Treat equipment with respect
7. Remain seated during snack
8. Before leaving, clean up what you are playing with
9. Quiet during naps and homework

Another poster displayed a poem, which said that the wounds from sticks and stones *will* heal, but those from words remain forever. A small white-board listed the kids who were prohibited from certain activities, such as playing particular games.

Several children were in the room and the boys quickly signed up for Nintendo. Soon after this, James sat down and loaded a game. He played to an audience of three boys who closely monitored his moves. A few minutes later, an aide prompted him to move, and he surrendered his seat to his brother. Robert gazed intently at the screen, careening down a racecourse on a virtual snowboard, the growing audience packed closely around him. The aide ordered the children to give Robert more room, but soon his time expired and another child took his place. He jammed his hands into his pockets and joined his brother who stood behind an audience of younger children watching a video in another corner of the room. Children and parents continued to arrive, some carrying bags of doughnuts or bagels bought on the drive to school. They ate alone before mingling with their friends.

The school prohibited violent computer games, but children would sneak in "fighting games" from home. Ethel, the day-care provider, would confiscate them, and she also closely monitored movie videos. While James watched the movie, he rummaged through a cabinet looking for one of his favorites. Ethel told him that it had recently been moved to the sixth-eighth-grade center when the school reorganized its day-care services. After searching further, James announced that all the good videos had been removed. He wandered back to the Nintendo, where he and Robert received another turn. They competed against each other in a snowboard race. They ended this activity abruptly at 7:45 AM, when Ethel dismissed them to go to class.

It was mid-morning when Mrs. Simitan planted her feet firmly and clapped "1-2-3," signaling her displeasure at the noise in her third-grade classroom. At first, only a half dozen students responded by rhythmically responding with their own "1-2-3 clap," and Mrs. Simitan repeated the signal. The clapping drowned out the talking and everyone, including Robert Carlsberg, looked at her. This had been an unruly morning, though Mrs. Simitan had restored order, at least temporarily. "Take out your math books," she instructed. The thirty-five children lifted their desktops, revealing a few well-ordered piles of supplies, loose papers, binders, and books, but many more in disheveled heaps. "Children, we're having a problem with listening again. Open to page 169." While the children rummaged noisily for the correct book, she handed out a homework assignment, explained how to complete the math book drill, and reminded them to tell their parents to attend a school meeting that night. "School is your job," she advised. "You have to do the best at *your* job, just like I try to do the best at *my* job." Mrs. Simitan passed out additional homework, explained the concept of "re-grouping" to a dozen students who did not understand it, and admonished several other students to do their work. Ten minutes had passed since she had last restored order; again she led them in "1-2-3" clap.

The rhythm of that day's class built up from cycles of instruction, admonishments to focus attention on an assignment, and sudden, jarring orders to put one thing away and take something else out. This was not a day of "group work" but of individual activities. Mrs. Simitan instructed students one-on-one or in small clusters, interrupted by a new cycle of clapping when the children made too much noise. As a rule, they spent less than twenty minutes on any one activity; then Mrs. Simitan shifted them abruptly to something else. Most of the time, she issued oral instructions one time only to compel the children to listen.

Robert was developing an acute sense of time and was especially happy with his new wristwatch. "This is digital, so just look at it and it tells you what time," he said. Robert considered this important, since he wanted to know how much more time he had until the school day ended. "If it's during a math test, I want to know how much longer till school's out. For the other ones [analog timepieces], it takes a few seconds. This one I just *see* it."

While Robert was attentive, his desk was messy. The reason, he said, was that he had so little time to switch materials between activities that he and others simply tossed books and binders into their desks. By day's end, any vestige of order had vanished. At 3:00 PM, the final bell rang, and the students quickly departed with their parents or headed off to the after-school program, happy to be free, but exhausted by their day of continual stops and starts to attention.

After class, Robert and James returned to the day-care center, where they ate cookies and drank some juice. Some of the children worked on their homework in a nearby classroom, while others played indoors or outdoors. Ethel said, "We try to keep it pretty unstructured, because the classroom has so much structure." Aides monitored their activities, policing the use of computers and carefully recording playing times, keeping in touch while watching the children on the playground, and coordinating the departures of children. Parents had to sign out their children, and they often chatted with Ethel about their children.

Ethel saw many symptoms of stress among the children, which she said extended "all the way down to first and second grade. I don't like to see it." While the school prepared the children well for high school, Ethel expressed concern, "When are they supposed to be kids?" She mentioned children who by age five or six had lost interest in school; the academic instruction had become too intense for them too early. To train the kids to listen carefully, kindergarten teachers sometimes gave oral instructions that differed from written rules. The children "zoned out" to protect themselves from the dual pressures that followed from high academic expectations and religious training. "These kids know the difference between right and wrong, and they get very upset."

For the Carlsbergs, day care had started out as a monetary transaction, but the line between family and school became blurred. They became friends with Ethel and several aides who helped out during the inevitable logistical crises of daily life. One time, Pat Carlsberg called Rebecca, an aide whose several children attended the school, to ask if she could take Robert and James home with her, since neither she nor Alex could get to the day care by 6:00 PM. Rebecca took the boys home with her and kept them until after 8:00 PM, when Pat picked them up. Rebecca transported the boys to and from school when Alex's father underwent surgery in a distant city. In turn, Alex and Pat strongly supported the day-care staff in their periodic disputes with school administrators.

Robert and James had their own ideas about day care. They were bored with the relatively impoverished entertainment infrastructure at day care compared with the array of computers, big screen television, and media and games that they had at home. "They have really bad games. I have better games," Robert commented. "We played there [at day care] because that was the only thing to do. Well, in first grade they had an air hockey table. They traded the air hockey table for a mini air hockey table and a foosball table that really sucks." James added that the only advantage of day care was they were exposed to older children who had been playing longer. The tougher competition helped them improve their own performance, although he and Robert had beaten their competitors because they used "more powerful strategies" in their play.

James and Robert typically spent 10–11 hours a day at day care and school, both important "activity settings," populated by classmates, younger and older children, teachers, aides, and other parents.[1] These people were available to them in ways that were patterned by rules of appropriate action and interaction, the daily routines of families and organizations, and the economic and social organization of the community. The activities that occurred there included play, schooling, care giving, discipline, and entertainment.

The activities reflected the often-diverse motivations of the personnel, and not surprisingly, personnel did not agree about the meaning or purpose of these activities, or about what was really going on. They learned and followed tacit and explicit scripts for performing tasks. Adults also organized and enacted larger cultural values, goals, and beliefs, so that the activity settings made sense within particular cultural frames of reference. Such settings were common, in the sense that many children found themselves in school and day care, but they were also idiosyncratic: the Carlsberg boys experienced a specific school and day care with particular people and activities.

For the Carlsberg boys, activity settings included several homes, automobiles, playgrounds, stores, and even a virtual realm accessible through the Internet. These settings were connected in a distinct way for each family and child. Many children attended the same school and day care as Robert and James, but their other settings were different.

During the summer and holidays, the family altered its child-care arrangements. One summer, James spent a month with Pat's family while attending a summer camp. Robert attended summer school, which served the function of child care. The combination of summer school and after-school care cost less than other forms of day care. Robert was strong in mathematics, so his parents sought out programs that emphasized verbal skills. This was difficult, since most summer school programs emphasized the mathematics at which Robert already excelled. During the rest of summer, Pat and Alex each provided day care by taking one vacation day a week. The boys also spent time with their grandparents.

James and Robert also experienced time in ways that were molded by busyness. During the school day, they alternated between intense activities, abrupt changes signaled by others, and waiting and watching. In day care, they spent more time watching other children play Nintendo than they did playing the game themselves. In class, they encountered abrupt transitions, which required them to pay constant attention to make sure they had the proper materials available. Their time proceeded in chunks. They learned to manage desks and binders while under pressure, a hidden curriculum that provided skills needed to thrive at school and beyond.

For these boys, and many others, control over time became more important than activities per se. When asked, the boys preferred to "hang" with their friends, with nothing planned or scheduled. James said, "Ride my bike, go to a park. Just like, hang out, talk about school. Like, any reports we have to do. And like, how hard they are. And, how strict is your teacher?" To arrange this "hanging out," the parents had to increase their busyness, racing here and there, making arrangements.

Yet busy work schedules had their benefits. James said that being in a family where both parents worked was "cool," because sometimes his parents "both have business to do and they just get us a game to play with and set us down and play with it while they go upstairs to do all their work." Excursions relieved the long days at school and day care. "It's like really fun 'cause we get to go to movies and play and do all this fun stuff. I think it doesn't happen as often [as in families where one parent works], but when it does happen, it is a *better* trip or whatever. Because the people who aren't working, they get to go out with their kids more often and do lots of stuff; they must be like little things. But like my parents, who are working, they get to do like big things, except it's like once a month or something." Such "big things" included visiting a miniature golf course, eating at pizza restaurants, going to a movie, or taking a day trip to the Monterey Bay Aquarium.

The boys spent time, not just in the moment, but thinking about past excursions and anticipating new ones. These treats provided islands of respite in days marked by regimented activities and the tedium of waiting. Newly liberated from day care, James mused: "While I'm in school I want to be in day care. While I'm in day care I want to be home. While I'm at home I want to be at Great America [amusement park]. While I'm at Great America I want to be at home watching a movie. While I'm watching a movie I want to be playing a video game with my cousin." He laughed, "Then I'm stuck at home complaining that I don't have anything to do." In saying this, James anticipated Bradd Shore's remark that the very modularization of life, exacerbated by busyness, has its own effect on attention and engagement, leading to a craving for the new and dissatisfaction with the moment.[2]

Robert and James relied on their parents to arrange "play dates," but the boys tried to influence these and control their activity settings. They constantly lobbied for sleepovers, and their strategizing could be quite sophisticated. One time, Robert was in the family room with Marco, a friend from class. James had been invited to a friend's house to play and spend the night. Originally, James had negotiated this sleepover and the parents had agreed that Robert could come too. But then Robert spied Marco at a church event and the latter asked if he could come over to play. So Robert negotiated the separate play date. However, while Robert wanted a sleepover, Marco's parents decided he was not ready to spend the night way from home. Marco's father said he would come to fetch his son as late as possible, but Alex and Pat wanted Marco to leave early so that they could drop Robert off at James's friend's house for the original sleepover. The result would be a quiet and restful morning for the parents. Alex also worried that Robert was avoiding his commitments when he abandoned the original invitation. But perhaps the boy was learning to "jump ship whenever you can get a better offer," a valuable skill for the future, Alex mused.

Robert and James had access to a technological infrastructure that in-cluded devices for communication as well as entertainment. The boys wanted to arrive at day care early to gain access to its Nintendo setup, but they also recognized its inadequacy compared to their home gaming setup, and this contributed to their boredom. Likewise, the relatively lean enter-tainment infrastructure at Pat's mother's house was a growing source of tension and resistance. Although elderly, she provided supervision on short notice and thus formed a critical buffer when the plans of Alex and Pat went awry. Her modest house contained a small television, but neither computer nor VCR, much less a DVD player. Ever vigilant and protective, the grand-mother refused to let the boys play in the street, so although the boys loved her, spending the day at her house was always an issue.

For Robert and James, entertainment devices were more than a distinc-tive environment; they used them creatively. They were a safe and, as far as the boys were concerned, interesting haven. They were critical compo-nents of their activity settings and the focus of much of their attention and emotion. The boys compared prices and knew the places to get the best bargains. When James showed off his new video, he remarked not about its content, but that he had bought it cut rate.

Were Robert and James victims of busyness, especially because of their parents' jobs? One time, Pat refused to take a vacation because of her in-creased responsibilities at work. Alex and the boys left her at home and de-parted for a Sierra cabin. Robert commented later: "She's always worried and she never comes home much. While we were gone she stayed there [at work] until 11:00 PM every day and when she came home she like stayed up three more hours doing work." He had studied his mother's patterns and noted that she was always ready to step in if someone asked, even if it was unnecessary. "Even if those people [i.e., her co-workers] were *really* going to do it, she probably would say, 'No, you do whatever you want. I'll do it.' She does that a lot."

James, too, understood that job pressures affected his own daily life. When asked about the difficulties of being in a dual career family, he re-sponded: "Probably if at least one or both didn't work, I'd probably get to know them [i.e., Alex and Pat] a little better, and they'd trust me more. My friend, his mom stays at home and his dad used to, too, because he like broke his arm. He got their trust, so he gets to ride his bike around the block. He lives way down there and he gets to ride his bike to my house. My mom won't let me ride my bike two inches from the house."

The Carlsberg boys were thus keenly aware that busyness constrained their lives, and they did not simply accept it passively. They speculated about their parents' motivations and aspirations. Robert recognized that his mother repeatedly assumed more responsibilities at work, and he asked why. When she did not join him and his brother and father at the vacation cabin, he sagely concluded, "Mom didn't come because work takes over her life."

While driving home with the trunk full of first communion glasses for Robert's class, Pat remarked that she had agreed to decorate half of them "because I'm stupid." Then she laughed and said other parents would also paint some glasses. James, seated behind her, chimed in that those parents would be "the ones that are willing to waste their time and have an excuse not to do their 'work' work." Pat asked if he did not appreciate what she did for the boys' classes. Would he prefer that she go to her workplace more? James replied that she did not volunteer simply for them or even their classes but to avoid her own work. She brought a lot of "work home from work" (i.e., her job) but then painted wineglasses or did other tasks for the classes rather than complete it. Stunned, Pat strained to see her son in the rearview mirror. "James, that was an insightful analysis," she said. Later, the boys told Pat that they wished she would avoid volunteering for the school, since it benefited all the children, and they would prefer her to devote more time to *them*.

On occasion the boys went from resigned acceptance or clever analysis to attempts to control the activity settings of their lives, to set things right as they saw it. Usually, they did not succeed, since adults largely created these activity settings. Still, the boys could stall adult plans. One day, Pat picked up the two boys after school and headed for a workshop in which she had enrolled a reluctant James. Usually, Alex drove him, so Pat asked James for the name of the workshop facilitator. James replied sullenly, "I don't know." Pat probed him, explaining that after several weeks he *must* know the man's name. James again denied knowing the name. The workshop rule was that when asking a question, you had to state the other person's name. He had deliberately not learned the name "so I can't call on him for questions." Pat, still trying to generate enthusiasm, commented, "I bet he knows your name." James's icy reply was, "He's paid to."

At other times, the boys tried to provision activities settings, as when Robert bargained for a private play date and sleepover. He also suggested the Christmas gift of a videocassette player to his grandmother, or perhaps a computer. His family laughed at this suggestion, and Robert, in spite of himself, joined in. But the laughter could not conceal his seriousness and urgency about manipulating this particular activity setting to his advantage.

Pat and Alex provided the transportation that allowed their children to travel safely between the islands of their daily lives.[3] They also often monitored their own and other children. For Pat and Alex, transportation and monitoring were connected to their notions of safety, referring, not simply to physical or psychic threats, but also to ways of doing things that validated them as responsible actors. They had to monitor the children in ways accountable to a visible or invisible audience of other adults, with their own idiosyncratic standards of acceptable care and reasonable monitoring. Of course, various legal and organizational standards also provided the context for monitoring. Using child care drew Pat and Alex and other adults into activity settings that helped define who they were as reasonable and responsible people. "Safety" related not only to the children but also to the parents and their reputations.

Busyness permeated the parenting of Pat and Alex; it affected both their daily logistics and their participation in myriad activity settings, for example, scouting. Alex said that participation in scouting had been an important part of childhood, so he made sure Robert and James had the best opportunities to do so. He was a den leader for one of his boys. He noted that all but one other boy came from divorced families. Most of them lived with their mothers and only occasionally saw their fathers. The kids were shuttled from place to place, and Alex often did not know how to contact a parent. He was unable to find a meeting time when the parents could attend. Scout guidelines required two adults at each meeting, both to control the kids and to provide accountability for each other, but this was not possible, so Alex held the meetings alone. While he was uncomfortable with this, he said, "I don't want my kids shortchanged." He found himself dealing with disruptive children and he banished several from a subsequent meeting or two as punishment.

Pat also was drawn into scouting through her involvement in projects and willingness to assist with miscellaneous events, such as hosting mass breakfasts. The couple said that they wished they could avoid the additional labor, but they were committed to providing their boys with "normal" experiences, like scouting, which would not happen unless they became involved. They also questioned the ability and willingness of many other parents to provide responsible care. Parents dropped off their children without a word. Once, they had been unable to track down a parent for two days: a "play date" had turned into an improvised sleepover when the parents left town.

The Carlsberg house also revealed assumptions about creating activity settings under conditions of busyness. Some of the rooms were stages for formal family events; others provided settings that made the space attractive for children. An obvious example was the big screen television with its array of video games. A hidden example was Alex's cache of Pokemon cards, which he gave to the boys as their allowances. Alex and Pat made the house a desirable destination for the friends and classmates of their children. They decided which items were acceptable and affordable, and which were not. In doing this, they became drawn into their sons' worlds, not just as monitors, but also as their creators. Their involvement became a family activity. Thus Alex memorized the Pokemon card delivery schedules at several area toy stores and their telephone numbers, and he mobilized his boys to capture as many as possible. He explained that some stores limited purchases to ten packs per person, and so his children simply went through the line again to buy more. "You gotta cheat to do this," he joked, explaining that the searching and running around was "just another one of those things you do for your kids."

Despite their efforts, Pat and Alex were uncertain how best to raise children under conditions of busyness. "We've lost it as parents," Alex reflected on a particularly frustrating day. He was awestruck by parents whose children obeyed instructions. "We beg and plead and yell at them, and they just don't do it. You're not supposed to spank them, although that worked fine in my day." Alex commented, "What would make us more effective parents would be to get rid of what makes us ineffective": television and video games. He had nothing against either, but "its when they become an obsession, they [i.e., children] don't pay attention." He was torn between providing his children with the things that society deemed valuable, at least in part so that they would fit in with their peers. He often asked himself whether he should "go along with the stuff in society or raise my children so they obey?" Ironically, he believed that the very things his children wanted, which he hoped would support their quest for friends, also undermined their behavior and his and Pat's authority. Yet he equally feared the consequences of restricting television and games, because his boys were so habituated to them. "My kids are really spoiled," he laughed, shaking his head. On weekends, they would wake up and immediately pronounce that they were bored. "Read a book," he would tell them, but he feared that he and Pat gave in too many times, and now they were unable to entertain themselves. In his view, children with a stay-at-home parent were advantaged. They had less temptation to buy things, since a parent was around. Alex and Pat both said that they felt pressure to make the most of their limited time with their children, and that this affected their parenting. Alex mused, "I can't tell you how many times we've done something that we know isn't the right thing, the best thing to do [for the kids] because of that."

Most of the parenting issues that concerned the Carlsbergs pertained to the present or the immediate future. But other important issues of busyness, for example, those connected to educational decisions, took longer to unfold. As described in Chapter 3, the boys attended a private school at which their parents volunteered hundreds of hours on various projects. Alex and his wife could have reduced these demands by sending the boys to public school, but both parents believed in the importance of an "Ivy League education." Alex and Pat had attended state universities. They said that they learned as much there as they would have at another school, but they missed the social networks of more prestigious schools. "Doors open for you," Alex said. "You get hired at graduation as a manager," rather than having to prove yourself as a line worker first. Education for Alex was more than a matter of skills and knowledge; it also involved connections, class, and power. "The race is on even in kindergarten," he said, shaking his head. He mentioned a particularly prestigious local elementary school available "for fifteen thousand dollars a year," and joked ruefully, "So you're already a bad parent because you didn't send your kid there." Gazing at the nearby hills, he reiterated, "The race is always on."

Childhood, as the historian John Gillis reminds us, has become a measure by which legions of adults mark their own life courses.[4] The Carlsbergs were drawn into their children's lives in ways that would likely have seemed alien to previous generations. Both how they were drawn in and how they responded reflected the idiosyncratic events of their lives and those of their children. It also reflected their own remembered childhoods. These assumed an importance, not only because they were so *different* from those of their children, but because Pat and Alex were compelled to think about childhood through their involvement with their children's activity settings.

Embedded Stories

THE SCHWARTZES: BARBIE WARS

Hettie Schwartz loved Barbie dolls, but her parents and older sister gently rebuked her for this. They preferred the world of highly educated professionals, and their activities and remarks reflected this. Hettie's dolls were not accepted in this world.

Arthur believed that adults should provide a model of how to work and live full lives, and he left no doubt what that model should be. "Sonya really likes the fact that she sees her mom out there working, doing stuff," he said. "She's a little sponge, absorbs the stuff and is really proud of her mom and of our life. She likes to be kept busy. Hopefully, it will motivate them to do something with their lives in society."

Linda wanted her daughters to understand that women could be professionals and fully capable people. When the sister of a family friend considered quitting her job as a teacher, the Schwartz family debated the issue over dinner. Hettie asked, "Doesn't her husband make enough money?" This irritated Linda, who had hoped that her daughter understood that work was not simply about money. She replied that this was not what women had been fighting for all her adult life. One Saturday morning, while Linda was folding laundry, Hettie was playing with her dress-up clothes. She asked if her mother felt like a princess, and Linda responded, "No, I feel like an indentured servant!"

Hettie was caught in a world of conflicting expectations that pitted her against others in her family. Her parents prized activities that developed the technical and social skills that highly educated professionals could use. Hettie, seven years old, did some things that her parents approved, such as working with computers and creating art. But she also liked "playing Barbies" with her friends. A central feature of her play life was using the computer to design fashions for her dolls. While tolerating her Barbie play, Hettie's parents tried to deemphasize it, for it led Hettie away from the directions they wanted her to take. They especially disliked the stereotypical gender role they felt was inherent in the play. Linda commented with horror that there was even a Barbie attorney, dressed in pink, a most unprofessional color.

In spite of their misgivings, the Schwartz adults converted the wet bar in their house into a play area densely populated with dolls. The banter of these parents was light and playful, but the undercurrent was to convey to their daughter that even in play, the stakes were high for the future. Sonya, Hettie's twelve-year-old sister, an intellectual and an athletic tomboy, took on the attitudes and demeanor of her parents. She scornfully dismissed Hettie's Barbie art as "not very creative."

The Schwartz family has a clear sense of how they view themselves and present the values they believe in. They have a strong story line connecting their past, tied to Jewish history, the present, exemplifying a cultured, worldly outlook, and an envisioned future of daughters who are professionals in a world of gender equality. As in many other families in America, if a child does not espouse preferred values and practices, other family members may use various degrees of persuasion to change that child's direction.

THE ALLEN / RODRIGUEZES: A CAR FOR PRIVACY

The long-standing disagreement over planning between Bill and Sophia versus her family spilled over into automobiles, perhaps the single most important piece of technology that impacts people's busyness. Bill and Sophia went shopping for a new car. Sophia's many relatives expected them to buy a large car. That way, Bill and Sophia could take her relatives on outings, for this was what family was about. Bill and Sophia felt the pressure to fulfill these family obligations, but they also wanted to draw boundaries that would give them some privacy. The problem was that no matter what they decided, the effects on them and their wider family would remain for years.

Bill and Sophia owned a pickup truck and a Ford Escort. The Escort simply could not meet the addition of two boys to the family, as well as the demands to transport members of Sophia's large family. In their search to buy a new car, they looked seriously at minivans and smaller sport utility vehicles, as well as at Mercedes and Porsches for fun.

Several weeks later, Bill opened his garage door with a laugh and pointed to a shiny, dark purple sports car with room for neither luggage nor a third person, making it a spectacularly impractical solution to their transportation problem. And that, said Bill, was the point. They would keep the old car and truck for hauling people around and use the new car for weekend cruising. Bill said that Sophia's sister and her husband, owners of a large SUV that seated nine, hoped that he and Sophia would buy a large vehicle so they too could drive the family, but Bill didn't want "to be the taxi driver" for the family. Bill and Sophia also realized that a sports car could be used to protect time alone with each other. Still, Bill observed that their decision had provoked his brother-in-law's anger. When Sophia said with a laugh that the car was "our vice," her sister's husband looked up from his dinner and said with mock sincerity, "See, I'm the practical one who *wants* to drive everyone around."

A spacious automobile could have been their means of keeping in touch with others. Instead, Bill and Sophia deliberately bought a two-seater to establish separation and to privilege their own relationship. Their car became the conscious symbol and reminder of the limits of extended family involvement.

THE TRANS: THE FAMILY CATERING TRUCK

The things that people use may become symbols of their families, their identities, their hopes and dreams for the future, and the stuff from which family sagas unfold. Such was Binh and Sheila Tran's catering truck. For sixteen years, the Trans, refugees from Vietnam, had scrimped and saved, working long hours to realize the dream of owning their own business. Binh was in construction and building maintenance, and Sheila worked as an electronics technician and cosmetologist, except when their three children were small and she had stayed home to care for them. Now that they were older, Sheila had persuaded her husband to quit his job and invest their life savings in starting a catering business with her. In 1997, they bought the truck second-hand for $53,000 and paid in addition for the exclusive rights to a sales route. This was Sheila's dream come true: an 18-foot sparkling silver vehicle, scrubbed inside and out every working day, outfitted with fresh food, with drinks resting on crushed ice. She could proudly tell her friends and relatives that she owned her own business, her husband was working with her, and her children were helping to clean the truck on weekends. The truck was the symbol of family unity as well as business success.

Sheila, thirty-eight years old and educated through the second year of high school, was born into a poor Catholic fishing community on Vietnam's southern coast. At the end of the Vietnam War in 1975, she escaped by boat with her family. She brought to America a willingness to work hard, and a strong attachment to her family. Her devout faith prepared her to believe that something good was possible for them all.

Her husband Binh, a high school graduate, was in his middle forties. When the Vietnam War ended in 1975, the victorious communists had incarcerated hundreds of thousands of former soldiers and administrators of the defeated government of South Vietnam, Binh among them, in reeducation camps, where they tortured and starved the inmates, and forced them to perform hard labor.

Binh recalled those days. "For the first two weeks, I was put in a large metal container, where water seeped in. I was wet all the time. For three years, at night, my legs were shackled with a bar to other men, so tight that I could only lie on one side. We had only a small amount of rice, so I became very thin, hungry. Only in the last two years have I been able to eat a little." After Binh was released, he fled Vietnam by boat. He met and married Sheila in America.

The catering business was hard work, but Binh and Sheila, no strangers to suffering, did not complain. By 4:30 AM, Binh and Sheila had left their rented house, driving their weathered Toyota to the lot fifteen minutes away, where they rented a space for their catering truck. The lot contained outlets for electricity and water, an icehouse, and a warehouse of several thousand square feet, where the caterers bought the food and drinks they sold to customers. While Sheila washed the inside of the vehicle, cut vegetables, and started up the grill, Binh brought back crushed ice, bought provisions, and placed drinks, chips, cookies, and fruit in the truck's side panels. By 6:00 AM, they were on the road. They would visit each site in the morning and again in the afternoon, not returning from their route until mid to late afternoon, after which they would hose down the truck in preparation for the next day's journey.

With seemingly boundless energy, this middle-aged couple threw themselves into making the most of the precious new opportunity that they saw in America. They did this not only for themselves but also for their children. They hoped to maintain the Vietnamese ideal of keeping their family together, while preparing their children to succeed in America. They worked mightily to strengthen their family. They stretched their meager budget to pay for their children's music and martial arts lessons. Binh remarked, "I put my children in martial arts to give them discipline, direction and control." Music lessons were for relaxation, and religious instruction was for moral training. Binh took martial arts lessons with his children, and the entire family participated in Catholic Church activities and camping events, which they saw as an integral part of their social lives. To teach them responsibility, Binh and Sheila assigned them household chores, including the washing of the catering truck on Sundays.

Each day, the truck reminded Binh and Sheila, as well as their children of what they should strive for: both economic and family success. One without the other would constitute failure. Binh and Sheila expected that two of their children, Ron and Ginny, would complete college, hold high-paying jobs, and in later years support the whole family. Sheila told her children: "Now I work and have money, which I spend on you guys. Later, when you get a good job, you'll buy us a house and car. That's the old custom. My parents did that for us."

Their plan was for their children to follow American values and practices in the workplace, while retaining Vietnamese values at home. They dreamed that when their children grew up and had their own families, all of them would live together in one house. A constant reminder of their dream was a poster hanging on the wall next to the kitchen table that showed a mansion on a cliff overlooking the sea and five expensive automobiles.

Ron, sixteen years old, had made this his dream too. "Dad hopes his dream house will be near the sea," he explained. "He'd buy the land and build it himself. One of my main goals is to make my Dad proud, to graduate college, go into a good company, make good money, live with my parents. He would build it for all of us, all our future."

Thus for Binh and Sheila, their hopes for the future depended on more than financial success; their family also had to remain close, retaining core Vietnamese values and practices: the respect of children for their parents, the limitless sacrifice of parents for their children, and the unquestioned financial and emotional support of each family member for the others.

First, however, Binh and Sheila needed to succeed in their new business enterprise. Although they were in a booming economy, they encountered difficulties almost from the start. The route they had bought was not a good one and did not bring in much income. Their business was extremely sensitive to wider economic downturns: customers dwindled as layoffs rose, while expenses for truck maintenance remained high. The rental fee for parking space plus insurance came to about $6,000 a year. Truck repairs cost another $3,000, and food another $5,000. The customers who took the food on credit cost them another several hundred dollars a month. According to city heath regulations, at the end of each day, all cooked food had to be disposed of, so Binh and Sheila would distribute it to street people who waited for it at the parking lot.

On this day in April 1999, they got a late start, because earlier drivers had taken all of the crushed ice and Binh had to break up a new block. Customers would be waiting, so Binh hurried to pack the ice into the truck. He hopped into the vehicle, sped twelve miles down the freeway, and careened into an industrial park, the first stop on his route. He tapped his musical horn, and a raucous tune announced his arrival. At the back of the catering truck, Sheila was cutting up onions next to the sizzling grill. Her eyes were tearing, and sweat was running down her arms. She had already grilled sausages, eggs, and ham, which she had made into sandwiches and then wrapped in cellophane. Later in the day, she would cook fish, noodles, and rice. One customer was waiting at the curb, and two more stepped out from the side door of the windowless company building. At this time in the morning, people bought coffee, fruit, sweet rolls, and an occasional sandwich.

With an easy familiarity, Binh called out, "Hello, Mr. Wonderful." A stocky man, sporting a large mustache and wearing a striped shirt and khaki trousers, returned Binh's greeting. Money slipped out of the man's hand and dropped to the ground. "Throwing money at you," he joked.

A woman asked, "Do I owe you? I don't remember. Can I have tea bags?" Binh replied, "Sister, I don't think so. You took food on credit in March and you haven't paid back."

Another woman said, "Hi, I want to pay my bill." Binh looked at his ledger and said, "Thirty-six dollars." She paid and ordered, "My favorite, orange juice and bagel with cream cheese."

When they left, Binh said, "She'll pay once a month, but a lot of people do not, and I'll never get it. They aren't happy if we don't extend them credit, but if we do, some people don't pay back for months, and some who are laid off never pay you back. Lots of people owe us 60–70 dollars. And at many of these companies, only a couple of people come out to buy when we show up."

The banter of Binh and Sheila with their customers masked their growing concern as their dream disintegrated day by day. As Binh drove, he picked up two ball bearings with his right hand and swirled them nervously in his palm. "These are exercise balls," he explained, "like Chinese Kung Fu." At one stop after another, only a handful of customers appeared. At one site, a manager of the company approached Binh and called out, "Hey man, you're the second truck today. Another one was here already. I thought this was your route. Watch out, or they'll horn in on you."

Binh replied, "It is my route," and after the manager left, he explained, "They push their way in. I'm expected to threaten them and say that it's my route. I don't like that, and I don't do it. This is a rough business, very competitive, and people push each other out."

Sheila had fried some fish, and they ate this for lunch. They discussed their business. Sheila noted that Mondays and Fridays were their slow days, but Binh added that everything was slowing down. "In the past, before the Asian crisis, business was a lot better. Then the Asian market fell apart, production fell, people were laid off, and few people come to the catering truck."

Binh and Sheila did not talk much while on the route, but when they did, it was often about economic concerns. They spoke in their native language, Vietnamese.

Binh said, "We've got to take in the truck for repair."

Sheila's voice rose with anxiety, "How long will it take?"

"Two hours. It needs realignment, cost two hundred dollars. If we leave it overnight, we've got to get more ice for the milk and juice."

They did not go to the last three stops, because there was no business. As they headed back to the parking lot, Sheila asked "How much did we earn today?"

"Two hundred something." Binh replied.

Binh's pager buzzed, and he called back on his cellular phone. A woman wanted to hire him to do some house repair. He told Sheila he would do this to earn extra money.

After cleaning and outfitting the catering truck, Binh drove it to the garage where it would be repaired while Sheila followed in their automobile. That day, they had brought in $240, $220 of which went to repairing the truck. To make the business successful, the Trans needed to bring in $400–600 a day, but all too often, days ended like this one. Within two years, they had used up their savings, their business was declining, and their route was unattractive to prospective buyers.

Binh worked on the truck with his wife for about the first year and a half. After that, he gave up on the catering business. He wanted to sell the truck, but his wife was unwilling to abandon her dream. Binh, meanwhile, took a job as the custodian of a housing complex in a town about twenty miles away. Each morning before going to that job, he helped his wife prepare the catering truck, which she then took out on the routes. Sometimes he would accompany her on the early morning stops, when business was best. In the afternoons, when business was slower, she drove by herself, and he went to his other job. In his spare time, he studied to pass the California construction contractor's license exam.

Sheila worried about the desperate circumstances they faced. She revealed this one Sunday when she brought Ron to help her wash down the catering truck for the following day. His younger sister, Ginny, was at the martial arts academy taking a proficiency test, while Binh was working as a handyman for a neighbor. Paul, a Down Syndrome child, was playing in the parking lot. Sheila directed Ron to hose down the truck. He sprayed it, used a long handled soft brush to apply the soapy water, and then rinsed it off.

Sheila inspected her son's work and complained loudly: "What's this? Why are there marks? You did not clean it."

Ron responded in an exasperated voice, "Yes, I did, Ma. Those are water marks."

Sheila insisted, "It cannot go out on the road like this." She pointed to the splotches.

Ron refused to back down. "Ma, it's water. I washed it. It doesn't come off." His tone said it was not his fault, and that she was overly demanding. The edge in her voice accused him of being sloppy and lazy. Her anxiety about the catering wagon's appearance was heightened because of their economic crisis, which she and Binh desperately tried to conceal from their children.

The children had already sensed that something was amiss. Each Saturday, after church activities, Sheila headed with the children to visit her sister's house a couple of miles away. Here, she relaxed a bit in the supportive atmosphere of her relatives before returning to the grim reality of the catering business. Binh never went. He was doing odd jobs and increasingly was off alone on his boat fishing for sturgeon and striped bass in the Delta.

Every couple of weeks, Binh visited his close friend Khanh, who had transformed his garage into a recreation room. On weekends, families visited the Khanh household. While the children went off to play in a corner of the house, the women clustered in the kitchen, where they gossiped and prepared boiled chicken, noodles with prawns, and barbecued beef ribs and pork.

The men, in the garage, drank beer and cognac and ate duck porridge and beef with vegetables. Throughout the day and well into the night, they played guitars and flutes, sang old songs, composed and recited poetry, told off-color jokes, and reminisced about the old days in Vietnam. They idealized it as a place where, unlike America, men dominated and women obeyed.

Khanh said that these drinking parties were like those they used to have in Vietnam, except that here in America, they lessened the pain and frustration of living in a strange new land. Khanh helped Binh through the dark days of the collapse of the Trans' dream for the future. He lent Binh money, they played music together, and above all, he listened as Binh poured out his heart. Binh said that when he was in a reeducation camp, tired, ill, and starving, he had despaired, but it was nothing compared to the despair he felt now. In the camp, there were others suffering the same fate; they shared that bond. But in America, while all of his friends and relatives were flourishing, his own family was in dire straits. He was ashamed to visit his relatives. Khanh listened and never lost faith in his friend.

"All week I am like the trash," Binh remarked. "On the weekend I let the trash out. I let go at places such as Khanh's house. For me this is like a valve releasing stress. You have to have the solution to your problems. If you don't, another cannot help you. By listening, Khanh helps me with my problems."

Sheila desperately tried to keep the catering business going, persisting long after Binh had written it off. Finally, she relented, they sold their truck and route, and Sheila went to work on another person's truck.

When they started their business, Binh had put up two signs next to the poster of the house by the sea. These signs, in gold letters on a red background, expressed good wishes for the new business. After they sold the truck, Binh took down the signs. He left the poster on the wall; their dream of the future remained.

Conclusions

As our fieldwork progressed, we were able to explicate more of the tacit work of coping and buffering. Calling this work tacit suggests that the results of busyness are hidden, if not invisible. Images may pop into mind of anthropologists squinting to see something that others cannot. There is an element of truth to this. We realized that the metaphors of juggling or balancing work and family obscured how much time people actually used to control daily life. As researchers, we were excited because we had found something that allowed us to see things in a different way, and it soon helped us to understand facets of the families' lives that had been unclear.

But not everything was hard to see. While busyness is about tacit work, it is also about the things people use. Material objects reflect the lives of people who have much to do. People also shape things as they attempt to cope with the world in easier and more effective ways. People take on many devices and ways of configuring spaces in the hope that these will lead to efficiency and productivity. This outlook is based on an instrumental view in which people value objects not for what they are but for what they might allow us to do. The study of busyness is inescapably about the material world.

People used material things to make their lives more efficient, but in doing so, they sometimes introduced new surprises into daily regimens. Regardless of the outcome, these activities required effort. People had to choose features of products, compare prices, and then learn things associated with each device. To configure devices into systems required more work. This does not mean that such material infrastructures cost more to develop, maintain, and use than their resulting benefits, only that we must not forget that these benefits came with prices. At times, the people we observed seemed only to convert one form of busyness into another, and sometimes they abandoned "costly" elements of their infrastructures.

Thus families developed material infrastructures that buffered the effects of busyness and facilitated coping. Whether or not people led more efficient lives, their buffering had two characteristics. First, it was not without costs and often required activities that families or individuals did not consider to be work. Second, it was fundamentally social, in that people involved in these activities agreed to act in certain ways.

Beyond the instrumentalism, objects also organize our experiences by allowing us to "reestablish a purposeful order"[5] Artifacts help stabilize and objectify our identities in several ways. They do so by demonstrating power and position in social hierarchies. Possessing devices is a mark of wealth, and the capacity to summon or compel others to help us is an act of power. Electronic devices that facilitate coping may seem egalitarian in the way they bind people together, but one person's efficiency-enhancing system can be another's burden and a reminder of one's own inability to summon assistance.

Second, they reveal our continuity through time by providing "mementos of the past, and signposts to future goals."[6] They remind us, and others who know us, of that continuity, as well as of who we are.

Finally, artifacts provide evidence of our places in wider networks of valued relationships. They are reminders that we are not alone and are related to people in the past and present, as well as suggesting directions for the future. Objects "magnify our power, enhance our beauty, and extend our memory into the future."[7] In this way, the pure instrumentalism of busyness takes us into a symbolic realm for which we may be unprepared. As symbols, objects do not simply provide a passive backdrop to our lives; rather, they become props in stories we tell about ourselves and others. Ruth Finnegan argues that we learn to compose narratives about cities and other places of our lives. Such stories provide temporal framing of those lives, the way good stories do, linking past, present, and future. They provide a plot that is intelligible to us because it helps us assimilate our experiences. They also provide images and themes that allow us to generalize about our stories and ask if they are the same or different from those of other people.[8]

Building a material infrastructure to buffer busyness is thus deceptive. There may be an instrumental practicality about its elements that leads us to believe they are merely utilitarian. Ironically, this very matter-of-factness may obscure the larger symbolism of objects and places in busy lives.

CHAPTER EIGHT

Connecting People

When we began our journey, we had a dozen destinations: we would participate in the busy lives of twelve families. Later, we added two more families, but the sample of fourteen dual-career families may still seem small. Yet this does not tell the whole story. We did not simply study *in* these families; rather, we studied *through* them. Each family could be viewed as a universe unto itself, but it simultaneously provided an entrance into the lives of countless other people. Each family was enmeshed in ties with extended family members, friends, neighbors, and co-workers. Other people who were usually marginal to a family could suddenly be swept into its latest crisis of busyness, only subsequently to fade into the background of its everyday life. In this way, we learned that we were not studying families separately and alone, but the fourteen families were *focal* families around which radiated other people. Those people, too, spoke to us and allowed us into their lives, and so their busyness was also revealed. Not surprisingly, the busy lives of these families were often interconnected, as when the activities of one could only occur with the assistance of another. Coping with busyness was not just a matter of individual responsibility and family efficiency. Connections to other people often formed the critical buffers that allowed people to cope, and some individuals and families were more effective at this than others.

Popular imagery of work and family balance often portrays organizations, such as companies, as drivers of busyness and family as a refuge. But we saw families using organizations as providers of resources that they could mobilize for their own coping. Employers were often the sources of goods, people, and ideas that could be transformed into buffers. Individuals, for example, could be valuable assets precisely because of their capacity to provide access to an organization's resources. It follows that individuals and organizations differed in their usefulness as buffers.

Growing Networks

RAJIV MOHAN: LIVING IN A WORLD OF NETWORKS

Elsewhere in this book are examples of families that played with their own boundaries, recasting distant kin into new roles and turning friends and paid employees into fictive kin. But there is another facet to this process of reaching out, bringing friends and trusted acquaintances into a halo of reliable people. People are recruited, nurtured, and pruned as they serve the needs of the family and as the members of the family in return reach out to them. Rajiv Mohan self-consciously reached out to relationships new and old to help him and his family. His wide-ranging and numerous networks both protected him from some of the effects of busyness and required his constant attention and efforts.

Rajiv could not believe his bad luck: laid off yesterday from a job he loved at a high-tech computer company and standing beside the freeway today staring at his stalled Mercedes. Soon a tow truck arrived to take the car to his mechanic, but the prognosis was not good: it needed a $7,000 new engine and so was not worth repairing. Rajiv needed a car and was a loyal Mercedes driver, but he was reluctant to spend the money following his layoff: "You have money, you know, but psychologically it's hard." So he called a friend in one of his networks and told him he needed to get a used car soon, preferably a Mercedes. The friend, who lived in southern California, told him to get on the plane to Los Angeles. When Rajiv arrived, his friend opened his garage doors; inside were five Mercedes. When offered the blue one, Rajiv replied, "This is a $60,000 car and I've just been laid off. I can't afford it." But his friend sold it to him for $9,000 because of all the favors and advice Rajiv had provided him with. In assembling a technological infrastructure with global reach, he had also created heterogeneous social networks that he could draw on for advice and information, money, and automobiles.

Rajiv spoke of his networks as discrete and separate, each for different uses. They represented both a snapshot in time of his connections and a personal history of his relationships and jobs. Learn about his networks and you learned about his interests, friendships, and activities over the past thirty years.

Rajiv described two networks formed when he worked at the high-tech computer company that later laid him off. The first developed out of the New Computing Group. He left the group and company with a good reputation, and people there continued to call him for advice. The second resulted from the many connections he had through the company, although relationships with Indians predominated. Rajiv ran a large corporate project in India that created a flow of workers to the United States; while many of them left the corporation, they consulted him later about possible career moves. Despite the layoff, he remained loyal to the company: he used its products and platform, toted a leather briefcase emblazoned with the corporate logo, and retained his collection of promotional T-shirts.

Rajiv's Indian network also included connections with classmates from several Indian universities, as well as with family members in India and Los Angeles. Rajiv came to the United States over thirty years ago, long before South Asians had come in great numbers to Silicon Valley. He had lived among non-Asians, and unlike more recent South Asian arrivals, he was not part of an Indian community. As a result, Rajiv was not well connected to them. Still, he talked to many Indians who sought his advice about their business prospects.

Another network connected him to venture capitalists. A year before his layoff, Rajiv told his manager that he wanted to learn more about venture capital. He then got opportunities to sit in on meetings evaluating proposals from start-ups, and this enabled him to learn how businesses are developed.

In effect, he provided technical expertise in exchange for the opportunities to learn more about the business end of entrepreneurship. These connections and the reputation he had built allowed him to put together a new business after his layoff. Working with this network required a tolerance for ambiguity and uncertainty; it was not simply a matter of summoning up cash through phone calls. "A lot is being willing to go into situations that don't have a specific objective," he said, "and you suddenly find out *something*." For example, he met one business partner at an international business workshop. Through it, he made friends with a Hong Kong–based entrepreneur, and while the three days of workshops proved less than helpful, the two men started a new company.

Rajiv developed other networks with individuals at major research universities. Some of these connections dated back to his school days and others from his high-tech employment, since he frequently attended conferences and meetings. He would give people advice about their commercial developments. In return, they provided him with information about emerging technologies.

Rajiv also was part of networks that reflected some of his past activities and interests. While he seldom used them, he considered himself part of them. One such group consisted of the people he had met through his education in systems theory. Many of these were significant intellectual mentors. Rajiv pointed out that Indians typically formed deep relationships of respect with their former teachers. To remain in touch with them, he would call them each year. Rajiv also felt a special loyalty to Mercedes, in part because the company had provided him, along with other Mercedes owners, with a free credit card and worldwide concierge service. But Rajiv's ties to the company were deeper, extending back to his graduate studies in public health. He had tried to form an Indian company that would provide mobile health clinics and became linked with Mercedes vans. The company failed to develop, but he made connections with a "community of people dealing with the high-end ambulances." He continued to draw upon that community when necessary. He developed another network during the 1970s and 1980s while he was at university and working on projects to improve Native American health care. As a consultant with both the Indian Health Service and U.S. Public Health Department, he had visited reservations many times to develop health care information systems, and he kept his contacts with people in the

Native American communities, although he seldom used them. Rajiv also developed a loosely connected network of friends in Australia, Hong Kong, the United Kingdom, France, and Singapore, as well as a local network assembled through his many business interests.

Rajiv's networks were important to him personally and professionally, for they enabled him to reach anyone necessary to the success of his many endeavors. The key was, not to have a single gigantic network, but rather to be able to reach people through those already incorporated into it. He could not predict which of those relationships would be valuable in the future, so he tried to nurture them all. But he had so many networks that he neglected some. A person in one such network was an expert on Picasso. Rajiv did not use this relationship, since he and his wife lived modestly and did not collect the works of great artists. But he joked that if ever he had a question about Picasso, he would know where to go. Whatever he needed to know, he could find out through his networks.

Rajiv's networks protected him from some of the effects of busyness. He was able to ask informed people for their expert advice and trust that they would not knowingly mislead him. Indeed, they often watched out for his welfare. They helped him scan the environment and process information about its threats and opportunities. He returned the favor and thus was part of a global network based on efficiency, productivity, caring, and genuine concern. They often spoke of themselves as members of a family. When a potential investor approached Rajiv in another country, a trusted member of his network cautioned, "We don't want *that* kind of money in our families." In a world of flux, where capital, people and ideas flowed freely, and where many institutions and organizations were transient, Rajiv's networks provided constancy, stability, and people he could trust. Still, he distinguished the people in these broad global networks from the handful of people who were essential to his everyday life: his wife, two coworkers, and two business associates.

Rajiv formed his networks in a deliberate, particular way. He described what he did as "nurturing—I don't burn bridges." To develop this, he would meet the needs of others, even if he did not benefit much in the short run. He responded to requests that might only have a payoff several years later. He did not try to calculate such payoffs, because he considered such thinking futile. He assisted because it was the prudent thing to do, not to seek immediate gain. One time, someone who was forming a new company called him to check on a reference of a prospective employee. While chatting on the phone, they discovered that they were from the same state in India. They met for lunch, and Rajiv provided informal advice regarding the start-up. Later, Rajiv was allowed to invest some money in the company's early round of funding. Usually, in this phase, only major institutional and affluent private investors are invited to invest. The man, he said, "got good value from me. This was his way of saying thanks." Such generosity also ensured that Rajiv would provide future consultation.

In truth, Rajiv spent much more time nurturing his networks in conversations that did not pay off, but, as he explained, that was the nature of networks. This raised another issue: Rajiv responded to the requests of others, but he also had to be able to limit the access of others to him. He had to balance control of his time with being a good citizen of his networks. He accomplished this through his technological infrastructure.

Because he could not predict future business needs, he tried to avoid making unnecessary enemies. He exclaimed that he did not understand leaders who went back on their word or took advantage of other people. He viewed himself as forceful and direct. Even when he had to deliver bad news or present analyses that others might not like, he believed that working relationships could endure and should not be damaged. When Rajiv's nephew asked him about trying to retain workers who expressed interests in leaving for greener pastures, Rajiv replied that he would make a reasonable counter offer, but if it looked very good for the person, then he would let them go and even try to support their decision to leave. It was likely that the person would go to work for a company that had connections with his, and having those connections would help his company. Rajiv continued to praise the company that had laid him off long ago. People who moved out of his company might return one day at a higher level, particularly in fast-changing companies. So he never tried to stop people from leaving and never disparaged them once they were gone.

Rajiv worked to develop his networks in large and small ways. People invited him to many conferences, seminars, and workshops; he joked that the most important thing he received from them was business cards and address lists, preferably with e-mail addresses. He filed away such information for future reference. He constantly assessed the skills and knowledge of individuals with an eye to their suitability for particular positions. While attending a university conference showcasing new technologies, he showed less interest in the eye-popping devices on display than in the advanced graduate students who had developed them. Such constant assessment allowed him to recruit talented individuals for positions in the companies in which he had an interest. Often, he made the connection between person and position months or even years later.

Rajiv's activities revealed both his heavy reliance on networks and his values and assumptions about the world. To achieve his goals, he was willing to use others and be used by them. But neither he nor the members of his network were simply manipulative or acting from selfish motives. They watched out for each other, and some of them became genuinely trusted friends. Acting within networks brought its own rewards. The networks revealed a glimpse of who Rajiv was, not merely what he wanted to accomplish. His goals were not purely financial, since they also supported new ideas. And for Rajiv, participating in the networks was enjoyable in and of itself.

Rajiv's networking also demanded of him a tolerance for ambiguity. He might set out to attend a recreational event or arrange for a visa, say, only to realize that doing so opened up other opportunities. Something work-related might become a family matter. Rajiv recognized this ambiguity, and that not everyone was comfortable with it; altering the use of an activity might offend some of the participants.

Rajiv's use of networks led him in two contradictory directions. The first was rational calculation and efficiency, which determined where he would spend or invest time for optimal future gains. He used a tacit, and sometimes overt, cost-benefit analysis to decide whether or not to grant or restrict access, since not all network contacts were equally useful for a particular purpose. The cost of inaccessibility to key people could be catastrophic, just as the benefits to access could be enormous. The difficulty was to know which relationships under a variety of conditions could be delayed without cost, which held a low probability of bringing great rewards, and which outcomes were likely to bring great benefit.

The second direction was responding opportunistically to new circumstances, engaging in activities without knowing where they might lead or what benefits might be gained. This required openness and exploration, infinite possibility, and taking risks, in conditions where it might not be possible to trace the results or realize the consequences for years. Rajiv's Native American network was currently latent, a result of educational experiences long ago. Yet the development of this network prompted his interest in cultural anthropology, which affected how he assessed the design and development of products: they were not merely devices to which people had to adapt, but rather perturbations to ongoing social systems. He was no longer passionately interested in Native American health issues, but his interests in design and culture remained.

Among the families in our study, Rajiv's networks were striking, both in their extent and diversity, and in his reliance upon them. They consisted of a variety of individuals, each unique and distinct in their relationship with him. Some were close, virtual extensions of his family, while others were distant, drawn upon rarely if at all. He also wove organizations into his networks: corporations, universities, and professional associations. Indeed, Rajiv used his connections with individuals to connect with organizations and their resources, and likewise, he used organizational connections to find the individuals who would become part of his networks. Although it may have appeared effortless, a mere by-product of his charismatic sociability, for Rajiv, networking was a complex set of activities. To develop, maintain, and grow his networks required largely tacit work that was one adaptation to busyness.

Rajiv Mohan said that the need to be constantly accessible and "in touch" suggested a misplaced arrogance. While dining at a professional conference, he chatted with a middle-aged man who was constantly taking calls on his cellular phone. The man shook his head, affecting the look of a harried, important person. Rajiv commiserated, and the man commented that he had to be in constant contact with his office or things fell apart. Rajiv playfully asked how he had managed before cell phones, and the man responded that back then, his subordinates had called his wife and left messages at his home. He would call home several times a day and retrieve the messages from his human answering machine. When the man excused himself for another call, Rajiv shook his head and said he was familiar with a number of heart surgeons; being in touch was a life-and-death matter for them. But for everyone else it was hubris to think they were so important that things could not run for a few days without them.

Rajiv practiced what he preached. In his work, he assessed and managed risk, communicating and traveling across national boundaries, and making decisions in the face of uncertain information and limited time. Despite this, he was calm and unhurried. He accomplished this by surrounding himself with a few trusted, responsible people, whom he had supervised for a decade when they worked elsewhere. *They* managed things so that he did not constantly have to intervene. In return, he respected their judgments and private lives. They demanded and provided stability and predictability, thereby allowing Rajiv his calm. He was very different from both of them, because he loved to go with the flow on short notice and did not mind changing plans "on a dime," but he was the first to admit that they allowed him his flexibility.

Rajiv's example also reminds us that flexibility is not merely an adaptation to unwanted events. The lesson is of broader applicability than to their individual lives. Flexibility need not just mean a reluctant, if civil response to the small disasters of daily life, much less to the big ones that can truly change a life. It is also closely associated with an opportunism in which surprises can bring benefits that otherwise would never materialize. Flexibility connotes openness to the vicissitudes of the everyday and the banal. Unexpected events may provide the doors through which opportunities, innovation, and enjoyment enter life.

Rajiv was a person whose work and temperament predisposed him to be on the lookout for opportunities. He held an Indian passport and used a visa service to facilitate his business travel. On this particular day, Rajiv sat in Angelo's small office explaining his upcoming trip to Hong Kong, Los Angeles, London, and Paris. He needed visas for the European leg of the trip but also needed his passport in Hong Kong, making it impossible to leave it with Angelo to obtain the requisite visas. Angelo carefully reviewed the itinerary, looking for places where he could get the visas while still allowing Rajiv to keep the passport when he needed it.

Angelo explained that he could get the visas because he was part of a nationwide network of independently owned offices. Each of 200 countries had its own visa forms, but the information they requested was widely distributed and it took time to bring it together for a visa application. He mentioned to Rajiv that they were working on a software portal that would automate the process by linking the visa forms with a client database, saying, "The software would revolutionize this business." Rajiv smiled and asked Angelo about the people who were preparing and investing in the business

plan. It was premature, replied Angelo. Rajiv then asked who was developing the software; again Angelo replied that they were not that far along.
"Do you know what I do?" asked Rajiv. He then explained that his company
"incubates start-ups" by developing the technology for "equity and a fee,
always both." Angelo perked up and said that a friend at a local bank was
developing the business plan "on the side." Rajiv's company used that bank,
so they agreed that Angelo's friend would call Rajiv's corporate controller to
explore how they might work together.

Later, Rajiv laughed and said he never knew when opportunities might
arise, but he was always ready. In this case, he might have discovered a new
company client that would develop the very service that would ease his
travel burden.

THE FLAHERTYS: THE SOCIABLE FAMILY

To build flexibility into his day, Jerry Flaherty deliberately blurred the compartments of his life, so that his relationships did not fall into any one domain. This allowed him to shift effortlessly between spheres of life by in-
termingling co-workers from his entire job history with friends, neighbors,
and fellow parents. Because these people were not trapped in any particular
compartment, they could help him address a wide range of issues in his life.
In his view, they amplified his capacity to "bend" and contributed to the
creativity of his responses.

For example, Jerry explicitly constructed the guest list for his fiftieth
birthday party so that it included people from these different compartments,
or as Jerry called them, "pages" in his life. The list contained current co-
workers and people met through work, as well as co-workers from previous
positions. Family members attended, as did neighbors, fellow parishioners,
and parents of his children's classmates. The criteria Jerry used, since he
could not invite everyone from all his life's pages, was that he had had a meal
with the person in the past year and that they knew some other guests.

In fact, Jerry was uncomfortable if he kept the pages separate. Previously,
he had done so, to such an extent that many close friends and family members did not know his future wife when they were dating. "Now they're one
page. The advantage is that you now shift emphasis on one page if problems

occur in one area." He valued this capacity to shift focus while paying attention to all parts of his life. Once, for a short time when Jerry was a community developer, a young boxer lived with him. The young man had a son while he was a teenager, and Jerry learned from him the difficulty of keeping pages separate. "He managed his life on separate pages. When something bad happened he put all his attention on that page and didn't pay attention to the others." The result was that just when things started improving, he would be surprised by something gone wrong. Merging the separate pages, said Jerry, amplified the benefits throughout his life. Jerry recognized that not everyone would want to or could organize thinking the way he did.

Typically, the people we studied pursued flexibility by both merging and isolating life's compartments, depending on the circumstances. Jerry, for example, blurred those compartments only under some conditions. While in the office, he kept family and work strictly separate. He focused on professional communications and tried to avoid personal telephone calls, with the exception of emergency calls from his wife, children, and two subordinates. His wife helped him maintain these distinct compartments precisely because she refused to make a strict separation between work and family. She always had *her* cellular phone on and with her, just in case her son or daughter needed to speak with her. She also made and received the myriad telephone calls with schools, friends, and family members that were a regular part of this busy family's life.

As organizational leaders, Jerry and Eleanor were able to utilize resources to build a seamless web between their home and workplaces. They drew on a technological infrastructure to handle much of their busyness and maintain their vast professional and personal networks. They kept several computers at home so that they could work there, and both of them carried Palm Pilots and cellular phones; Jerry also carried a pager. Their jobs also supported their technological infrastructure. When Jerry decided to get a personal digital assistant, he directed his department's technical assistant to investigate them. When a home computer failed and Jerry or Michael could not get it running, they called on the same technician. Jerry also used his organizational resources to fend off crises. When Jerry, in a rush, forgot his briefcase, he called and instructed his staff to begin the meeting without him. He commented that because his staff were excellent, they would hardly notice his absence.

Clearly, Jerry and Eleanor Flaherty depended on extensive relationships of friends and acquaintances to make their everyday life work. The Flahertys used these people for specific, practical purposes, but they also felt affection for them. They referred to themselves as a sociable family, they clearly enjoyed the company of others, and they put a great deal of effort into maintaining their networks and developing the trust that enabled them to work.

They understood that, in spite of their efforts over the years to arrange and rearrange their individual work schedules to move children around and make sure they were safe, they could not do this alone. Jerry explained, "I think probably for us, the success side of it is being able to have options and to have several different potential answers to where the kids are going to go." How they would get there was equally important. The Flahertys paid some people to help them. While Eleanor had no local family members, Jerry's large family lived in the region. "Having my own family—my brothers and sisters, the aunts and uncles—provides another set of alternatives," he said.

Eleanor discounted the importance of this extended family, since they lived far enough away to make it difficult for them to help and had their own obligations to deal with before helping Jerry and Eleanor. This led Jerry and Eleanor to rely heavily on neighbors and the parents of their children's friends. They drew on this core group of families when needed, which constituted the center of the family's social life. Yet they could not take it for granted that these people would assist them. Jerry and Eleanor needed to make an effort to keep them willing to help. Jerry reflected, "It's kind of like there's a larger support network that provides other alternatives, and you've got to feed that network if you're going to go take from that network." When Jerry or Eleanor stayed home, they welcomed their children's friends in the house and often hosted weekend sleepovers. They invited their children's friends along when they took recreational trips to their mountain cabin. They helped other parents without calculating how this would benefit them in the future. One day, Eleanor had to pick up their son Michael and help him get ready for a ski trip. "I had to get Michael and Chris at three o'clock, which happened to be when [their daughter] Mary and Paula were coming out of school, and I said to Samantha [the mother of Chris and Paula], 'I'm available. I'll take them if you want.' And it happened to be a day that she really needed that."

The Flahertys did not find this extra work onerous, and they did not complain about it. This sociable couple enjoyed the company of others. More than a decade before, Jerry had organized a Labor Day camping trip in which over sixty friends, family members, and co-workers journeyed to the mountains and took over a campground. Over the years, the event grew, as some families dropped out and others joined. The adults prepared food communally and acted as a single "parent" for the packs of children who roamed the campground and forest. Jerry also organized the annual purchase of Christmas trees displayed in the front yards of his street. Jerry and Eleanor hosted many large and small dinners and parties; their house became a well-known local gathering spot. They described themselves as gregarious and clearly enjoy the social life they have created. Yet they acknowledged that it also connected them with people who were then willing to help out by watching or driving a child somewhere.

Jerry and Eleanor had jobs that drew on their sociability. "Both Eleanor and I have been pretty extrovertish in our professional lives. We have jobs that cause us to go out, so we get introduced to other things that are possible solutions." They were each "willing to make [phone] calls and were not shy about saying, 'I want to meet you.'" Their work allowed them to be actively involved in the community, which further nurtured their networks. "I have had the good opportunity of having a lot of relationships with a lot of people that I still feel close too. Same with Eleanor. I think both of us have done a lot of community work and have done a lot of things for other families that is reciprocated."

On occasion, their networking "work" was clearly identifiable, as when Eleanor joked, "I'm getting off easy this summer." Originally, Eleanor had brought people together in a carpool for their children. The other parents had more flexible schedules and were willing to do most of the driving. They let Eleanor "off easy," she said, "because I organized this."

There was also a hidden aspect to the networking work of the Flahertys: calculating the exchanges involved in these activities, even if sometimes they were not fully aware that they were doing this. One day, Jerry rushed to a meeting that had an agenda relevant to the work of his organization. But there was more: a long-term colleague of his had organized this. She sat on the advisory board of Jerry's organization. Over the years, the two of them had collaborated on numerous projects. Jerry had to "pay her back by attending her things," he joked. This was simply what you did for friends.

Here Jerry tacitly acknowledged the importance of what anthropologists call balanced reciprocity: he attended her events because she attended his.

Such internal work, thinking about reciprocal exchanges, was the foundation of the Flahertys' network. Eleanor described it as a "balancing act," one that had to be carefully managed. One day, their daughter Mary remained at her friend Paula's after camp. Both girls were in the car pool, and they had been close friends since they first began school. Since Eleanor and Samantha, Paula's mother, also were close friends, Eleanor was comfortable asking Samantha to watch Mary for several hours. The women often helped each other out, and Paula participated in many Flaherty family activities. Eleanor had comparable relationships with other mothers. She did not calculate repayment of the favors, because the families had known each other a long time. "It would just work out."

A different situation arose when the families did not have a history of friendship. Eleanor met Kay through work, but did not know her well; nor did their daughters know each other. In negotiating the car pool, they paid more attention to the balanced reciprocity of a ride for a ride, but Eleanor noted that "Kay was really great" because she offered to take the kids to camp every day. She could do this because she and her husband worked from home. Eleanor appreciated such generosity, although she did not expect it. Eleanor had been in few car pools over the years, because her schedule prevented her from committing to a regimen of balanced reciprocity. Because she did not want to let others down, she assumed the burdens herself. This required her to negotiate some work hours and on occasion ask Jerry for help. Since he was in a similar position, he assisted when he could.

Jerry and Eleanor thus fluctuated between using their network and simply assuming the burden of arranging their family tasks. The network was *there*, but they were careful not to abuse it. When one neighborhood family agreed that Mary could spend time after school with their daughter at home, Eleanor was grateful: "I brought them a plant at Christmas, but with all of those situations you really need to bend over backwards not to abuse them." They did this by doing small favors that acknowledged the services rendered. She commented, "I think it's probably easier than it might be for others, because we naturally sort of do things for people. We'll invite them over or take them things." When they dropped Mary off at her grandmother's house near school to wait until classes began, Jerry and Eleanor reciprocated by inviting her to dinner or doing small repairs on her house, "so there's enough give and take."

For many families, busyness is best managed with a little help from friends, acquaintances, and co-workers, who provide direct, immediate help that makes the days easier and also form a potential buffer against surprises. Whenever people meet, they may use this encounter to add to their network, and many people are always "on," searching for useful connections and people. Some people develop these relationships for utilitarian purposes, for their usefulness in accomplishing other goals, not because they are intrinsically satisfying. In turn, people may allow others to use them. Such reciprocal ties may be the foundation of real community. The limitation of such communities is that they are built on immediate practical considerations and not on enduring commitments.

Organizational Resources

THE MENDOZA / JONESES: USING WORK ORGANIZATIONS
TO ABSORB FAMILY BUSYNESS

Humberto Mendoza and Suzanne Jones respectively worked for public and private sector employers, and both of them used their work organizations to absorb some of the effects of busyness. Their organizational resources were so deeply integrated in their lives that it was difficult to tell the boundaries between work and family. A striking example was the way they wove technological devices into the fabric of their daily life.

Since their own personal computer lacked a modem to connect to the Internet, they used Suzanne's corporate laptop computer to connect to the Internet. "She has those resources," said Humberto. "I mean that's another benefit from her working at a private company: they provide her those things." Her company also provided her with the technical support to keep equipment operating, whether for company or personal use. For example, when she wanted to use her laptop over the weekend, but it wasn't working, Suzanne called Fred, a company technical support specialist in whom she had great faith. He came to her house to fix the laptop. She explained that he would do "what is necessary to get the job done." In return, she took him to lunch.

Humberto's public sector employer did not provide the array of equipment of Suzanne's high-tech employer. He received a pager, which he used for the family's technological infrastructure. He disliked it and cellular phones because they led to constant interruptions, but he carried the pager while on the job so that Suzanne could reach him in an emergency. Significantly, fire department personnel did not page him. If the department requested that he return the pager, he would not buy another one but would use Suzanne's company pager.

Humberto and Suzanne also used their employers as sources of information to locate goods and services that they used at home. Suzanne planned the party for her younger daughter's baptism for several weeks and made several inquiries from her cubicle. One day she called the number of a corporate caterer, provided by a nearby administrative assistant, and asked if he did catering on weekends, explaining that she had a baptism coming up on Sunday. "We tasted your brie and fruit plate and would like to serve that," she explained. She got his e-mail address and said good-bye. She also sent an e-mail to the corporate cafeteria downstairs asking if they would cater the baptism.

Humberto, too, used his job as a source of personal services. Humberto purchased his family's used car from a man whom he had met while doing a fire inspection of the man's diner. When the man encountered unrelated legal difficulties, Humberto interceded on his behalf. "I told him he owed me for that. He owed me big time." The man moved from the city, opened a used car lot, and reciprocated by finding Humberto and Suzanne the right car. Similarly, Humberto had met his mechanic of many years while performing fire inspections. "He maintains my cars, and as a result of maintaining my cars, we have a very good relationship. He offers door to curb service: I can drop the car over there and he'll drop the car back and I pay him. If we've had mechanical problems, I've been able to call him and tell him, 'Get the car towed down there.'" Humberto had likewise found his landscaper, tile setter, and house painter through the fire department, and even tried to furnish his home office with furniture he saw being installed at fire department headquarters.

Suzanne also drew on organizational resources to achieve family goals. Despite her excellent salary and job share, she was dissatisfied with her job and employer, but she decided not to leave for another few years. She joked, "I want to stay for another kid. They pay full maternity, so I want to stay and use that. I've paid lots of disability for years." Only after a third child would she move on hoping to find a more engaging position. Meanwhile, her employer provided other services that supported her family. The company maintained a listserv of its employees, who exchanged information about family issues. She found the girls' pediatrician off the list and shared information about children's services and products. The participants were restrained; they stayed away from "hot button" issues. For this reason, Suzanne did not mention that her children had not been fully vaccinated. "There's such a stigma about it in society right now," she commented. "My child is biting other kids" was about as "far out" as the discussions went because, "people know issues can unleash a firestorm." They knew one another and realized that if they provoked anger, it could affect their personal reputations on the job. Suzanne seldom responded, except when she felt very strongly about an issue, such as home birthing, midwifery, or breast-feeding. Furthermore, her employer's human resources department monitored the discussions. When a lively debate began about the company's maternity leave policy and its interpretation of federal law, people suggested ways around the policy. A representative from human resources then began "dropping in," presenting the company's legal interpretation. Some concurred, others disagreed on legal grounds, and still others argued that regardless of legalities, there were moral issues of right and wrong.

Suzanne used organizational resources in her efforts at self-improvement. Two decorative candles sat in her cubicle, gifts from a mentor. "We go to lunch every four or five weeks to talk about how to manage our lives according to the *Seven Habits of Highly Effective People*," she said, referring to the popular self-help book by Steven Covey. Suzanne had taken a workshop based on the book at a previous employer, but the trainer had been incompetent. Suzanne's mentor had just returned from a similar workshop offered by their company. The woman sent an e-mail message out asking if anyone else had taken the course: she wanted to meet them and discuss the issues raised in the workshop. Since the Covey program recommended finding a "learning partner" to help incorporate the ideas into daily life, Suzanne responded to the message. The two women had lunch and continue to discuss the book and their lives.

The use of organizations for personal gain can also extend beyond the boundaries of a specific employer and into larger realms of professionalism.

Humberto explained that, by virtue of his professional training and service as a firefighter, he had resources that could be mobilized in the case of a family crisis. He did so when Suzanne's sister was killed in a bus accident in a midwestern city. Humberto immediately called a national professional association in which he was active and asked them to alert the local branch that he would be requesting cooperation from the local police and fire departments. Several people had died in the accident, and the wrecked bus was stored on an unsecured lot where anyone could tamper with it. By the next day, he said, "everything was cleaned and sanitized," and so, in accordance with his training, Humberto approached the site of the accident as a crime scene. By mobilizing his resources to ensure local cooperation, he was able to obtain videotapes of the accident scene that helped the family win a substantial settlement from the bus company. He insisted that what he did could have been done by anyone, but he was able to do it faster, and in this case, time was of the essence. "I learned a lot back there. You learn how the system works." He also drew upon the advice of his cousin, a policeman with lengthy experience, who taught him to "never assume anything at an accident scene."

THE CARLSBERGS: WORK AND SCHOOL

Much of the busyness of the Carlsbergs is hidden, and its implications for their lives are not obvious. It is easy to visualize this family of four standing before us, posed for a family portrait. But imagine each of them instead as a portal opening onto the organizations that stand behind them and you get a truer look into their busyness.

Alex's employer was one organization that exerted a powerful influence on his life. He was a highly ranked employee, but that would not protect him from a corporate move, something the company was pondering. Within the organization, he had to be attuned to the peculiarities of different departments and the contracts he sometimes audited, as well as the company's decisions about the software programs he would use. Through the company, he was connected to its training courses and credit union; *because* of the company's indecision, he was connected to an association of retired business people, who were advising him on developing a plan for his business, an escape from corporate America. The latter was an entrance to an alien world of financial and legal institutions and manufacturers and distributors that he knew primarily through the Internet.

Pat, too, connected to a workplace, and while it was important in her life, it was very different from Alex's. Because of her supervisory duties, she needed to be knowledgeable about personnel policy and terms of employment. The nature of her work, typically conducting research in education and for government agencies, linked her days to the minutiae of grants and contracts and the regimens of attorneys and government compliance officers. Years of experience had honed her skills in navigating bureaucracies at a remove and obtaining the cooperation of people who had minimal incentive to provide it.

Their sons, Robert and James, and Alex and Pat's parents were the bookends to their lives. The boys linked Pat and Alex to their school, which was both fundamental to their dream of betterment and progress and uniquely vexed, disturbed, and angered them. Because it was a religious school, Pat's prodigious professional knowledge of public schools was of scant help, for the rules of the latter had little relevance here. The fact that the school was embedded in the affairs of their church only exacerbated the sense that things could and should be better, and the deep frustration that they were not. The boys also connected Alex to a web of organizations offering the products and services of contemporary suburban childhood, such as Cub and Boy Scout troops and arcades for children's parties.

Alex and Pat also encountered organizations through Alex and Pat's parents and Pat's mother. The latter spoke English fluently, but Italian remained her language of choice in sensitive medical matters, and Pat translated for her. The couple helped Alex's parents, too, because they dealt with bureaucracies. During fieldwork, they helped them maintain insurance on their rental property and to deal with a lawsuit that resulted from an accident caused by Alex's father. On account of his father, Alex plunged into a world of hospitals and medical care when he arranged for surgery for his father's Parkinson's disease. Because his HMO performed such surgery only at selected sites, Alex repeatedly endured a 200-mile round trip and helped his parents make the decisions that would affect the quality of their lives. Their involvement in a municipal senior citizen center drew Alex and Pat in as technical assistants and producers of media for the center's various celebrations. Pat and Alex also assisted an elderly couple who had befriended Alex's parents.

When the husband died, they suddenly found themselves settling an estate and dealing with lawyers, accountants, insurance agents, and bankers.

Collectively, the family dealt with dozens of organizations that, in different ways, affected their lives. Health care providers, schools, government offices, and retailers were the backdrop to daily life, and at any moment, one could assume sudden prominence and come to intrude for days or weeks. Purchasing items led inevitably to mistakes and disagreements, and settling these could require repeated calls that challenged their ability to figure out the locus of responsibility. These seemingly small errors—an erroneous listing on the jury roll, a discrepancy of pennies between two accounts—concerned the Carlsbergs. They feared the errors might indicate even more troublesome problems that could not be ignored.

Each organization was in effect a separate universe that operated slightly differently from others, with implications for how it was navigated. Each had its own rhythms and purposes. It could be reached or contacted only through particular channels. It would recognize and even answer some questions, but not others. Sometimes, it seemed to serve a Carlsberg, and at other times, they seem destined to serve it.

The Carlsbergs' busyness is impossible to imagine apart from the organizations that they encountered. Being able to work effectively on them, through them, and with organizations is part of the hidden work of managing busyness; not everyone does it equally well.

In his capacity as a systems analyst who reconciled pennies on multimillion-dollar government contracts, Alex was well prepared to deal with many organizations that affected his family. Pat was particularly adept at figuring out standard operating procedures and individual motivations, and she exhibited a patience honed by years of dealing with distant partners. Yet neither could really figure out what it took to work smoothly with the school their sons attended.

As with all families, the Carlbergs lived connected to large and small organizations that performed a variety of functions. The Carlsbergs had to interact with these organizations, and these activities affected their busyness. The skills and knowledge needed to work effectively with them were unarticulated, and so they were part of the tacit work of managing busyness. People in our study had to deal with organizations that were as much a part of their life as family or community.

THE LE FAMILY: A "TRADITIONAL" VIETNAMESE PRESCHOOL
BECOMES A TRAINING GROUND FOR BUSYNESS

One day, without warning, the Le family's day-care facility closed. Dan took off several days from work, taking care of the boys, until he found an alternative: an elderly Vietnamese woman who ran day care out of her mobile home. There the children heard and spoke Vietnamese, ate Vietnamese food, and learned the proper behavior for Vietnamese children: dependence on adults and compliance and submissiveness to elders, in return for which they received affection and approval.

The Le family drew on religious and community organizations as it tried to adjust to the closure of Ben's preschool. Dan and Fern Le, concerned that their oldest son was not receiving enough instruction in Vietnamese traditional values and practices, sent Ben to what they considered a traditional Vietnamese Catholic preschool. People often think of tradition as opposed to modernity, but the schooling of Ben Le shows how these may become totally entangled. The irony goes far beyond the fact that there was nothing traditional about preschool for the Vietnamese. The nuns themselves, symbols of tradition, had internalized a lifestyle of busyness. Along with teaching the children to respect their elders and to respond to questions in both English and Vietnamese, they led these three- and four-year-olds to perform activities that were segmented in briefly timed intervals. The kids learned not only how to become good Vietnamese but also how to accommodate to busyness at the same time.

Both Dan and Fern expressed concern that the nuns would have a hard time disciplining their rambunctious son. They need not have worried. The nuns at the preschool followed a routine for discipline that quickly brought both the children and their parents in line. This began with a no-nonsense obligatory orientation for parents. Two nuns handed out a detailed printed list of regulations for children and parents and informed the parents that the nuns would tolerate no deviation. To emphasize their point, they read the regulations out loud:

1. Parents must drop off their children between 8:00 AM and 9:00 AM, when the gates are shut and locked; a late child is not admitted, and the nuns are too busy to look after a child who comes too early.

2. Parents must sign their child in and out by name and room number. For an additional fee, the children may remain at the school until 6:00 PM. Late pick-ups cost $20.

3. During the school period, parents are not allowed in the classroom.

4. Parents must keep their children home if they are ill and notify the school by phone of their absence.

5. At school, the children must wear uniforms, and they are not allowed to bring toys or chewing gum from home.

6. The school provides milk and snacks, but the children should bring their own lunch from home.

7. The school will not tolerate children or parents who fail to follow the rules.

The children learned immediately that they had to conform to a highly regimented schedule and rigorous mental workout. If they obeyed and did their work correctly, they were hugged and received encouraging words. If they misbehaved, the nuns spoke to them harshly, after which they would comfort them. If the children did not finish their tasks, the nuns would urge them to continue, but if their attention wandered, the nuns would shout at them. When a nun asked a question and a child failed to respond, the nun would call out, "I did not hear you. Oh, aren't you a baby. Class, say he is a baby for not answering." While impatient with disobedience, they were patient with children who were slow or unable to finish a task. Still, the children could not dawdle, for every few minutes, the nuns turned to a new assignment. At lunchtime, they hurried the children, while helping them learn how to eat properly and how to clean up afterward.

In class, the nuns spoke to the children in a combination of English and Vietnamese and gave instruction separately in the two languages at different times of the morning. In addition to basic conceptual tasks, the nuns taught the children how to show respectful behavior toward parents and teachers, to share toys with fellow students, and to clean up and put away items after using them.

Dan and Fern Le were delighted with the changes the school effected in their son Ben. The nuns told Dan that for the first couple of days, Ben had been silent, but now he fitted in well. Dan said that the nuns loved Ben. The nuns told Dan that Ben did not speak Vietnamese and was a very picky eater.

Dan told them that they were sending him to the school for that reason. According to Dan, Ben was happy at the school. He had learned a lot, the letters of the alphabet, colors, numbers, and how to write his name. Dan showed off some of Ben's work, several papers with letters and drawings fastened by a magnet to the refrigerator at home. Ben had learned proper behavior and spoke some Vietnamese. Dan asked Ben to bow with his arms crossed and express a respectful greeting. Ben did it once, but then pulled away. He didn't like being on display.

Ben, nearly four years old, had learned more than a few academic skills and proper Vietnamese deportment. He had taken the first steps in learning to accommodate to busyness. Adults had organized Ben's time in specific segments that conformed to their notions of what they needed or wanted to do and what he must do. In the morning, his parents hurried him to get ready to commute with his father, who dropped him off at day care on the way to work. They had to be on time. In the afternoon, he returned home at the convenience of his parents. At preschool, he followed a schedule that was strict and unyielding, where the nuns hurried him through myriad tasks, all timed in short blocks. He learned to march to the toilet and finish quickly, to eat lunch fast and to eat everything, after which the nuns praised him. Using both Vietnamese and English, the nuns taught him numbers, shapes, colors, gender distinctions, letters, and words, both spoken and written. He learned motor skills, songs, prayers, moral teachings and respect for elders, sharing, hygiene, cleaning up, and keeping track of his own things. He also learned to pay attention and to respond quickly when the nuns asked him a question. Ben learned to perform certain activities in particular spaces too, and, at different times, to use the same space for different activities. Finally, he learned to respond to adults other than his parents regarding modules of timed tasks other than those his parents had taught him. Both at home and at preschool, Ben was becoming socialized to a world of American-style busyness with a Vietnamese flavor.

As we have seen elsewhere in this book, Dan and Fern Le were able to function effectively in the work organizations that they dealt with. Dan had learned to operate skillfully within a large hierarchical organization, which he used to further his family as well as personal entrepreneurial interests. Fern's experience as an office worker revealed a different kind of flexibility. When the workload became oppressive, she quit and found better conditions and pay elsewhere. The couple were thus well prepared to navigate the explicit and implicit rules of American organizations, with the necessary tacit knowledge. But they also were willing and able to turn to organizations related to their ethnic heritage when American organizations failed them. This was what happened with Ben's education. What the parents did not realize, however, was that at the Vietnamese Catholic preschool Ben would receive, not only a heavy dose of Vietnamese values and practices, but also those of American busyness as well.

Conclusions

Successful coping requires people to have access to a variety of resources, including information and ideas about coping practices. People who can provide services that reduce various burdens, such as after-school care, a ride to the airport, or "covering" at a meeting are another important resource. As the stories in this book have shown, the challenge lies in knowing in advance what specific resources will be needed. To be sure, some are quite predictable, such as the need for childcare during specific hours. But it is in the very nature of busyness that resources may be required suddenly and desperately, perhaps never again to be needed.

As we watched families seek resources to help them cope with their daily lives, we found that people often did not know which persons, things, or ideas they would need to draw on for a particular problem. Furthermore, families differed in the range of their needs and the variety of resources they needed. In addition, people often needed help at precise times and particular locales. People who were *willing* to help them might be unable to do so because of the timing. This included other family members. Finally, resources varied, in that some could only be provided by a handful of people with particular expertise, while in other cases, such as transporting a child to school or house-sitting, a wider pool of people could perform the task.

People cope by responding to specific needs, which in turn influence how they use social networks. One way is to cultivate deep ties with a handful of reliable people who can be counted on for assistance. This works when the needs are fairly predictable. While important, strong ties are typically limited in their scope. They may not be useful for accessing a broad range of resources. More useful here are networks of weak ties. The "strength of weak ties," says Mark Granovetter, is that they involve connections to people an individual may not know personally.[1] Although the linkages through weak ties are indirect, they have the potential to mobilize resources beyond what is immediately and directly available to a person.

The distinction between strong and weak ties does not address everything that is important about social networks, but it establishes the importance of the texture of those networks. It is all too easy to consider strong ties as good and weak ones as irrelevant, but they are in fact complementary and useful for different purposes. Strong ties bind us to people we know and often care about, but they encapsulate us in the self-confirming security and comfort of the predictable. Because the resources needed to cope with busyness are often unpredictable, weak ties are especially necessary for effective coping.

Social networks involve more than connections between people. Individuals are also connected to organizations, and they may use these to cope with busyness in their daily lives. Organizations can provide technology and technical assistance, as well as sources of information about services. People also use organizations to gain access to the services of other groups. Organizations are sources of practices, such as project management skills, that people use at home to cope with their personal busyness. To be sure, organizations and employers can be adversaries of families, but organizations can also provide important resources that people import into their families to buffer the effects of busyness.

CHAPTER NINE

Remaking Family

It is only fitting that we end our ethnographic journey where we began: with families. They consist of individuals, and yet it was often difficult to determine when someone was "in" their family. Sometimes people were surrounded by family members but lost in cyberspace. Of course, they were still members of the family, but not in the same way as others in the room who were perhaps discussing an upcoming vacation or a relative's health. At other times, individuals were physically apart from their family members, yet firmly "in" the family. A few key strokes on a computer at work could take someone from planning a marketing program for a new product to searching the web for places to park a child after school for a few hours. How people are in their families can change from hour to hour, or even minute by minute.

The complexity that results from the interplay of people, places, and activities that make up real families begs for simplification, and it is tempting to generalize about "the family." Strong feelings are held on the subject.

Everyone seems to know something, if not everything, about it. In the abstract, family often seems an unrealizable ideal, and it is not difficult to elicit passionately articulated predictions about its future.

The fates of individual families are played out in the myriad details of everyday life. Despite predictions of the imminent demise of the family, we found that belonging to a family was central to the lives and identities of the people in our study. It was in their families that they talked about what was occurring that would affect their lives today and tomorrow, and what they could or should do about it. It was also where they were sheltered against the effects of a changing world, in which they were obliged or empowered to take on more and more. We suspect that these families are not exceptional. They form sites where present realities and future expectations are negotiated and may be reconciled.

We have described the different situations of the families we studied, what created their busyness, and what they did about it. Sometimes we saw people follow corporate models and "outsource" activities that formerly occurred in their family. We also saw them draw upon the metaphors of family to create "pseudo-families" among friends, neighbors, and co-workers. Above all, these families were much more than sources of obligations and activities; they were resources for coping and buffering. They used the idea of family itself to buffer. Family in this sense was dynamic and malleable.

Outsourcing Family

THE MENDOZA/JONESES: CHOOSING DAY CARE TO IMPART VALUES AND SKILLS

One of the most widely used outsourcing practices is day care. We have previously described how Suzanne Jones and Humberto Mendoza sent their daughters to day care and preschool. Significantly, they did this not only because of their own work schedules but also because the girls learned important everyday routines there. Humberto called day care a "child development social skill program. It's an activity where our kids are learning, but at the same time, it's where they can play and be with kids of their own age." In his view, it was not an expense, but an investment in the social skills and character of their girls. He contrasted this with other families. "I don't hear them saying, 'Yeah, it's a social development where they're learning this and this and that and they come back well-mannered. They're learning yes sir, no sir, yes ma'am.' You hear about expenditures on child-care costs. What really I hear is, 'It's an expense.' I don't hear it as an enhancement of their character."

The couple specifically chose providers that taught civility and table manners, which they considered important. They wanted them to learn to ask, to say thank you and excuse me. Suzanne insisted that children could learn to share at a young age if they were in the proper environment. Angela's preschool emphasized sharing. Children would ask each other when they could play with a toy: "How many minutes?" Suzanne said that in other facilities, children impulsively grabbed toys from each other. One time, a little boy came across the street and pulled a fistful of Nicole's hair. Nicole looked shocked; she had learned not to do that in day care.

Even when their parents stayed at home, Angela and Nicole went to day care. Humberto and Suzanne felt no guilt or reluctance about this, because they valued the continuity that it provided their girls, along with valuable training in social skills and companionship. Of course, this also freed Humberto and Suzanne to pursue their own projects several days each week. Suzanne insisted that day care benefited both her children and herself.

Humberto and Suzanne could have provided such a learning environment at home, but in their view, this would have been difficult, involving constant work on their part. Good day care inculcated important skills and values when both parents were working. "I think sometimes the preschool–day care helps us to manage that part of our life."

THE SCHWARTZES: DISPERSING FAMILY CHORES

The Schwartz family evolved a distinctive strategy that involved dispersing some family chores so that they could have more time to spend doing other things together. Linda Schwartz commented: "I like to use the word 'delegate.' When you are working, how else do you get things done? And you have the money to buy someone else's time so you can spend more with the family. Frankly, I hate cleaning the toilet, mowing the lawn, and driving kids all over town!" Even ordinary activities could teach larger lessons.

When parents and children gardened together, they did so in a way that broke it into smaller, manageable components. One weekend, they planted flowers. Linda had new pots they had brought from Mexico. "Pull out dead plants and save the dirt," she told her children, showing them how to plant the new flowers. She taught them to enjoy gardening by breaking it down into particular tasks, which were then assigned to either family members or professional gardeners, who did the bulk of the landscaping and the more difficult work for her. Only some simple activities became defined as gardening for this family.

Creating Pseudo-family

Perceptions of who belongs to the family vary greatly among families, as do what are considered to be family issues. Extended family can merge with fictive kin, nonrelatives who are treated as family. Fictive kin may include close friends or even people such as day-care providers or others hired to perform family functions. The Flaherty, Scott, and Mendoza/Jones families are among those in our study who played with the boundaries and functions of family.

THE FLAHERTYS AND THE BRODYS: EMPLOYING FICTIVE GRANDPARENTS

Fifteen years ago, the Flahertys made a momentous decision about child care. Six months before Michael was born, Jerry and Eleanor were working full-time. They discussed what child-care arrangements would allow them to continue their careers. One of Eleanor's co-workers mentioned a couple that provided such care to only one or two children at a time, and somewhat to their surprise, Jerry and Eleanor found themselves auditioning for the role of responsible parents in the living room of Ray and Flo Brody. As Flo interviewed the couple, she told them her rules, which ranged from no pacifiers to proper table manners.

Ray recalls, "You could see Jerry's wheels turning: Am I gonna meet her standard as a parent?" Eleanor says that Flo was relentless in her questioning and told them, "We don't adopt the kid; we adopt the family." The two couples reached an agreement: The Flahertys would deliver their new son to Flo each weekday and then pick him up after work at a precise time. The expectation was that this was not a short-term contract but the start of a long-term relationship. Flo, and to a lesser extent Ray, would help raise the boy through childhood. This arrangement would continue only if the Flahertys met Flo's conditions. The Brodys would take care of Michael during weekends only if convenient or if the child accompanied them on their prized camping and hunting trips.

Over the years, the arrangement grew into a relationship between the families, and when the Flahertys' daughter Mary was born, she became the first girl Flo had "adopted." Although, according to Jerry, the Brodys adored and "would die for" Michael and Mary, the relationship between the two families was not always comfortable. The Brodys were politically conservative, worshipped Rush Limbaugh, and denigrated all Democrats. Ray was especially outspoken in his denunciations, and even Flo admonished him to tone down his rhetoric around the children of these Clinton Democrats. Later, Eleanor wondered if he'd "turned our kids into Republicans."

While Jerry and Eleanor were paying for a needed service, and occasionally wondering if it was worth the hassles and frustrations, their children developed independent relationships with the Brodys and came to view them as grandparents. After all, Jerry acknowledged, "they spent more time growing up with Flo and Ray than with Eleanor and I." Over the years, the bond between these four adults grew, though it always centered on their mutual love of the children, Jerry says. Flo celebrated her birthday at the Flahertys as a family event, while Christmas, the children's birthdays, and Halloween took place first at the Brodys', and only later at the Flahertys'.

As the children grew up, the arrangements and relationships changed. When Michael entered elementary school, he attended its after-school daycare program. Later, when Mary entered school, the Brodys drove the ten miles to pick up both children and then return to their house, where they took care of them until a parent arrived after work. As Michael and Mary grew older, they became more vocal in their preferences. They no longer wanted to be shuttled to different places. When he was in high school, Michael was able to negotiate more independence. He took an after-school job twice a week, used public transportation, and finally drove a car home.

In 1999, Flo died, and relationships and arrangements again changed. Jerry and Eleanor had organized her final birthday party, and months later Mary and Ray organized a garage sale to clear out some of the items in Ray's crowded house. Jerry and Eleanor transported things of their own to his house to be included in the sale. One evening, after Ray had driven the children to their house and dined with the Flahertys, he and Mary sat at a computer and created the invitation to a party commemorating Flo's life. A few weeks later they co-hosted the event in Ray's backyard. Ray continued to pick up one or both of the children when called upon and convenient to him. Eleanor remarked that whatever he could do was helpful, and besides, it was good for the children to see him.

Michael Flaherty and Ray Brody sat in the Brody kitchen. Michael made a flippant remark about something, and Ray sharply rebuked him: Michael's friends had caused him to be impertinent. If it continued, he warned Michael, "We're not gonna go duck hunting or pheasant hunting this year." After an awkward silence of several minutes, Ray lightened up. He described a shot Michael made last year during hunting season. The pair had one pheasant left to their limit as they headed back to the trailer after a day of hunting; they would use it the next day. Then they spotted a large bird several hundred yards away, and Ray's dog gradually worked it toward them. The bird suddenly took off, and Michael made a great shot to bring it down. Ray beamed with pride as he recounted the tale.

Later, Ray drove Michael and Mary to a fast food restaurant for lunch. During the drive he talked about manners and standards, about being a lady and expecting boys to be gentlemen. "Don't lower yourself to them," he told Mary. He commented that he and his wife had taught Michael and Mary proper manners, but the two youngsters would forget them when they went home and ate with their friends or wolfed down food in hurry.

As he lamented their behavior and expressed longing for the good old days, he sounded like a grandfather who cared deeply about his grandchildren. And indeed, as Mary told one of her friends, Ray was "my adopted grandpa sort of guy," reflecting the unlikely amalgamation of two very different families.

After fifteen years of attachment to the two children, Ray, Jerry, and Eleanor were inextricably bound, and yet the relationship remained ambiguous. "He won't depend on us, although he considers us family," Eleanor observed. Ray distributed money-saving coupons and cash before entering the fast food restaurant, and then collected the meal receipts afterward to write off his taxes. He also wrote off a portion of his utilities as a business expense, and occasionally a bill would arrive at the Flahertys. "I don't even ask what it's for," said Eleanor. "I just pay it."

Jerry and Eleanor paid for a service and then found that the very definition of their family and its values were changing. At one level, the Brodys' values were similar to their own. Both couples agreed that it was important for Michael and Mary to develop a sense of right and wrong and to behave properly. But they differed greatly in the particulars of what they thought was right and wrong, acceptable and unacceptable. Ray and Flo were avid pheasant hunters, and Michael and Mary accompanied them and so became hunters. Ray believed everyone should have a gun and know how to use it safely. Jerry reluctantly accepted this, but at the same time lamented, "My son has four guns now." He continued, "Each one was a real issue, since these aren't our values. They are Brody values—Ray and Flo's—and Brody values *are* part of Flaherty family values." He concluded that the Brodys had become like grandparents to his children, and "the grandparents just have different values."

The relationships between the Flahertys and Brodys continued to change as the children entered and left high school. Ray still provided care when needed and convenient, but his life, too, altered rapidly after the death of his spouse. He developed a new romantic interest. The Flahertys wondered whether she would accept Mary and Michael, and how long Ray would continue to help out. Their concern also was profoundly intimate, for Ray's girlfriend had replaced Flo, a woman Mary considered to be an additional, fictive grandmother. This new romance mattered to Jerry and Eleanor, because they worried about their daughter's feelings. The contractual arrangement for child care, signed so long ago, was now only a distant memory.

THE SCOTTS AND THE ROMEROS: SATELLITE FAMILY

Rosie Romero, the Scott family's nanny, influenced the Scott girls regarding beliefs and religion, television programming, foods, and the rhythms of the Romero extended family. Additionally, the young Scott girls were from time to time included in Romero family activities. In turn, the Scotts had an impact on the education of the Romero sons. But unlike the Flaherty-Brody relationship, the Scott-Romero connection did not endure, thereby revealing the limitations of pseudo-family.

Roy and Michelle Scott had originally hired Rosie Romero to be their housekeeper; she did this for three and a half-years. When Crystal Scott was born, the Scotts asked Rosie to be Crystal's nanny and hired Rosie's sister to take over the once-a-week housekeeping chores. A year and a half later, April was born, and Rosie also became her nanny. Roy and Michelle took care of their two daughters in the early mornings, evening, and at weekends; Rosie watched them in between, as well as every other Wednesday night.

As with the relationship between the Flahertys and the Brodys, that of the Scotts and Rosie started as an economic transaction but became an emotional one that bound the families together. In a sense, they became pseudo-kin, though in other ways, they preserved a distance that reminded them that the relationships might cease at any time.

Rosie's eighteen-year-old son Rod was studying computer-aided design at a community college and did his homework on a computer that the Scotts had given him. On occasion, Roy tutored him. Rosie's eleven-year old son Alberto attended a school near the Scott family home. He could do this because Rosie listed the Scott's residence as Alberto's home address. Rosie dropped Alberto off on the way to work, which shortened her commute time.

When three-year-old Crystal and April, aged one and a half, stayed at the Romero household, the distinctions between the two families blurred further. Rosie's refrigerator displayed pictures of Alberto and Rod, but also of Crystal and April. Rosie would ask Crystal, "How many babies do I have?" holding up four fingers. Crystal would answer, "Rod, Alberto, me, and April." One year, the Scotts and the Romeros took a joint trip to Hawaii. One condo was reserved for the children and the Romeros and another for Michelle and Roy.

Because of Rosie, Roy and Michelle could have flexible schedules. Rosie increased her child-care hours when Roy or Michelle left on business trips or fell ill. During the day, Rosie straightened up the Scott house, but her primary task was child care. She earned slightly less money than she had done as a housekeeper, but the work was more predictable, easier to schedule, and gave her more time to be with her family. Besides, she loved the

Scott girls. She said, "It isn't just a regular job. It is like raising children. People tell me not to get so attached to the girls, but show me a way not to love them!" Her son, Alberto "loves the girls so much and they love him." Alberto and Crystal joked together like siblings. Crystal bossed him, saying, "Sit down, you are grounded!"

One lack of fit between the two families was religion. The Romeros had converted from Catholicism to a nondenominational Protestantism several years before. Rosie's older son, Rod, was deeply involved in the Christian community in his early teen years and was taught to believe in the dangers of rock music. Rosie cautioned him about MTV: "Studies show it produces violence and drug-taking in teenagers."

Michelle Scott had been raised a Catholic and was considering a Catholic education for the girls. While she was comfortable with Christianity, Roy was uneasy about religion, and he adamantly disapproved of parochial education for his daughters. He said, "Neither of us are religious at all, and Rosie is, and so she provides a counterbalance in some ways. I guess in the last six months, she has started taking Crystal to Bible School one day a week and so Crystal is now doing a lot of 'Who made the sky blue, Daddy? Do you know?' And I said, 'No, no.' 'Well, it's God.'" Rosie did not involve the girls as deeply as she would her own children, but she told the children about Jesus and the Bible and prayed for them to become "God's daughters."

Rosie realized she was an employee, not a relative, yet her duties thrust her into a role similar to that of parent. When she took April to a children's exercise class or the park, she watched April closely because the girl would bite other children. Once during class, April grabbed a boy and accidentally scratched his face. The boy's mother, visibly upset, rushed him to the bathroom, and Rosie apologized profusely. She feared that the staff would ask her to leave, but they assured her that April was only a baby and that it was not a problem. Rosie felt particularly vulnerable to criticism about injuries to the children and her possible legal liability. She was disturbed by the high-profile coverage of a British nanny who was accused of murdering a baby by shaking it. Accordingly, she took care to explain every injury to the children to Roy and Michelle.

Rosie's husband Mario was less trusting than Rosie of the close relationship with the Scotts. He disapproved of moving Alberto to the posh school near the Scotts, even if it offered his son a better education. He would have preferred to see Alberto in a neighborhood school, surrounded by Latinos, not in a school in which he was a minority student. Mario also felt uneasy about his wife's emotional attachment to the Scott girls. "When the children grow up or the Scotts move away, where will that leave her?" he asked.

His concerns were prophetic: the Scotts moved to southern California. They tried to persuade Rosie and her family to accompany them. Michelle said, Rosie "is just part of us, and if we move we'd love her family to move too." Rosie and Mario declined, since her roots were in nearby rural Monterey County. Before they departed, though, the Scotts were able to arrange a new job for Rosie.

THE MENDOZA/JONESES: CREATING AN EXTENDED FAMILY

Humberto and Suzanne reshaped their relatives and close friends into a consciously constructed extended family. This required work. It was a strategy that both buffered and created busyness, because it generated both new supports and new obligations.

Humberto had an uncle and aunt who acted like grandparents for the girls, according to Suzanne. The couple, who were in their seventies, had their own grandchildren, who lived elsewhere. Angela and Nicole had visited them and were eager to go back. Suzanne said that this aunt and uncle had time to pay close attention to "talking about the girls' lives." The Mendoza/Jones family visited these relatives about once a month.

Suzanne and Humberto also created pseudo-kin with unrelated families who had young children. Humberto said, "We have associated with a couple of them, and I'm finding that we are having extended family. We're kind of creating a microcosm family." He explained: "We're developing these relationships, or liaison relationships with these other couples and we're getting together, we're communicating and sharing, and we're trying to maintain contact with each other as the kids are growing up."

Humberto and Suzanne formed another pseudo-family connection with Marvin and Alison, a couple who lived in a coastal town about seventy miles away. Alison once worked with Suzanne at a high-tech company, and her husband worked at a defense plant. They had one son. Marvin's parents were in New Jersey, while Alison's were in southern California, so they were removed from their closest relatives. Humberto found it unusual that Alison and Suzanne had stayed friends long after they had left their common employer. "As a result of that, I got involved in the relationship with Marvin and Alison by barbecue, dinners, playtime with the kids at the park, and things like that. What we're finding is that we like each other's company, that we've even talked about going up to the mountains and renting a cabin together for the kids, get together with the snow, but we like each other's company." Humberto concluded: "So what we're seeing is that there's this pseudo-family type atmosphere developing with other couples. Something needs to be filled. And it's kind of unique because it happens even though they're dual careers and all this other stuff. It kind of reaffirms the anchoring of family. It takes effort to do it, but the rewards are there."

A New Instrumentalism?

THE HOPKINS / JOHNSONS: SUPPORTING EACH OTHER'S BUSINESSES

The families we studied played with the limits and functions of family and the relationship of families to the world of work. Companies, for example, typically hired individuals with little thought as to their spouses. But within the family, husbands and wives often treated each other as tacit partners. These partnerships took many forms, of which one such arrangement was that of Kent Hopkins and Peggy Johnson. They helped each other, not only with paid work, but also with the work of future business development.

Kent and Peggy served as consultants to each other. Their ability to do this effectively depended on their particular skills and knowledge and how they corresponded with each other's "job" requirements. Both in their early thirties, they held jobs in separate companies. Each was also developing a separate start-up company. Peggy was one of four partners in a small company, in which she ultimately would have little role. The other three partners were on the East Coast. Kent assisted by providing general advice about dealing with partners at a remove. Kent's business idea was to develop an online company that would allow people to build office environments. The possible clients ranged from facilities managers to secretaries, with the service scaled to the customer's expertise and the size of projects. Peggy helped Kent organize the business, and one reason she was pursuing a graduate degree was to develop skills relevant to her husband's business venture. The couple believed that the idea had the potential to attract venture capital funding and succeed, but because of the competing demands on their time of jobs, child, and house, they had not developed the business plan. They also believed that each needed the expertise of the other for their business plans to succeed.

When Peggy Johnson was unable to keep work from overtaking her life, Kent stepped in to cover her domestic tasks. They accepted the reality of all-consuming projects and deadlines as part of each other's lives and helped out when they saw the need.

They had developed assumptions and values in their marriage that were so taken for granted that they no longer needed to deal with each case when it occurred. Both of them were committed to starting businesses, and they supported each other without question. Peggy recalled an example. "I was a little stress puppy in March," she said. She was the chief operating officer of the start-up she was forming with three East Coast partners and she had assumed responsibility for developing the business plan. At the same time, she was receiving physical therapy for an injured knee and working intensively on a course in her graduate program. Peggy was up until 2:00 AM some nights, faxing material to her partners and then calling them to discuss it as they began their workdays. Despite fatigue, Peggy completed the business plan, but she did little for the partnership after that. From Kent's perspective, Peggy's duties were an unexpected burden that required an adjustment from him. He took care of their son, Sam, in the evenings while Peggy worked on the plan, and he tolerated Peggy's moods. "I suspect I was relatively emotional and demanding, and that Kent was accommodating," she said. Peggy said she would do the same for him. "We're pretty good at covering for the other if there's a need. By that I mean cooking, washing up, putting Sam to bed. We're not good at it when we can't see the value of the other's activity or we think, 'my activity is more important than yours.'" However, Kent valued entrepreneurship too, and Peggy's business activities clearly reflected their values. "It was a potential moneymaker," Peggy added, "and that's something he supports. It may have outweighed any inconvenience." Kent agreed that March was a difficult month for the family, but as far as he was concerned, there was little to discuss or negotiate, since they were committed to supporting each other's entrepreneurial projects.

Flexibility is not just a matter of personal temperament or accommodating to unexpected occurrences. People sometimes try to create conditions that support flexibility in their immediate surroundings, although one person's flexibility can easily be a constraint on others. Flexibility may be difficult to publicly oppose, but it may be privately resisted until doing so is futile.

THE FLAHERTYS: A FAMILY "JOINT VENTURE"

Jerry and Eleanor Flaherty developed a tacit "joint venture" even as they passed through different employers. Their complementary skills and outlooks enabled each to help the other in significant ways. Their partnership was based on a deep commitment to building the community in which they lived.

The work partnership of the Flahertys extended to and included family. When Eleanor's co-worker Norma handed her a copy of their organization's latest report, on how children in the region perceived jobs and careers, for example, Eleanor looked puzzled; she had already seen the report. Norma explained that Jerry, Eleanor's husband, who worked in another organization, wanted a copy but had been unable to download it off the web site because the report had been "embargoed" and not formally released. Norma knew Jerry professionally and was happy to let him see an otherwise restricted copy, but she reminded Eleanor that it was for his eyes only: he must not show it to his staff. Norma released the report to him because he was Eleanor's husband.

Eleanor and Jerry, working for different employers, had jobs that were conducive to helping each other out. This ranged from listening sympathetically to complaints after bad days to professional consultation. Sometimes, Eleanor and Jerry appeared to be a single entity that produced a specific kind of work: hire one of them and you also got the services of the other. While keenly aware of responsibilities to their individual employers and the pitfalls of conflict of interest, they were nonetheless bound together by common values from their work, and these mutual understandings were important in their marriage.

This arrangement was not accidental, experimental, or recent. The couple had met while Jerry was working as a community organizer and Eleanor for the city in the parks and recreation department. Jerry went on to work as an economic development consultant for different cities, including Eleanor's. Their jobs, though different, dealt with issues of youth, community development, education, and job training. Jerry noted that these jobs intersected and supported each other. "I was working for a school district doing community organizing; she was working at a park site. But the school district's funding came from a criminal justice grant to curb juvenile delinquency, so you think of park site, you think of kids; there's something there: same community, different ways of approaching something. I came to work for the city; she went to work for the school district." Later, the city hired Eleanor, where she held a succession of positions. At one time, she was the interim director of a job training and development program. When she resigned to spend more time with their son, the city hired Jerry to take her place. Eleanor later joined a nonprofit organization that fostered private-public partnerships to enhance the regional economy.

Jerry used the Silicon Valley rhetoric of innovative entrepreneurship to describe how they helped one another as they took on different jobs. "Eleanor and I have a joint venture—truly—and there's times those ventures support each other and there's times they can stand alone without dragging down each other." Jerry continued: "There's a lot more commonality. There's a lot of mutual benefit to each other in what we do." Simple proximity and unforced interaction fostered casual information sharing. While reviewing their plans for the next few days, Eleanor mentioned that her organization was convening an important workshop; Jerry said he would attend. No representatives from County Social Services had signed up to attend, although the workshop addressed issues that affected them. Eleanor asked Jerry to call them because of his good connections there. Jerry, too, used Eleanor's connections for organizational ends. His organization needed a keynote speaker for an upcoming event, and someone asked Jerry which of two influential regional leaders he knew best. One was a longtime professional colleague who had a contract with Jerry's outfit; the other worked for Eleanor's nonprofit organization. Jerry responded, "Familiarity isn't an issue." Because he felt comfortable approaching either, he advised the person to focus instead on choosing the most appropriate speaker.

Together, Jerry and Eleanor offered access to wider regional networks essential to their work than they might have had alone. Eleanor commented that Jerry's connections made her work much easier. "It provides me credibility and avenues. It's a conduit for relationship building and it gives you that little extra edge of credibility that creates an openness to hearing your story."

Often, Jerry and Eleanor helped each other informally, but on occasion, they made a formal arrangement. For example, Jerry brought home a grant proposal and asked her, "You want to be partners on this proposal?" She agreed, knowing also that when agencies work together, they have a better chance of receiving funding.

Sometimes, their consulting assistance was specific and focused. Jerry explained: "Eleanor's doing a retreat today with her staff, for which I gave her a lot of overheads and things on strategic planning. I talked through a process about how you get people to talk about the business of the organization, the work of that organization, and how people contribute toward that work. How do you build an organizational structure that is organized around the work you need to do?" Eleanor was new to her executive position and her organization was facing a budget shortfall, "She gets into cycles of desperation about this isn't working right," Jerry said. "We'll talk about things, partially kind of just like 'cause I just want to talk about it, partially like do you have any ideas on what to do about it?"

Similarly, Eleanor helped her husband. She had learned how to deal with a very large board of trustees, and so when Jerry's advisory board doubled in size, he asked her, "How do you organize around a larger board, because it's something I've never had to do before?" He explained: "She's much, much better about doing the methodical things, about doing the incremental things that create a stronger base, and I'm much better at jumping up here than trying to backfill the void that I created with that jump there." She coached him on how to "backfill" the organizational voids he had created through his own eagerness.

Jerry and Eleanor based their partnership on more than shared and complementary skills. They had a deeper and broader commitment to work based on building community. Jerry said it was symbolic that he and Eleanor had met while she was working in a park and he was doing community development. "Both of them were around community development of some sort, people development. I think there's common, there's shared values about what the work is, the purpose of the work and how the work is achieved. There's a lot of commonality on valuing the importance of what we do for similar reasons."

Eleanor and Jerry extended their partnership to their children's education. When she was required to volunteer at each private school, Eleanor agreed to analyze data for each school and prepare reports required for accreditation. But she did not know how to do the analysis quickly, and she was running out of time. She asked Jerry to help. The couple argued over how to proceed, since Eleanor had already invested time and effort in her approach. Normally, Jerry would have let her do the report her own way, but in light of the looming deadline, his greater experience in this area, and his wife's plea for help, Jerry took over the analysis. The two of them viewed the report as another consultation in which the person who had the specific expertise completed the project.

Jerry and Eleanor agreed on values and goals but not on how to implement them. Because of this, they brought tensions into home life that ordinarily would remain in the workplace. Just as Jerry and Eleanor had created common grounds of agreement, so too, they indicated its limits. Each partner typically read materials prepared by the other, but they carefully guarded their comments and especially their criticisms. As Jerry observed, the overlap between their professional lives also necessarily required "firewalls" that disentangled their fates from each other. Knowing the limits to their collaboration was as important as being able to work together. Their overlap between jobs and careers also risked blurring separations between larger domains of work and family. For Jerry and Eleanor, the way they helped each other created vigilance and helped prevent inappropriate boundary crossings that might threaten their careers or family.

THE JACKSONS: CONTRACTING WITH GRANDMOTHER

When it came to big issues, Vic and Karen Jackson planned far ahead. This had been part of their life together from the start. They had met several years before in another California town, where they were married. At that time, Vic was working but also attending engineering school, and Karen, who had completed her college degree, was working as a hospital administrator. As newlyweds in 1992, they decided that, while both of them would work, Vic would be the primary earner. Karen explained: "His career had to come first, because he would be able to dominate more with his degree, higher salary, and career path. We agreed that for a certain number of years, we would follow his career wherever that took us."

At the same time, however, Karen's twice-divorced mother had raised her to be independent, and Karen was raising her own daughter in a similar fashion, to have "a self-assurance about her, to feel that she can do whatever she wants to put her mind to and does not need a man to take care of her." She expected this attitude to rub off on her daughter "just by the way I live my life. I mean, Vic and I negotiate and we discuss things a lot. One of us does not run this marriage. It's a shared thing, fifty-fifty."

The Jacksons, as much as any family in our study, exhibited an instrumentalism in their family life, which they imported from the corporate workplace. Each weekend, the Jacksons held a formal family meeting, at which they discussed conflicts, scheduling, and their determination to retain family time, "with as few interruptions as possible." Out of these meetings came their decision to declare dinnertime off limits to outside interruptions and to devote it primarily to their daughter, Tina. For two hours each night, they turned off their phones, PDAs, and computers. The one exception was one week in the month when Karen was on call for twenty-four hours to her company to monitor hotline computer emergencies for hospitals throughout North America.

Vic and Karen also used their weekly meetings to make plans for the future, including major family decisions. It was at one such meeting that they decided to invite Karen's mother Sarah to move in with them to help with child care. This was not a spur of the moment decision but the result of long-term planning and negotiation. Before agreeing to have a child, Vic and Karen invited Sarah to visit them on a trial basis for a couple of weeks. When Sarah was preparing to go back home to Colorado, Karen asked her if she would come back for two years if and when Karen became pregnant. Sarah would live in their house and provide child care, in return for a small salary.

Sarah said she would do so. This initial agreement was only the beginning of the process. Vic put together various charts to determine the costs for Sarah before she moved to California, assessing whether or not she could afford the change in prices. One chart showed the agreements between the three adult family members about work, caring for the child, Tina, and the prospective time allotted for the different activities of each member of the household. A second chart showed payments to Sarah: the wage per hour and the number of hours per week. A third chart showed Sarah's expenses, including rent and one-fourth of the household bills: electricity, gas, telephone, garbage, phone, long-distance phone, cable TV, and water. Since Sarah would do some housecleaning, Vic and Karen would cancel their housecleaning service. A fourth chart showed the coordination of the activities of the three adults and the days and times of day that they would each take care of Tina. The list included various activities associated with the baby: milk, feeding, wet diaper, dirty diaper, laundry, naps, temperature, and so on. They would continue to use such charts while Sarah lived with them.

Sarah returned home and sold her house. Assured that her mother would help her with child care, Karen became pregnant. Shortly before Tina's birth, Sarah returned to Karen's house. At this time they negotiated and finalized the details of the agreement. Karen says, "All of this was carefully planned, but even so, each person had to make adjustments." Despite their carefully laid plans, conflicts finally escalated to such an extent that Sarah moved out.

In their daily lives also, the Jacksons consciously developed businesslike rules and routines to guide them. These included a division of labor, written in charts such as those used with Sarah. As with Sarah, these were a form of contract. Vic explained that this helped to forestall miscommunication. They followed the agreed-upon plan when Tina was born. Karen took care of her in the early evenings, while Vic, along with Sarah, did this late at night and in the early mornings. Sarah did much of the housecleaning. After Sarah left, Vic alone awakened Tina and prepared her for day care, now at another woman's house.

Sarah's departure profoundly affected household routines. Karen recalled: "A negative impact of my Mom moving out was that she really helped a lot with the cleaning. I'm having a hard time staying on top of the clutter, cleanup, and the hard-core cleaning. I'm spending more time than I'd like to. I'd like to re-propose having a cleaning service, which we always had done before. If they came in once a month and scrubbed the floors and the bathrooms, and stuff, then I could maintain it."

Karen observed that the housecleaning contract with Vic was an example of plans that failed. "What we do is we have our assigned cleaning duties right now, and every week that they fail, I just put a note on it and after about three weeks of Vic attempting to do his half of the list, he gives in and allows me to hire somebody to come in and do it. We always have to try this strategy first, though—Okay, we're gonna do it ourselves. We're gonna save money. Let's divide up the list again."

Karen explained the principle they used for their division of labor. "We pick things up we like and don't like and kind of divide it that way. He's a kitchen man. I can comfortably leave this kitchen like this [in a mess], because when we come home, he'll have it clean. He's a kitchen guy. I'm more of a clutter, dust, floor person, like those areas bother me more. Right now, we're just splitting the bathrooms fifty-fifty."

About twice a year, Karen and Vic met to renegotiate their division of labor. "Vic and I have known each other for eleven years now and the list is not going to change," Karen noted dryly. "I still hate to unload the dishwasher, and he doesn't fold laundry, so his job is to wash all the clothes and sort them. My job is to fold them and put them away. Most of the handyman stuff Vic does. I tend to cut the front grass and he usually cuts the back, or we alternate it. I do most of the flowers."

With regard to cooking, Vic and Karen shared the tasks, though Karen did about two-thirds of it. "I really enjoy cooking," she said. "It saves us money for me to plan out menus and shop for a week at a time and cook. And I enjoy doing that. I am more the kitchen engineer, and he's the mechanical and materials science engineer. Technical engineer is his job. He can really think something out before he does it. That's why he's better at home improvement projects than me."

Vic agreed that he divided up household tasks along the lines outlined by Karen. They began to put together lists of household tasks before Tina was born, when both he and Karen were working long hours. "We try and develop an equal weighting of time and also allow each other to pick things that they like most and hopefully, the task you like least are the ones that the other person doesn't mind. Our natural styles are kind of at odds with each other. Karen likes to wake up early in the morning, turn on loud music, open all the windows, and start creating clouds of dust. I, on the other hand, do things after dinner, on Sundays, or something like that." Vic remarked that both he and Karen disliked doing household tasks, "so it can result in tension if we don't do it together. It works out best if we do things at the same time."

The instrumentalism of the Jacksons in their family life does not signify the disintegration of family bonds, but quite its opposite. The contractual style they have developed works because they want it to work. It is not simply an import from the workplace. It depends on their mutual love and affection, a recognition of each person's likes, dislikes, and foibles, a commitment to respect these and negotiate compromises, but above all the recognition that they share a common goal, frequently and explicitly articulated, to create a strong family in a changing and uncertain world, in which families, with few set guidelines, increasingly find that they must remake their own destiny.

THE CARLSBERGS: THE SWITCH

"We did a switch in how we're doing things," Pat Carlsberg commented. Alex, her husband, now was getting up by 4:00 AM and racing down the empty freeway to work, thereby cutting 30–45 minutes off his usual morning commute. He was able to leave work by 2:45 PM, beat the evening rush hour, and pick up his sons as their school day ended. After a short drive home and a nap, Alex was occupied with the boys. "I spend a lot more time with the kids because now I work with them with their homework." He prepared dinner and afterward, "we'll do something at night. At least I'll read to them, because they still love stories at night."

For Pat, the switch or role reversal, as she called it, had different results. Alex used to take the boys to school; now that duty fell to Pat. She dropped them off shortly before the 8:00 AM start of school and then entered the freeway at the height of the morning commute, typically arriving at work after 9:00 AM. Thanks to a supportive supervisor, she received increased recognition and pay increases, but her workload also increased: she was managing four projects, each with their distinctive requirements and separate staffs. Because of her supervisory duties, her days were long and she usually returned home between 7 and 8 PM. Often, she ate alone and missed the evening's activities with her sons. And, she complained, "I'm still bringing work home." Alex and the boys would head for bed around 9:30 PM, but Pat would stay up to work a little more. "We can't even get to the kitchen table anymore," said Alex, because it was covered with project-related paperwork and her company-provided laptop computer. "She's up till 11, 12, 1 o'clock working" he added. "Not only is she working longer now, but she's bringing it home and it's consuming her."

The busyness and the schedule switch of Alex and Pat affected their children in complex ways. Before the switch, the boys had to depart for school early and return late from day care. They spent the time in between with paid caregivers. When Alex and Pat rescheduled their work hours, the need for day care evaporated, much to the boys' approval. "I have more time to play now. I can do my homework," said James. While the day care offered him a homework club, "the little kids don't listen, so they just make a lot of noise. And you can't concentrate as much and you can't ask for that much help, 'cause they only help you with one or two problems and then they have to help everybody else and they won't help you anymore." Robert, too, was relieved. Although he had earlier begged to get to day care by 6:30 AM, he later confided, "I hated day care." If he *had* to go to day care, then he wanted the most opportunities to play Nintendo, the center's only redeeming feature.

The change that brought relief from day care for the boys came at the cost of convenience for Alex and Pat. That Alex was allowed to arrive at work before anyone else and be productive reflected corporate downsizing. It also led to his growing isolation within the firm. If business improved, then he might have to meet more with other employees, thus eliminating the "early bird option." His early arrival was hardly a permanent solution. For Pat, the late departure to job after delivering the boys to school meant a lengthier commute. Since she started work later, she stayed later and later to complete tasks and answer questions. As a supervisor, her presence was mandatory.

The new regimen affected the family in unfamiliar ways and created new and different tensions. Alex was exhausted from his early departure, and while he was able to pick up the boys after school, he often fell asleep when he got home with them. James, when asked about seeing his father, replied with a laugh and mimicked the man speaking to his sons: "Good morning. [pause] Go to bed." He then continued, "My mom and dad, when they get home from work, they have a lot of stress. And my dad, he always takes a nap because he's always really tired. He gets up at four and does work and he's stressing. So he always takes a nap. And my mom is really always stressed 'cause she works from way early to way late to like seven o'clock or eight or ten. Because she likes to work overtime, which I don't know why."

Pat and Alex agreed that the decision to switch was motivated by the increasing traffic, which lengthened Alex's commute. He went in early a few times, discovered he could get to work in fifteen minutes, and so the experiment became the new routine. "It's for him, to be able to make it easier for him," Pat said. Always concerned about Alex's health and the stress in his life, she agreed to the routine knowing that "there would be some give and take." She paused and thought carefully about the latter words, for despite the clear motivations, the switch had influenced them in unforeseen ways.

For Alex, the benefits of time with his sons proved significant. "I'm feeling much better myself about that," he reflected, "and I'm finding out that you can have a really good time with family life and work isn't as important as it used to be." He was surprised to discover that the boys did not miss day care. "I thought they liked being in day care because they got to play with kids and stuff. I find that they actually prefer to come home." The switch allowed him to make some small steps toward achieving "normalcy" in daily life, the elusive condition that he so prized. He hoped the family's life could progress "just to where any given day has some kind of pattern that is recognizable. It's like every day there's something that screws up your normal life." His working hours and his sleep patterns were now more predictable, and he felt more energetic, although Pat's erratic workdays limited family normalcy. He prepared and served dinner at a regular time, since he could not predict when Pat would arrive. He said he was sad that Pat was missing the pleasures of family due to her commitments at work, and he worried about her chronic headaches and sleeplessness.

Pat, too, described the role reversal as an experiment with mixed results. She had coincidentally cut back on volunteering at the boys' school, theoretically freeing up hours each week, but she said that about 75 percent of the time had been absorbed by work. Both her projects and the illnesses of several key co-workers had increased the demands on her time, as had her sense of commitment to work deadlines. Alex concluded that the peer recognition at work, too, had become more important to her. Pat acknowledged that the 25 percent more time she had devoted to the family was insufficient, "but at least it was something more that I could give." She was frustrated, however, that those hours were only available in the morning, "so it's not, from their standpoint, quality time with Mom, it's more the mandatory, 'Gotta get dressed, wash your face, comb your hair.' But it added about two hours a day of being able to have little conversations that wouldn't have normally occurred." The boys simply wanted her home earlier. She said that her son James "thinks that my not being around is an impact and that bothers me, 'cause I'm not able to give them what they think they want from me." Although her priorities were husband and children, "you don't always have the opportunity to put them first on your list of priorities. Sometimes the job *has* to be the first priority."

Both Alex and Pat continued to think extensively about their individual and collective busyness. Alex felt more secure in his job now and was less concerned about developing his Internet business. The "rewards" he received from his children were what mattered, and that validation was grounded in an emerging view of family and time. He realized "that just a little bit of recognition from your family is worth all the peer recognition together. You want to have that sense of being proud of your kids and getting along with your kids." The result, he hoped, was that "when they are teenagers they will still like you and they're not running with some gangs or whatever, and they feel a bond with the family." Yet the new routine also raised concerns in Alex's mind. He worried that his wife was becoming "jealous because the kids are bonding very heavily with me" due to the time he spent with them in the afternoon and evening. And while he thought he must have saved time by shortening the commute, "I used to get some help with the kids at night, with the dinners, with the homework, with the stories and stuff," and the result was that "my time is being dragged away." The time he spent with his children had thus increased, but much of it was filled with activities that he now performed unaccompanied. The results were at best confusing, and he still complained that he and Pat could find no time to plan anything. "We're stuck in the classic work situation where you don't have the time to sit down and plan it and do it right."

Pat said that she had not devoted the necessary time to family, but added "if I haven't been able to change something I've at least been *aware* of where things really should be but aren't. I think it's also the realization that life is too short and there are too many bad things that can happen that can just change everything so dramatically." She asked, "Why aren't we spending all of our quality time together? I think I've had that philosophical discussion with myself a lot more frequently in the past six months. What am I really doing here at 6:30, 7:00 at night at work?" Often, she then left for home, but she admitted that she still lugged papers home. "I don't know why I feel compelled to have to bring something home, but it's that if I have five minutes I want to know that it's close by, that I can look at it if I have to." She was especially disturbed by the lack of time she spent with Alex, joking, "Occasionally, he'll say, 'Hey, do I know you?'"

For the time being, she tolerated the routine and her increased work-load as necessary inconveniences and burdens. She said she felt guilty and expected things to be *different* in the future, but not necessarily *easier*. She accepted busyness as a condition of her life and saw few ways to lessen its impact, except by retiring. In fact, she was both threatened and relieved by the occasional rumors that her employer would close down its local office.

The Carlsbergs' switch was an experiment that reflected the particular circumstances of their lives and their habitual ways of addressing what they saw as problems. Their new routine was likely temporary, less an ultimate solution to their busyness than their latest attempt to control it. Family obligations were at the core of Pat and Alex's lives, but family was not immutable. In fact, it was malleable, and they could stand apart from it and ask how best to change it in ways that might allow them to cope better.

In making the switch, Alex, Pat, and their children made choices whose implications became clear only after the initial decisions had been made. They based their choices on what they thought was good for themselves and their family, and the effects that their decisions would have on it. While the switch led them to discuss efficient commutes, peer recognition, control of family time, and domestic labor, it also compelled them to address larger issues. Alex reversed the importance of his roles as parent and employee and found that he approved of the change. Pat recast the American Dream, with work taking precedence over family, at least for the moment. However, the question persisted of whether the switch enabled the Carlsbergs to control busyness or simply changed the form it took.

Conclusions

Busyness may be with us throughout our lives, but the Carlsbergs' role switch, the Flahertys' familial agreement with the Brodys, the Jacksons' instrumental settlement with Grandmother Sarah, and all of the other family experiments with living arrangements illustrated in this chapter remind us that as we cope with busyness, we are refashioning not only ourselves but our society as well. What kind of people do we become, what sort of society do we create, and where do we turn, individually and collectively, if we are dissatisfied with what we see?

PART FOUR

Continuing Concerns

CHAPTER TEN

Why It's So Hard to Say No

Our Journey Through Busyness Revisited

This book has documented a journey that we undertook because we had some questions about conventional views of the relationship between work and family. We quickly realized that there was much more to daily life than we and other scholars had assumed. This prompted us to expand our focus to include what we call busyness. In doing this, we were following a time-honored anthropological practice: to challenge our initial assumptions and questions as a richer description emerges from prolonged first-hand contact.

As we explored how family and work connect with busyness in people's lives, we found that busyness occupied many facets of people's lives, with varying degrees of emphasis. For some people, volunteerism loomed large every day, while for others consumption, education, or medical and health-related activities were prominent. Regardless of where busyness appeared in their lives, individuals were at the center of the lifestyles they were creating, while they were simultaneously swept into the lifestyles of others.

Like many other scholars, we at first assumed that what we should look at was how people balance or juggle work and family obligations, but we soon realized that balancing and juggling are dubious metaphors. Simply counting time in familiar categories such as work or family fails to capture the constraints and choices confronted by people in their everyday lives, or the ways in which these realms overlap.

What we found was that family and community obligations and activities penetrated workplaces because of the time spent in them and the availability of information technologies that blurred their boundaries. Similarly, work migrated home and was interwoven into the rhythms of family life. While such intrusions may seem pathological to some people, including social analysts, families can also be viewed as preparing adults and children for the realities of life in a new economy. The radical separation of work and family in America, so taken for granted by the post–World War II generation, may prove to be an exception to their close relationship in most societies.

Our journey revealed that work could not automatically be assumed to be a source of stress, for it is also a source of the very resources people use to manage their obligations. Families may be less a refuge from an often hostile or indifferent world than sources of busyness for their members. Ironically, the workplace may provide respite.[1] And the interface of work and family may simply be the visible arena where problems are manifested and experienced, even if their causes lie elsewhere.

The busyness we found ourselves describing transcended work and family. We became sensitive to another set of activities that were part of everyday life. These involved the management of other daily tasks. The purpose of these extra activities was to bring about efficiency and productivity in daily life, yet they themselves required considerable effort. In other words, they constituted an added-on busyness in people's lives. Ironically, people frequently ignored their very existence and seldom calculated their costs and benefits. This tacit work of busyness could be public in the sense that other people could see it and assess it, even if the busy person was oblivious to it, yet it also involved private, internal work occurring in the consciousness of individuals. We came to realize that people were frequently preoccupied with how they should manage or organize their work and family obligations.

Because coping took so many different forms, the individuals we studied did not see these behaviors as a unified, interrelated set of practices in their lives. This is why we speak of them as tacit. Thus we found ourselves observing seemingly empowered, responsible individuals juggling myriad daily and weekly demands, continuously looking for opportunities to improve on their use of time. This led them to be often "on," looking to improve their practices of coping and buffering. Being "on" in this way is another facet of the tacit work of busyness.

A complement to being "on" was the quest for settings for being "off" in ways both large and small. The goal of such quests was sometimes that of respite from having to think about what would or might happen. It could also be reflection about the content and direction of life, either individual or collective. Sometimes, the escape thrust the individual or family into a set of activities different from those of routine everyday life. Such activities were sometimes distinctive, or they were protected from intrusions and interruptions. It was difficult for people to find the time, and a chore for them to step aside from everyday life, and scheduling this came at the cost of spontaneity. This price was especially high when people tried to reflect about life, since these thoughts often occurred at unplanned moments.

Trying to cope alone is difficult, limiting, and often expensive. Because of this, the people in our study created systems of things and people, which they used to buffer the effects of their busyness. These buffers were social in that they created relationships among people. They also were intended to last: they were constructed for the future.

Such buffering suggests that busyness is more than an individual problem that can be managed by acting alone. Yet the buffering we saw suggests much more. It suggests that people do not just respond to external busyness; instead, they try to create lifestyles in which coping is more effective and perhaps less intrusive. In the extreme, it also demonstrates the possibilities of everyday life: people have choices and can radically rearrange their obligations and activities.

Our ethnographic journey through busyness has taken us through a complex web of everyday destinations. It also has a larger significance beyond drivers, coping practices, and buffer building. Our study documents some of the specific conditions that affect how work and family play out. The people we met did not work or have families in general. They worked in particular ways and had particular families. The details of their lives had consequences for how they were busy, how they assessed and interpreted their busyness, and what they could do about it.

To grasp what busyness is about, we need to do more than document the practices of everyday life. By explicating the minute and the contingent, we may inadvertently portray the patterns of individual lives as more unpredictable and idiosyncratic than they are. When we capture the fine-grained texture of everyday life, we run the risk of presenting it as a miracle of ordinary creativity, as the individuals we describe navigate the apparently uncharted terrain of the new day.

The power of ethnographic journeys comes, not simply from attention to the microscopic, variable, and creative, but also from linking apparent minutiae with the larger context. The details of busyness might be interesting to read about, or bothersome when we experience them, but they are also important because they link daily life with wider social structures and processes that may at first glance seem distant and removed.

Our journey through busyness revealed such linkages. The proliferation of activities, our daily practices of coping, and how we attempt to create stable, useful connections with things and people are reflections of social, cultural, political, and economic changes that are both writ large and manifested in everyday life. The sources of busyness in various spheres of life, and the processes that drive that busyness, are often far removed from the families who try to cope with their effects. Changing ideas about the proper role of government, the emergence of new industries, the workings of a global economy, and new technologies occur "out there," and yet their effects reverberate through the choices we make and the constraints on them. They remind us that we must know what is going on *beyond* our own lives in order to understand what is happening *in* them.

The meaning of our journey is therefore not found in amassing data about everyday life, but in allowing us to reflect upon and critique it. Busyness is not simply about time or even activities, but about the possibilities inherent in an experiment we are collectively performing on our lives, our families, and our workplaces.

As a result of our study, we have come to question certain conventional assumptions about workers, jobs, homes, and families. We consider it misleading to juxtapose the workplace as the location of work with the home as the place for leisure. The place of employment is a context of leisure for many workers. We also know that accounts of hours spent with nose to grindstone often exaggerate hours *working*. Additionally, we cannot assume that the tasks performed at work are mandatory, especially in an era when workers have learned the necessity of being perceived as busy in order to protect their jobs.

The conventional assumptions about households also do not hold up. Households have taken on many of the characteristics of workplaces; maintaining them has become another job. Yet allocating tasks at home may be more ambiguous than at work, and the tasks can be less predictable, stable, or sequential. A child's last-minute revelation of a homework assignment or need to investigate some esoteric topic can upset evening plans, but so, too, can canceled insurance policies, demands for information about personal health, and troubleshooting malfunctioning devices. In such circumstances, the home becomes a place of multitasking and real work, precisely because the stakes are higher and slack is nonexistent.[2]

We are left suspecting that talk about time and its management distracts us from the sources of our busyness only to enable us to take on more. A more sinister view is that the apparent time bind is a function of the very notion of efficient management that creates or enacts it.

Back to Families

We began our journey as an exploration of work and family, and especially of how the latter was being affected by the demands of an economy in which dual-earner families are common. Our fieldwork quickly suggested to us the limitations of a narrow focus on work and family, and on the insufficiency of the familiar juggling and balancing metaphors to understand it. Nevertheless, we wish to return for a moment to this conventional or received view. Work, and fear of it disappearing, is indeed a powerful driver of busyness. And while families are not simply shelters in a harsh world of workplace demands, they are at the heart of busyness.

The greatest danger in trying to understand the busyness of families is to consider them as timeless, essential forms. The anthropologist Stevan Harrell documents that the family as a social institution is far from immutable.

In different societies, it has performed several basic functions, but how it does so varies from society to society, at least partially because of their different institutions.[3] It is worth familiarizing ourselves with the scope of family functions. This enables us to recognize that our own family system is but one of many, that a variety of family forms exist within our own society, and that families well adapted to some conditions may be poorly adapted to others. Most important, it allows us to see how families can be other than they are.

Through history, the family has acted to procure resources, either by being a work group or the group in which all members share the goods obtained through the labor of one or more members. It has also been a basic economic group that processes the resources needed for survival, such as by preparing food and constructing shelter. The family often monitors and regulates the sexuality of its members, and it socializes children by transmitting the skills and knowledge expected of society's members. The family is often the basic property-owning group in society, and families both manage wealth for today and transmit it across generations. Families may represent their individual members, whose identities depend on the place of their family in society. Likewise, people's families may enable them to maintain their position in society. Lastly, Harrell points out that the family provides emotional support to its members.[4]

Modern families have typically shed sole responsibility for most of these functions, relinquishing aspects of them to other institutions in society. Relatively few families continue to act as work groups, and individual members may not pool the results of their individual labor. Family members typically purchase more products for final consumption than raw materials to be further processed within the family or household. Regulation of sexuality is no longer exclusive to the family; it is shared with other institutions, and sexual mores themselves have changed. Much socialization has shifted to schools and mass media, and even socialization within the family is often focused on preparing self-actualized children to be able to survive in a world apart from that of their parents. The ownership of property remains an important source of income for some segments of society, but wages and salaries are more important for most people. Individual identity is less about place in a family than defined by rights as citizens of a state, while social status rises and falls apart from that of family and often is tied to levels of education.[5]

The remaining basic function of the family is that of providing emotional support, and this function becomes prominent as societies undergo the transition to modernity. The emotional relationship of husband and wife becomes critical to the very survival of the family, as does the capacity of parents, typically the mother, to create an environment in which their children become independent, self-fulfilled individuals.[6] In this way the family is expected to be "a place of love and happiness where you can count on other family members,"[7] making its essential role in society that of a shelter from harsh external realities.

In *Centuries of Childhood*, Philippe Ariès argues that childhood as understood today emerged in the early modern period with the development of the conjugal family in which the ties between husband and wife became more important than multigenerational family lines.[8] Modern notions of privacy emerged simultaneously, and the family became distinct from (and even opposed to) the community of which it was part. *Centuries of Childhood* inspired a generation of social historians to investigate the origins of a family form that people in modern societies take for granted as natural and basic to human nature. Summarizing this scholarship, the historian Tamara Hareven describes the characteristics of the modern family.[9]

First, the modern family is a private realm, isolated from the community. The latter may take the form of institutions that provide services to families and so are connected to families in ways similar to private companies. Family members may regard the community as another external actor, to be judged on the quality of services, and not as a social unit of which the family is part. The privacy of the modern family is, however, even broader. The nuclear family is isolated from extended kin and nonrelatives alike so that it is sheltered, not just from the community, but also from specific kin, friends, and co-workers. Although Americans may express nostalgia for what they imagine to have been the large multigenerational families of the past, the nuclear family has been predominant in anglophone North America since the seventeenth century. Although these *families* lacked extended kin, their *households* often included unrelated individuals such as lodgers, boarders, apprentices, servants, and other people from the community. Today, the boundary around the family is generally isomorphic with a household. Home, it goes without saying, is where the family is to be found, a private refuge that is penetrated only by invitation. This makes it less flexible and adaptable, for it has become a single-purpose entity. Ariès argues that preceding forms of family exposed children to a greater diversity of role models than today's families, since a broad and shifting array of people were likely to pass through the household. The modern family also became the focus of individual privacy, as well as of the emotional nurturing and ties of sentiment that prepare individual members for life in a wider bureaucratic society. We can also speak of the modern family as individualistic, since it is a site of individual economic activities, but the family seldom acts as a collective economic actor. It is individualistic in that decisions regarding education, employment, consumption, and residence that in the past were collective ones are now largely made by and for individuals.[10]

Hareven argues that one consequence of the isolation of family is its weakened capacity to act in political arenas to influence relevant legislation. A second result is that family itself has emerged as an entity with its own lifestyle that exists apart from community and society. Such lifestyles underlie the widespread belief that family is a primordial building block of society, and that individual families are worlds unto themselves, whose circumstances are incommensurate with those others around them.

These changes in family structure follow a dramatic shift in the functions of the family. Family members used to provide services for each other. Their ties of mutual dependency were largely instrumental. Marriage and parenthood were based on reciprocal ties of assistance and mutual obligations within the family. The household was an important site for economic production and so its membership changed according to financial needs and opportunities. The result was the shifting array of outsiders found by family historians.

Gradually, instrumental kin relationships have declined as the basis for modern families, with the exceptions of first-generation immigrant families and working-class families. In fact, the rise of the nuclear family predated the Industrial Revolution, so that the latter did not shatter extended families, for the three-generational family of U.S. mythology is just that—a myth. It is what the sociologist William Goode calls the "classical family of Western nostalgia."[11] Other researchers, such as Peter Laslett and Richard Wall, and John Demos, have concluded similarly that the composition of the American family has long been nuclear, although it has been embedded in a variety of households under different conditions.[12] What have changed dramatically are, not the structure or composition of the family, but the functions it serves in society and for its members.

While we speak of the family as a human universal, the forms it takes are thus varied, as are the functions it serves. It cannot be understood apart from those functions. To speak of a family as modern is not to claim that it is better, only that it has formed under certain conditions. For example, the state as a geopolitical entity has accompanied the emergence of the modern family, and not just coincidentally: it has changed many of the conditions under which families exist. Educational systems have transformed enculturation within the family. Individual citizenship rights supersede family standing as a basis for representation in society. Legislation limits the power of families to be the sole regulators of their members' sexuality.

The people we have met in these pages are members of families that have developed under particular conditions—and that will continue to change and adapt as those conditions change. Enormous challenges face families today, and the issue is much more than just good time management. As governments shed functions, more and more obligations and activities are taken up again by families, as we have seen in this book. Performing these activities takes time, and so the logics of efficiency and productivity are both useful and readily imported into families from workplaces, many of which aspire to high performance or at least high *enough* performance to remain competitive in a global economy.

The paradox is that the modern private family, an emotionally supportive group bound by ties of sentiment and stripped of instrumental interdependencies, is the site of a new instrumentalism. That instrumentalism is based on coping and buffering the drivers of busyness and, more generally, of making sense of realities that seem to change almost daily. The work of deciding how to adjust to immediate realities and distant futures is both largely tacit and enormous in its consequences. It affects family members both individually and collectively. It can seem especially vexing because the family remains for many the sole refuge in a precarious, or at least trying world. It is not surprising that families that have been stripped of real interdependencies and that are based on facilitating the potential of their individual members may seem overwhelmed by the challenge.

Historically, families are not just passive respondents to changed societies, but are active in cushioning the effects on their members. Hareven documents the central role families and kin networks played in organizing migration from rural to urban centers in America in the late nineteenth and early twentieth centuries, as well as their role in facilitating settlements and helping people to adapt to new living conditions. Families and extended kin often acted as intermediaries between new workers and industrial employers, taught their members industrial discipline and how to use machines, and offered protection within factories.[13] Stereotypes of passive agricultural families being impacted negatively by industrialization and urbanization are misleading, for those families often responded creatively to new circumstances. Family obligations, far from invariably being a burden to individuals, were also resources that helped with adjustment to the new realities. In the process of adjustment, the functions of families changed, as did their place in larger networks of kin.

Despite the active agency of families to protect or cushion members from the effects of change, whether and how they do so is always an open question. Success is not assured. We also should not assume that families act collectively to adjust. The family is not just a collective unit but a group comprised of members who, under some conditions pursue their own strategies. For example, our fieldwork revealed that people are not simply in a family; some of their activities are related to it, while others are not. What might be most adaptive for the family collectively might be inconsistent with what is best for its individual members at different junctures of their life courses, and the decisions they make for themselves shape the family as much as acknowledged "family decisions." We may thus speak of family strategies for adaptation without concluding that they are pursued consciously and collectively, much less that they are successful.

Further complicating the relationship between the family and society is the delay or lag between the changing lives of people and the social structures in which they live. Adjustment is not instantaneous, and so actual families always represent adaptations to various conditions that have changed over time. Talk about the family goes beyond description, however, for it is also embedded in cultural norms and values. We assess individual families insofar as they conform to those cultural expectations and judge them, and perhaps their members, as good or bad. How to balance familiar sentiments, often rooted in conditions of a distant past, with new realities can be contentious and confusing. Guideposts are typically missing, and families have long acted as quasi laboratories in which people try to make sense of new conditions while simultaneously protecting their members from their effects.

The busyness we have seen reflects disjunctions between familiar cultural expectations for the family and a rapidly changing political economy. Many of those expectations were forged in the late nineteenth century, and they are not necessarily well adapted to today's conditions. The ideal of female domesticity consisting of motherhood and homemaking as full-time activities is inconsistent with increased participation by women in the labor force. The private family is separated from community and society, thereby making it more vulnerable to the very conditions that buffet it. Diminished interaction between the nuclear family and wider kin networks cuts off families from the reciprocal exchanges of assistance that have long been the basis of marriage and family.

Yet families are far from monolithic, and their traditional patterns also serve as resources for adaptation. Although the nuclear family and household are often seen as culturally expected, living arrangements with people who are not family members and extended kinfolk also occur and provide alternative models for family. Similarly, nuclear families and extended kin *do* establish instrumental relations of interdependency, and they, too, allow us to think about how families can be arranged. As we have seen in these pages, social networks that include kin and surrogate kin are important resources for many families, as is the closer integration of the family with the community. Even alternative timing of life-course transitions, such as marriage, parenthood, education, and retirement, can provide families with resources.

A Larger Universe

Ethnography is arguably compelling because it allows us to act as voyeurs gazing at the minutiae of other people's lives; indeed, doing so becomes a scholarly virtue. When the distance between our lives and theirs is close, ethnographic detail has an almost magnetic attraction, pulling us into comparisons of how our lives are similar and different from the lives of *those* people, who we hope or fear may really be like us. A function of ethnography is not just to reveal more and more about them, but also to allow us to ask ourselves questions that we might not pose otherwise. While reading about the busyness of others may in this way provide a guilty pleasure, it can be a profound experience as well, for those other lives can help us think about our own circumstances and perhaps act to change them for the better. What is important is not whether their busyness is the same as ours, or whether they coped and buffered in the best ways, but rather what it allows us to learn that is useful in our lives as individuals and members of families.

There is, however, a danger in the attraction of the richly detailed perspective available through ethnography. Such rich descriptions also provide windows onto processes that may be changing entire ways of life, but that seem removed from everyday experience. Complementing the ubiquitous ethnographic microscope is the need for a "macroscope" that connects everyday life, and its immediate exigencies, with a larger meaning or significance. Doing so might sound like an academic thought experiment, but in fact it is profoundly practical. We can imagine, for example, reconfiguring our daily lives and our families to gain better control over busyness, but the effects of busyness would still reverberate through society, changing its very texture.

Busy lives might be firmly grounded in daily obligations, but how we handle those obligations, and even how we think about our lives, affects and is affected by moral visions of how we should live. As we have seen, one way to think about our busy lives assumes the importance and simplicity of time and pays scant attention to the content of our activities. Ideas about a time bind, or life speeding up, or of "fitting it all in" assume the centrality of time. They treat activities and how we categorize them as natural, necessary, and taken for granted. They are not problematical and they remain unexamined. Only the challenges of efficient organization or the productive use of time seem noteworthy. There is a matter-of-factness to this approach, one in which techniques of time management are paramount. Moral issues may arise, as when we choose among obligations or ask what activity-filled days are doing to families and our children, but the moral sense is typically muted. The focus on time takes for granted a world that presents alternatives and compels us to ask ourselves how to adapt or cope, but abundant alternatives are taken as inevitable. Morality lurks at some distance behind the minutiae of daily life, for the latter is largely defined by technique and mastery.

The perspective from busyness frames different questions regarding morality. The focus from busyness is less about mastery or exploring alternative techniques than about the very content of our lives and how we are connected to other people. There is uncertainty to the morality, for we cannot assume the inevitability and naturalness of the alternatives we confront, much less the activities they entail. From this perspective, we lack firm guidelines for even knowing what we should be doing and how we should be engaging other people in our everyday lives. The morality, far from lurking in the background, infuses our every action; organizing a car pool or using technology to limit and enable our relationships to other people become the stuff of morality, and not just matters of efficiency and productivity. The contrast between focusing on time versus focusing on activities is not merely an academic nicety but transforms the questions we can meaningfully ask about our lives and society.

The morality of busyness is inherently entwined with ideas about what it means to lead a good life. Such a life varies, of course, from circumstance to circumstance; there is no single good life. But as Alasdair MacIntyre argues, we can view the good life as a whole or a unity that is created through the narrative histories we create of ourselves and our settings. Everyone undertakes the work of creating such narratives, for humans are storytelling animals, and through those stories we aspire to truth. This truth is the unity of an individual life, and the question is: "How best might I live out this unity and bring it to completion?"[14]

Our narratives are not simply composed about or by us as lone individuals. In the narrative perspective, in MacIntyre's words, "my life is always embedded in the story of those communities from which I derive my identity. I am born with a past; and to try to cut myself off from that past, in the individualistic mode, is to deform my present relationships."[15] Those communities and societies into which we are born provide the settings in which we live, and those settings, too, have histories. In order to understand our actions, we are always inserting particular episodes into the narrative histories of ourselves and those settings. We place someone's intentions in causal and temporal order with reference to his or her history. We also place them in their role in the history of the setting or settings in which they belong. Such narrative history is basic and essential for characterizing and comprehending actions.[16] An action is always accountable in the sense that it is possible to ask a person for an intelligible account of it, and those accounts connect specific actions to larger intentions.

Through this dual process of constructing narratives of both self and settings, we connect our individual lives to cultural traditions; we are not just the authors of our own stories, for those traditions provide us with stories in which we make sense of ourselves. In the narrative view, a life is always embedded in the story of the communities from which we derive identity. We are born with pasts and futures, and a living tradition is our argument about what is good and worth pursuing.

If a human life constitutes a unity, then creating that unity is done under difficult conditions in modern societies. Such societies create compartments into which we and our behavior are placed. As we learn roles, we also learn to compartmentalize our actions and our identities. For example, we may inculcate the virtue of honesty at home while practicing deception elsewhere. Even the continuity and unity of the life course is broken up; old age and childhood are placed in different compartments from the rest of life. The challenge to a good life is evident: distinctiveness is emphasized over unity, but the virtues that define it are manifested in many or all situations for individuals. Exercising these virtues requires effort, and modern life can seem designed to thwart such unity.

Busyness exacerbates the difficulties inherent in creating the unity in life that social philosophers such as Charles Taylor and Alasdair MacIntyre argue is so important. As we have seen, the drivers of busyness provide a surfeit of alternatives from which to choose, as well as partitions between spheres of life and uncertainty about long-term intentions. Busyness is organized, not around virtues that integrate and unify a life, but around skill in managing competing demands on time. Busyness is less progress toward completing a unity than it is ceaseless movement that we hope will prove significant.

If, then, we see narrative histories as essential tools for living because they bind present to past and future, and collective traditions to individuals, then one way to characterize society is in terms of how it provides settings and practices conducive to the good life. At least from this perspective, in which morality is part of lived, daily experience, busyness threatens those conditions.

These questions surrounding the good life are important to individuals and families, but how they are resolved will reverberate throughout society.

The sociologist Alan Wolfe points out that capitalist economics and liberal democratic policies have freed many citizens from both concern with "the nitty-gritty of survival" and "the struggles for power taking place around them." In this sense, they have "freedom from economics and liberation from politics."[17] The result is a key paradox, in that we are largely free to make choices about how to live our lives irrespective of the actions of other people. But because of the social and economic complexity of our societies, we are interdependent with others in making those societies work. We may aspire to be free, yet freedom means being unencumbered by obligations to others, while economic growth, democratic governance, and freedom are produced through dependencies on other people: "To be modern is to face the consequences of decisions made by complete strangers while making decisions that will affect the lives of people one will never know," Wolfe writes. One resulting dilemma is that the more we depend on others (and they on us) owing to the web of obligations, the fewer are the agreed-upon moral rules that can account for those obligations.[18]

Wolfe argues that markets, the state, and civil society have provided moral regulation. The market approach begins by assuming that people will rationally maximize their own self-interest, so that their individual moral obligation to others is to do what is best for themselves. Economists who base moral regulation on self-interested individuals acting in markets typically develop explanations of why such action based on self-interest best discharges moral obligations to other people. An enduring challenge is to explain how what is desirable for larger collectivities is best obtained through the uncoordinated action of individuals, each relentlessly pursuing what is best for him or her.

The state provides an alternative means of moral regulation, based on the argument that individuals will in practice attempt to escape obligations to others, and so unbridled individual desires must somehow be restrained. Political processes operate to ensure that obligations to larger communities are met, and the state and its laws and regulations become the instrument through which collective obligations are defined and met. The state is not omniscient, but it is authoritative and relies on the power and knowledge of experts to act on behalf of distant strangers.

In their different ways, both market and state simplify the complexity of social coordination, the market by locating it in the actions of individuals and the state by promulgating universal solutions. Each operates independently of the people who might be directly involved in the actions of others. Because of this simplification and the apparent complexity of alternative means of coordinating obligations, we often think of market and state as the only forms of moral regulation in society. Yet liberal democracies have discontents precisely because neither the individualistic morality of the market nor the collective morality of the state can successfully address all of the issues confronting society. And despite their obvious differences, liberal markets and democratic states are based on some shared assumptions about moral obligations and codes. Both see social obligations as resulting from the action of individuals. They prefer present benefits to making sacrifices for the future. Both value the operation of simple mechanisms over paying attention to the ultimate purposes of action. The result is that markets and states are limited in their effectiveness as moral regulators of society.

A third way of providing moral regulation is through the operations of civil society. While civil society is less prominent in contemporary discourse than state or market, it is an enduring source of defining and meeting obligations. Civil society requires individual restraint, ties of solidarity between people, the expression of community norms, and voluntary altruism. It occurs because we are invariably brought into contact with others in ways that force us to recognize our dependence on them. Morality is based on and in these interactions. "We are not social because we are moral; we are moral because we live together with others and therefore need periodically to account for who we are," Wolfe explains.[19] This morality is negotiated among individuals who reflect on what they have done and are doing in order to decide what they should be doing next. Morality here is dynamic, emerging from the actual occasions when people interact. It is not simply a matter of applying the correct rule and following it. Such moral reasoning is ubiquitous, for tacit knowledge is embodied in every social interaction, and much of this knowledge is moral. There is no relief or "time out" from the need to account for what we do and why we do it.[20]

Busyness is occurring, not only in modern societies, but also in ones where the taken-for-granted regulators of social obligation are being transformed. Civil society has had little place in a world where the state and market duel for primacy, but these pages have revealed that busyness is found virtually everywhere and is affecting our everyday interactions. How it does so cannot be contained within the procrustean beds of work and family. But the drivers of busyness, our reliance on coping practices, and how we create buffers that enhance our resilience thrust us into social interactions with obligations, standards of conduct, and rules that have not yet been fully written. How busyness affects us individually and as family members is likely to be where we are most immediately aware of its effects, but it is the longer, often indirect effects on society that will arguably be more important to our futures.

We should not be uncritically confident about the possibilities of a civil society with renewed functions. Alan Wolfe and Charles Taylor remind us that any moral obligations and codes that emerge will be generated by the content of our interactions and our capacity to place them in larger narratives about ourselves and the settings that give them meaning.[21] Busyness neither eliminates the possibilities for such narratives and the unities they create nor is particularly conducive to constructing them.[22] For example, we have seen the quest for opportunities for reflection that is necessary for good stories to think with, but we have also seen the difficulty in finding them. Far more common are occasions for mastering techniques, the goals of which are not always evident.

An ethnography of busyness allows us to understand the poverty of simply looking at time as the sine qua non of busy lives, and to instead refocus our gaze on the activities that make us busy and those that we embrace to manage our everyday lives. Ironically, time reemerges in importance, albeit in different ways. We have seen its importance through the experiments individuals and families conduct over days and years to best live their lives. Time also reasserts itself in the possibility of constructing narrative histories that unify our pasts, presents, and futures into a good life. And we are also reminded that those lives are being led at a historical moment when market, state, and civil society are shifting their functions in society. There are few reliable guideposts in such a world, and reasons for concern and even despair loom large. Yet also possible are new forms of family, workplace, and community that can help us explore and meet the obligations we have to one another, and the sort of society that will allow us to lead our own good lives in the company of others.

Reference Matter

Acknowledgments

The research on which this book is based was supported by generous grants from the Alfred P. Sloan Foundation, to which we are deeply grateful—especially to program officer Kathleen Christensen for her commitment to bringing anthropologists into the study of work and family. Without her constant support and encouragement, this book would never have been written. We were also welcomed into a community of scholars through the Alfred P. Sloan Foundation Centers on Working Families, which created an environment in which we could play with and test our ideas; in particular, we thank center directors Tom Fricke, Elinor Ochs, and Bradd Shore.

Many people read parts of the manuscript or otherwise helped in its preparation, and they, too, have our gratitude. Mark Auslander, Marietta Baba, Steve Barley, John Gillis, and David Krantz, in particular, read and commented in detail on complete drafts of the manuscript, and their suggestions helped make the book what it is. Of course, we bear ultimate responsibility in this respect.

Kate Wahl at Stanford University Press believed in the project. She did what any author hopes their editor will do: steadfastly support the book, while offering guidance to make it better.

Charles N. Darrah drafted parts of the manuscript while he was a visiting professor at the Center for Work, Technology and Organization at Stanford University. He and J. A. English-Lueck were also supported by sabbatical grants from the College of Social Sciences, San Jose State University. English-Lueck thanks, in particular, her colleagues at the Institute for the Future.

Of course, our greatest debt is to the families, our own and those who permitted us to join them on their daily rounds—and far beyond. We were yet another complication in their already busy lives, but they uniformly welcomed us and tolerated our presence and questions with grace and good humor. Without them, there would have been nothing to write about.

Families

This list includes family members featured in this book and nonrelatives who play a significant role in it. The occupations listed are those of the major income earners in a family at the start of this study. Some family members used different surnames to refer to themselves in different situations, such as at work or in their neighborhood. Rather than hyphenate their names, which would denote a more consistent practice on their part, we have chosen to identify these families by use of a backslash to indicate ambiguity.

ALLEN / RODRIGUEZ

Bill Allen   Adoptive father of Esteban and Ricardo; husband of Sophia
Occupation: Parts expediter for a high-tech company

Sophia Rodriguez   Adoptive mother of Esteban and Ricardo; wife of Bill
Occupation: Data entry clerk for a public agency

Esteban   Adopted son of Bill and Sophia

Ricardo   Adopted son of Bill and Sophia

CARLSBERG

Alex   Father of James and Robert; husband of Pat
Occupation: Systems analyst for a large corporation

Pat   Mother of James and Robert; wife of Alex
Occupation: Researcher for a private research company

James   Son of Alex and Pat

Robert   Son of Alex and Pat

CARSON / KLEIN / ROGERS

Martin Klein   Current husband of Debbie; stepfather of Ethan andDerek
Occupation: Management and information systems specialist

Debbie Carson   Mother of Ethan and Derek; current wife of Martin;
former wife of Jason
Occupation: Historical interpreter

Derek Rogers   Elder son of Jason Rogers and Debbie Carson

Ethan Rogers   Younger son of Jason Rogers and Debbie Carson

Jason Rogers   Father of Ethan and Derek; current husband of Alys
Occupation: Computer engineer

Alys Rogers   Current wife of Jason Rogers

FLAHERTY

Jerry   Father of Michael and Mary; husband of Eleanor
Occupation: Executive director of a public agency

Eleanor   Mother of Michael and Mary; wife of Jerry
Occupation: Executive director of a chapter of a nonprofit youth
organization

Michael   Son of Jerry and Eleanor

Mary   Daughter of Jerry and Eleanor

Ray Brody   Fictive grandfather of Michael and Mary

Flo Brody   Fictive grandmother of Michael and Mary

HOPKIN / JOHNSON

Kent Hopkins   Father of Sam; husband of Peggy
Occupation: Facilities manager of a software company

Peggy Johnson   Mother of Sam; wife of Kent
Occupation: Internal process consultant in an American subsidiary of a Japanese company

Sam   Son of Kent and Peggy

JACKSON

Vic   Father of Tina; husband of Karen
Occupation: Electrical engineer in a large high-tech company

Karen   Mother of Tina; wife of Vic; daughter of Sarah
Occupation: Health care applications specialist in a medical technology
   company

Sarah   Mother of Karen
Occupation: Discount store department manager

Tina   Daughter of Vic and Karen

LE

Dan   Father of Ben and Steve; husband of Fern
Occupation: Aircraft parts supplier for a branch of the U.S. military; small
   businesses

Fern   Mother of Ben and Steve; wife of Dan (Fern also has a daughter by
   a previous marriage, who resides with her father)
Occupation: Office manager in a small high-tech company

Ben   Older son of Dan and Fern

Steve   Younger son of Dan and Fern

MENDOZA / JONES

Humberto Mendoza   Father of Angela and Nicole; husband of Suzanne
Occupation: Firefighter with supervisory and investigative duties

Suzanne Jones   Mother of Angela and Nicole; wife of Humberto
Occupation: Job-sharing high-tech marketer

Angela   Older daughter of Humberto and Suzanne

Nicole   Younger daughter of Humberto and Suzanne

Uncle of Humberto   Fictive grandfather of Angela and Nicole

Aunt of Humberto   Fictive grandmother of Angela and Nicole

Marvin   Pseudo-family connection

Alison   Pseudo-family connection

MOHAN

Rajiv Father of Frank; husband of Nita
Occupation: Business developer and entrepreneur in high-tech industries

Nita Mother of Frank; wife of Rajiv
Occupation: Environmental consultant; currently exploring new career directions

Frank Son of Rajiv and Nita

SCOTT

Roy Father of Crystal and April; husband of Michelle
Occupation: High-tech executive

Michelle Mother of Crystal and April; wife of Roy
Occupation: Executive financial officer for a nonprofit organization

Crystal Older daughter of Roy and Michelle

April Younger daughter of Roy and Michelle

Rosie Romero the nanny Mother of Rod and Alberto; husband of Mario

Mario Romero Husband of Rosie; father of Rod and Alberto

Rod Son of Rosie and Mario Romero

Alberto Son of Rosie and Mario Romero

SCHWARTZ

Arthur Father of Sonia and Hettie; husband of Linda
Occupation: Attorney

Linda Mother of Sonia and Hettie; wife of Arthur
Occupation: Attorney

Sonia Older daughter of Arthur and Linda

Hettie Younger daughter of Arthur and Linda

Reta The nanny

SMITH

David   Father of Mardi and Mirella; husband of Janelle
Occupation: Student life professional, working as a residence director

Janelle   Mother of Mardi and Mirella; wife of David
Occupation: Speech pathologist

Mardi   Older daughter of David and Janelle

Mirella   Younger daughter of David and Janelle

TENTORI

Tom   Father of Josh; husband of Fran (Tom also has a daughter from a
    previous marriage, who resides with her mother)
Occupation: U.S. Postal Service employee

Fran   Mother of Josh; wife of Tom
Occupation: Office manager in the law office of a U.S.government agency

Josh   Son of Tom and Fran

TRAN

Binh   Father of Ron, Paul, and Ginny; husband of Sheila
Occupation: Catering truck business; home repairs

Sheila   Mother of Ron, Paul, and Ginny; wife of Binh
Occupation: Catering truck business

Ron   Older son of Binh and Sheila

Paul   Younger son of Binh and Sheila

Ginny   Daughter of Binh and Sheila

Notes

CHAPTER 1. A JOURNEY THROUGH BUSYNESS

Full details are given the first time a reference appears in any chapter, as well as in the list of Works Cited at the end of the book.

1. Much of the writing about the relationship between work and family has centered on time. But it would be a mistake to take time too literally. Time is a central cultural concept and is a primary metaphor by which parents talk about their involvement in their families and with their children. See Kerry Daly and Anna Dienhard, "Negotiating Parental Involvement," in *Challenges for Work and Family in the Twenty-first Century*, ed. Dana Vannoy and Paula Dubeck (New York: Aldine de Gruyter, 1998), 111–13.

2. While many writers continue to talk confidently about achieving a balance between work and family, that notion has become increasingly problematic. Ellen Galinsky, president of the Work-Family Institute, writes that navigation, rather than balance, is a much better metaphor for discussing the interaction of work and family. See Galinsky, *Ask the Children: What America's Children Really Think About Working Parents* (New York: Morrow, 1999), xvi.

CHAPTER 2. HOW ARE WE BUSY?

1. See Phyllis Moen and Shin-Kap Han, "Gendered Careers: A Life-Course Perspective," in *Working Families: The Transformation of the American Home*, ed. Rosanna Hertz and Nancy Marshall (Berkeley: University of California Press, 2001), 44–45, and Marcia Brumit Kropf, "Part-Time Work Arrangements and the Corporation: A Dynamic Interaction," ibid., 155.

2. James M. Freeman, *Hearts of Sorrow: Vietnamese-American Lives* (Stanford: Stanford University Press, 1989), 392–93. For details of Vietnamese family values and roles and how they are changing in America, see id., *Changing Identities: Vietnamese Americans, 1975–1995* (Boston: Allyn & Bacon, 1995), 87–107.

3. John Hall and Charles Lindholm, *Is America Breaking Apart?* (Princeton, N.J.: Princeton University Press, 1999), 130.

CHAPTER 3. WHY ARE WE BUSY?

1. John P. Robinson and Geoffrey Godbey, *Time for Life: The Surprising Ways Americans Use Their Time* (1997; 2d ed., University Park: Pennsylvania State University Press, 1999).

2. Toby Parcel and Daniel B. Cornfield, *Work and Family: Research Informing Policy* (Thousand Oaks, Calif.: Sage Publications, 2000); Marcie Pitt-Catsouphes and Bradley K. Googins, eds., *The Evolving World of Work and Family: New Stakeholders, New Voices*, Annals of the American Academy of Political and Social Science, vol. 562 (Thousand Oaks, Calif.: Sage Publications, 1999), 8–211.

3. Juliet Schor, *The Overworked American: The Unexpected Decline of Leisure* (San Francisco: HarperCollins, 1991).

4. Jerry Jacobs, "Changing Hours of Employment in American Families" (paper presented at conference, "Workforce/Workplace Mismatch: Work, Family Health, and Well-Being," Washington, D.C., June 16 2003), 2–3, www.popcenter.umd. edu/conferences/nichd/papers/jacobs.pdf (accessed August 22, 2006).

5. Robinson and Godbey, *Time for Life*.

6. In 1970, 48.2% of male workers and 48.5% of female workers worked a 40-hour week, percentages that dipped for each 41% in 2000. Concurrently, 26.5% of men worked at least 50 hours a week in 2000, compared to 21% in 1970. For females, the percentage increase was even greater: 5.2% in 1970 to 11.3% in 2000. See Jacobs, "Changing Hours of Employment," 4.

7. Ibid., 6

8. National Research Council and Institute of Medicine, *Working Families and Work Policies*, ed. Eugene Smolensky and Jennifer A. Gootman (Washington, D.C.: National Academies Press, 2003), 11.

9. Ibid.

10. J. F. Sandberg and S. L. Hofferth, "Changes in Parental Time with Children." *Demography* 38 (2002): 423–36.

11. National Research Council and Institute of Medicine, *Working Families and Work Policies*, 32–36.

12. Harriet Presser, "Toward a 24 Hour Economy," in *Challenges for Work and Family in the Twenty-First Century*, ed. Dana Vannoy and Paula DuBeck (New York: Aldine de Gruyter, 1998), 39–48; id., "Work Shifts in a 24/7 Service Economy: Facing the Challenges" (paper presented at the Annual Blue Cross Blue Shield of Massachusetts Invitational Journalism-Work/Family Conference, Boston, May 12–13, 2005).

13. Kropf, "Part-Time Work Arrangements and the Corporation," in *Working Families*, ed. Hertz and Marshall, 154.

14. Harriet Presser, *Working in a 24/7 Economy: Challenges for American Families* (New York: Russell Sage Foundation, 2003).

15. Michael Wallace, "Downsizing the American Dream: Work and Family at Century's End," in *Challenges for Work and Family in the Twenty-First Century*, ed. Dana Vannoy and Paula Dubeck, 23–38 (New York: Aldine de Gruyter, 1998).

16. Helen Jarvis, "Moving to London Time: Household Coordination and the Infrastructure of Everyday Life," *Time and Society* 14, no. 1 (2005): 133–54.

17. Henk Overbeek and Kees van der Pijl, "Restructuring Capital and Restructuring Hegemony: Neo-Liberalism and the Unmaking of the Post-War Order," in *Restructuring Hegemony in the Global Political Economy: The Rise of Transnational Neo-Liberalism in the 1980s*, ed. Henk Overbeek (New York: Routledge, 1993), 2.

18. Katherine Newman, *Falling from Grace: Downward Mobility in the Age of Affluence* (1988; Berkeley: University of California Press, 1999); see also id., *Declining Fortunes: The Withering of the American Dream* (New York: Basic Books, 1993).

19. Brian Gill and Steven L. Schlossman, "Parents and the Politics of Homework: Some Historical Perspectives," *Teachers College Record* 105, no. 5 (2003): 865.

20. Sally Woodhouse, "Parental Strategies for Increasing Child Well-being: The Case of Elementary School Choice," University of California, Center for Working Families, Working Paper No. 7 (1999).

21. Penny Edgell Becker and Phyllis Moen, "Scaling Back: Dual-Earner Couples' Work-Family Strategies," *Journal of Marriage and Family* 61, no. 4 (1999): 995–1007.

22. Barry Schwarz, *The Paradox of Choice: Why More Is Less* (New York: HarperCollins, 2004).

23. Ulrich Beck, *Risk Society: Towards a New Modernity*, trans. Mark Ritter (Thousand Oaks, Calif.: Sage Publications, 1992); id., *The Brave New World of Work*, trans. Patrick Camiller (Malden, Mass.: Polity Press, 2000); Ulrich Beck and Elisabeth Beck-Gernsheim, *Individualization: Institutionalized Individualism and its Social and Political Consequences*, trans. Patrick Camiller (Thousand Oaks, Calif.: Sage Publications, 2002).

24. Hall and Lindholm, *Is America Breaking Apart?*, 130.

25. See John R. Gillis, *A World of Their Own Making: Myth, Ritual, and the Quest for Family Values* (1996; paperback reprint, Cambridge, Mass.: Harvard University Press, 1997), 238n71, citing Jon Bernardes, "Do We Really Know What 'The Family' Is?" in *Family and Economy in Modern Society*, ed. P. Close and R. Collins (London: Macmillan, 1985), 192–95. For a discussion of the idealization of the American family, see Stephanie Coontz, *The Way We Never Were: American Families and the Nostalgia Trap* (New York: HarperCollins, 1992), and id., *The Way We Really Are: Coming To Terms with America's Changing Families* (New York: HarperCollins, 1997).

CHAPTER 4. THE HIDDEN WORK OF THINKING AHEAD

1. ISO (International Organization for Standards) 9000 sets international standards of quality for business-to-business dealings.

2. Anthony Giddens, *Modernity and Self-Identity: Self and Society in the Late Modern Age* (Stanford: Stanford University Press, 1991).

CHAPTER 5. MAKING MANAGEABLE WORLDS

1. John Blair, *Modular America: Cross-Cultural Perspectives on the Emergence of an American Way* (Westport, Conn.: Greenwood Press, 1988).

2. Bradd Shore, "Knowledge in Formation: The Machine-Modeled Frame of Mind," *Technology in Society* 18, no. 2 (1996): 231–51.

CHAPTER 6. WHEN THINGS GO WRONG

1. Giddens, *Modernity and Self-Identity*, 114.

2. A further discussion of this point is found in Robert Perrucci and Earl Wysong, *The New Class Society: Goodbye American Dream?* (2d ed., Lanham, Md.: Rowman & Littlefield, 2003).

3. For a further discussion of parenting concerns in America, see Ann Hulbert, *Raising America: Experts, Parents and a Century of Advice About Children* (New York: Knopf, 2003). See also Ellen Galinsky, *Ask the Children: What America's Children Really Think About Working Parents* (New York: Morrow, 1999), 226–29, 243–44.

4. John Saul, *Second Child* (New York: Bantam Books, 1990).

5. Hulbert, *Raising America*.

6. The risks faced by the American middle class are discussed in detail by Elizabeth Warren in "Rewriting the Rules: Families, Money, and Risk," Social Science Research Council, 2005, http://privatizationofrisk.ssrc.org/Warren/ (accessed August 22, 2006); and Elizabeth Warren and Amelia Warren Tyagi, *The Two-Income Trap: Why Middle-Class Mothers and Fathers Are Going Broke* (New York: Basic Books, 2003).

7. Beck, *Risk Society*; Mary Douglas, *Risk and Blame: Essays in Cultural Theory* (London: Routledge, 1992); Giddens, *Modernity and Self-Identity*.

CHAPTER 7. USING THINGS

1. For a discussion of activity settings, see Jo Ann Farber, "Activity Setting Analysis: A Model for Examining the Role of Culture in Development," in *Children's Engagement in the World: Sociocultural Perspectives*, ed. Artin Goncu (Cambridge: Cambridge University Press, 1999), 99–127.

2. Bradd Shore, *Culture in Mind: Cognition, Culture, and the Problem of Meaning* (New York: Oxford University Press, 1996).

3. For a discussion, see John R. Gillis, "The Islanding of Children: Reshaping the Mythical Landscapes of Childhood" (paper given at conference, "Designing Modern Childhoods: Landscapes, Buildings, and Material Culture," University of California, Berkeley, May 2–3, 2002).

4. Gillis, *A World of Their Own Making*, xv.

5. Mihaly Csikszentmihalyi, "Why We Need Things," in *History From Things:*

Essays on Material Culture, ed. Steven Lubar and W. David Kingery (Washington, D.C.: Smithsonian Institution Press, 1993), 23.

6. Ibid.

7. Ibid., 28.

8. Ruth Finnegan, *Tales of the City: A Study of Narrative and Urban Life* (Cambridge: Cambridge University Press, 1998).

CHAPTER 8. CONNECTING PEOPLE

1. Mark S. Granovetter, "The Strength of Weak Ties," *American Journal of Sociology* 78, no. 6 (1973): 1360–80.

CHAPTER 10. WHY IT'S SO HARD TO SAY NO

1. See Arlie Russell Hochschild (1997), *The Time Bind: When Work Becomes Home and Home Becomes Work* (New York: Metropolitan Books, 1997; 2d ed., New York: Holt, 2001).

2. Charles N. Darrah, "Ethnography and Working Families," in *The Handbook of Work and Family: Multidisciplinary Perspectives and Approaches*, ed. Marcie Pitt-Catsouphes et al. (Mahwah, N.J.: Lawrence Erlbaum, 2006).

3. Stevan Harrell, *Human Families* (Boulder, Colo.: Westview Press, 1997).

4. Ibid., 468–90.

5. Ibid.

6. Ibid., 488.

7. Robert N. Bellah et al., *Habits of the Heart: Individualism and Commitment in American Life* (Berkeley: University of California Press, 1985), 87.

8. Philippe Ariès, *Centuries of Childhood: A Social History of Family Life*. New York: Vintage Books, 1962.

9. Tamara K. Hareven, *Families, History, and Social Change: Life-course and Cross-cultural Perspectives* (Boulder, Colo.: Westview Press, 2000).

10. Ibid., 14–15.

11. William J. Goode, *World Revolution and Family Patterns* (New York: Free Press, 1963), 6.

12. Peter Laslett and Richard Wall, eds., *Household and Family in Past Time*. (London: Cambridge University Press, 1972); John Demos, *A Little Commonwealth: Family Life in Plymouth Colony* (New York: Oxford University Press, 1970).

13. Hareven, *Families, History, and Social Change*, 16

14. Alasdair MacIntyre, *After Virtue: A Study in Moral Theory* (1981; 2d ed., Notre Dame, Ind.: University of Notre Dame Press, 1984), 218.

15. Ibid., 220.

16. Ibid., 208.

17. Alan Wolfe, *Whose Keeper? Social Science and Moral Obligation* (Berkeley: University of California Press, 1989), 1.

18. Ibid., 3.

19. Ibid., 215

20. Ibid., 213.

21. Ruth Abbey, *Charles Taylor* (Princeton: Princeton University Press, 2000).

22. Richard Sennett, *The Corrosion of Character: The Personal Consequences of Work in the New Capitalism* (New York: Norton, 1998).

Works Cited

Abbey, Ruth. *Charles Taylor*. Princeton: Princeton University Press, 2000.

Ariès, Philippe. *Centuries of Childhood: A Social History of Family Life*. New York: Vintage Books, 1962.

Beck, Ulrich. *Risk Society: Towards a New Modernity*. London: Sage Publications, 1986.

———. *The Brave New World of Work*. Translated by Patrick Camiller. Malden, Mass.: Polity Press, 2000.

Beck, Ulrich, and Elisabeth Beck-Gernsheim. *Individualization: Institutionalized Individualism and Its Social and Political Consequences*. Translated by Patrick Camiller. Thousand Oaks, Calif.: Sage Publications, 2002.

Becker, Penny Edgell, and Phyllis Moen. "Scaling Back: Dual-Earner Couples' Work-Family Strategies." *Journal of Marriage and Family* 61, no. 4 (1999): 995–1007.

Bellah, Robert, Richard Madsen, William Sullivan, Anne Swidler, and Steven Tipton. *Habits of the Heart: Individualism and Commitment in American Life*. Berkeley: University of California Press, 1985. Reprint, New York: Harper and Row, 1986. Rev. ed., Berkeley: University of California Press, 1996.

Bernardes, Jon. "Do We Really Know What the 'Family' Is?" In *Family and Economy in Modern Society*, ed. P. Close and R. Collins, 192–95. London: Macmillan, 1985. Cited in John R. Gillis, *A World of Their Own Making: Myth, Ritual, and the Quest for Family Values* (1996; paperback reprint, Cambridge, Mass.: Harvard University Press, 1997), 237n71.

Blair, John G. *Modular America: Cross-Cultural Perspectives on the Emergence of an American Way*. Westport, Conn.: Greenwood Press, 1988.

Caplan, Pat. *Risk Revisited*. London: Pluto Press, 2000.

Coontz, Stephanie. *The Way We Never Were: American Families and the Nostalgia Trap*. New York: HarperCollins, 1992.

———. *The Way We Really Are: Coming to Terms with America's Changing Families*. New York: HarperCollins, 1997.

Csikszentmihalyi, Mihaly. "Why We Need Things." In *History from Things: Essays on Material Culture*, ed. Steven Lubar and W. David Kingery. Washington, D.C.: Smithsonian Institution Press, 1993.

Daly, Kerry, and Anna Dienhard. "Negotiating Parental Involvement." In *Challenges for Work and Family in the Twenty-First Century*, ed. Dana Vannoy and Paula Dubeck, 111–22. New York: Aldine de Gruyter, 1998.

Darrah, Charles N. "Ethnography and Working Families." In *The Handbook of Work and Family: Multidisciplinary Perspectives and Approaches*, ed. Marcie Pitt-Catsouphes, Ellen Ernst Kossek, and Stephen Sweet. Mahwah, N.J.: Lawrence Erlbaum, 2006.

Demos, John. *A Little Commonwealth*. New York: Oxford University Press, 1970.

Douglas, Mary. *Risk and Blame: Essays in Cultural Theory*. London: Routledge, 1992.

Farber, Jo Ann. "Activity Setting Analysis: A Model for Examining the Role of Culture in Development." In *Children's Engagement in the World: Sociocultural Perspectives*, ed. Artin Goncu, 99–127. Cambridge: Cambridge University Press, 1999.

Finnegan, Ruth. *Tales of the City: A Study of Narrative and Urban Life*. Cambridge: Cambridge University Press, 1998.

Freeman, James. *Hearts of Sorrow: Vietnamese-American Lives*. Stanford: Stanford University Press, 1989.

———. *Changing Identities: Vietnamese Americans, 1975–1995*. Boston: Allyn & Bacon, 1995.

Galinsky, Ellen. *Ask the Children: What America's Children Really Think About Working Parents*. New York: Morrow, 1999.

Giddens, Anthony. *Modernity and Self-Identity: Self and Society in the Late Modern Age*. Stanford: Stanford University Press, 1991.

Gill, Brian, and Steven L. Schlossman. "Parents and the Politics of Homework: Some Historical Perspectives." *Teachers College Record* 105, no. 5 (2003): 846–71.

Gillis, John R. *A World of Their Own Making: Myth, Ritual, and the Quest for Family Values*. 1996. Paperback reprint, Cambridge, Mass.: Harvard University Press, 1997.

———. "The Islanding of Children: Reshaping the Mythical Landscapes of Childhood." Paper given at conference, "Designing Modern Childhoods: Landscapes, Buildings, and Material Culture," University of California, Berkeley, May 2–3, 2002.

Goode, William J. *World Revolution and Family Patterns*. New York: Free Press, 1963.

Granovetter, Mark S. "The Strength of Weak Ties." *American Journal of Sociology* 78, no. 6 (1973): 1360–80.

Hall, John, and Charles Lindholm. *Is America Breaking Apart?* Princeton, N.J.: Princeton University Press, 1999.

Hareven, Tamara K. *Families, History, and Social Change: Life-course and Cross-cultural Perspectives*. Boulder, Colo.: Westview Press, 2000.

Harrell, Stevan. *Human Families*. Boulder, Colo.: Westview Press, 1997.

Hochschild, Arlie Russell. *The Time Bind: When Work Becomes Home and Home Becomes Work*. New York: Metropolitan Books, 1997. 2d ed. New York: Holt, 2001.

Hulbert, Ann. *Raising America: Experts, Parents and a Century of Advice About Children*. New York: Knopf, 2003.

Jacobs, Jerry. "Changing Hours of Employment in American Families." Paper presented at conference, "Workforce/Workplace Mismatch: Work, Family Health, and Well-Being." Washington, D.C., June 16, 2003, www.popcenter.umd.edu/conferences/nichd/papers/jacobs.pdf (accessed August 22, 2006).

Jarvis, Helen. "Moving to London Time: Household Co-ordination and the Infrastructure of Everyday Life." *Time and Society* 14, no. 1 (2005): 133–54.

Kropf, Marcia Brumit. "Part-time Work Arrangements and the Corporation: A Dynamic Interaction." In *Working Families: The Transformation of the American Home*, ed. Rosanna Hertz and Nancy Marshall, 152–67. Berkeley: University of California Press, 2001.

Laslett, Peter, and Richard Wall, eds. *Household and Family in Past Time*. London: Cambridge University Press, 1972.

MacIntyre, Alasdair. *After Virtue: A Study in Moral Theory*. 1981. 2d ed. Notre Dame, Ind.: University of Notre Dame Press, 1984.

Moen, Phyllis, and Shin-Kap Han. "Gendered Careers: A Life-Course Perspective." In *Working Families: The Transformation of the American Home*, ed. Rosanna Hertz and Nancy Marshall, 42–57. Berkeley: University of California Press, 2001.

National Research Council and Institute of Medicine, Board on Children, Youth and Families, Division of Behavioral and Social Sciences and Education. *Working Family and Work Policies*. Edited by Eugene Smolensky and Jennifer A. Gootman. Washington, D.C.: National Academies Press, 2003.

Newman, Katherine. *Falling From Grace: Downward Mobility in the Age of Affluence*. 1988. Berkeley: University of California Press, 1999.

———. *Declining Fortunes: The Withering of the American Dream*. New York: Basic Books, 1993.

Overbeek, Henk, and Kees van der Pijl. "Restructuring Capital and Restructuring Hegemony: Neo-Liberalism and the Unmaking of the Post-War Order." In *Restructuring Hegemony in the Global Political Economy: The Rise of Transnational Neo-Liberalism in the 1980s*, ed. Henk Overbeek, 1–27. New York: Routledge, 1993.

Parcel, Toby, and Daniel B. Cornfield, eds. *Work and Family: Research Informing Policy*. Thousand Oaks, Calif.: Sage Publications, 2000.

Perrucci, Robert, and Earl Wysong. *The New Class Society: Goodbye American Dream?* 2d ed. Lanham, Md.: Rowman & Littlefield, 2003.

Pitt-Catsouphes, Marcie, and Bradley K. Googins, eds. *The Evolving World of Work and Family: New Stakeholders, New Voices*. Annals of the American Academy of Political and Social Science, vol. 562. Thousand Oaks, Calif.: Sage Publications, 1999.

Presser, Harriet. "Toward a 24 Hour Economy." In *Challenges for Work and Family in the Twenty-First Century*, ed. Dana Vannoy and Paula Dubeck, 39–48. New York: Aldine de Gruyter, 1998.

———. *Working in a 24/7 Economy: Challenges for American Families*. New York: Russell Sage Foundation, 2003.

———. "Work Shifts in a 24/7 Service Economy: Facing the Challenges." Paper presented at the Annual Blue Cross Blue Shield of Massachusetts Invitational Journalism-Work/Family Conference, Boston, May 12–13, 2005.

Robinson, John P., and Geoffrey Godbey. *Time for Life: The Surprising Ways Americans Use Their Time*. 1997. 2d ed. University Park: Pennsylvania State University Press, 1999.

Sandberg, J. F., and S. L. Hofferth. "Changes in Parental Time with Children." *Demography* 38 (2001): 423–36.

Schor, Juliet. *The Overworked American: The Unexpected Decline of Leisure*. San Francisco: HarperCollins, 1991.

Schwartz, Barry. *The Paradox of Choice: Why More Is Less*. New York: HarperCollins, 2004.

Sennett, Richard. *The Corrosion of Character: The Personal Consequences of Work in the New Capitalism*. New York: Norton, 1998.

Shore, Bradd. *Culture in Mind: Cognition, Culture, and the Problem of Meaning*. New York: Oxford University Press, 1996.

———. "Knowledge in Formation: The Machine-Modeled Frame of Mind." *Technology in Society* 18, no. 2 (1996): 231–51.

Wallace, Michael. "Downsizing the American Dream: Work and Family at Century's End." In *Challenges for Work and Family in the Twenty-First Century*, ed. Dana Vannoy and Paula Dubeck, 23–38. New York: Aldine de Gruyter, 1998.

Warren, Elizabeth. "Rewriting the Rules: Families, Money, and Risk." Social Science Research Council, New York, 2005. http://privatizationofrisk.ssrc.org/Warren/ (accessed August 22, 2006).

Warren, Elizabeth, and Amelia Warren Tyagi. *The Two-Income Trap: Why Middle-Class Mothers and Fathers Are Going Broke*. New York: Basic Books, 2003.

Wolfe, Alan. *Whose Keeper? Social Science and Moral Obligation*. Berkeley: University of California Press, 1989.

Woodhouse, Sally. "Parental Strategies for Increasing Child Well-being: The Case of Elementary School Choice." University of California, Center for Working Families, Working Paper No. 7 (1999).

Family Index

Subject Index